GROWING CATTLE MANAGEMENT AND DISEASE NOTES

PART II - DISEASE

A.H. Andrews, BVetMed PhD MRCVS

(Presently Dr Andrews is Senior Lecturer, Department of Medicine, Royal Veterinary College.)

First Edition 1986

ISBN 0 9508820 2 X Growing Cattle Management and Disease Notes Part II - Disease

ISBN 0 9508820 3 8 Growing Cattle Management and Disease Notes Parts I and II - Management and Disease

Printed in Great Britain by: Centre Graphics Ltd, 12 Summer Walk, Markyate, Hertfordshire, AL3 8NF.

Published by: A.H. Andrews, ~~11 Aran Close, Harpenden, Hertfordshire AL5 1SW.~~

FOREWORD

Following the production of my book 'Calf Management and Disease Notes', it is logical now to turn my attention to the next stage in development of cattle. The period dealt with in the calf book was from birth to three months old. In this next study we observe the animals from about the three-month stage until they are slaughtered for beef or are entering the dairy or suckler herd as downcalving heifers.

Unlike the calf stage, this next period includes the potential for a large number of different management systems as well as disease conditions. Thus, for ease of use, it has been necessary to divide this second book into two volumes, the first concerned with management but hopefully also indicating some of the nutritional, genetic and disease considerations. The second part deals with the diseases and other conditions which can affect these growing cattle. It is intended that the two halves of the book should be used together, and they complement each other.

There are some other excellent books which cover the diseases of growing animals, but they do not concentrate on these specifically. The volumes include:-

ANDREWS, A.H. and GILES, C.J. (1984) The Henston Veterinary Vade Mecum (Large Animals) Edited by Evans, J.M. 1st edition. CBA and Associates Ltd, Richmond.

BLOOD, D.C., RADOSTITS, O.M. and HENDERSON, J.A. (1983) Veterinary Medicine. 6th edition. Bailliere Tindall, London.

The two parts of this book deal with management and disease, and so do not in any way compete with the above.

It is hoped that this present book will be of use to veterinary students and practitioners. Although there are many technical words I would hope that the two parts will have some relevance to farmers, stockmen and agricultural advisers. As information changes so rapidly, in many parts of the book space has been left to allow notes to be added by the owner.

DR A H ANDREWS
25 MARDLEY HILL
WELWYN
HERTS AL6 0TT
Tel: WELWYN (043871) 7900

CONTENTS

CHAPTER 1

ENDOPARASITIC CONDITIONS

Fascioliasis

Liver fluke infection, liver rot.

Aetiology

A trematode parasite, *Fasciola hepatica*, with a complex life-cycle involving an intermediate host, usually *Limnaea truncatula*, the mud snail.

Occurrence

The adults are found in the bile ducts of ruminants. Infestation occurs more commonly in sheep than cattle or goats. Other species can be infested including other ruminants such as deer, and also pigs, horses, donkeys, rabbits and hares. In unusual hosts, such as horses and man, the parasites tend to be erratic in their distribution and may be found in blood vessels, etc.

It is a relatively frequent parasitic condition of cattle and sheep although many cases of infestation are only revealed at the abattoir. During the years since the mid 1970's when the hot summer of 1976 killed off large numbers of the intermediate host, less infestation has been recorded. The hot summer of 1984 also helped reduce levels of infestation.

As transmission of infestation is dependent on successful completion of the life cycle, infestation is acquired in habitats where the intermediate host can survive. The snail tends to be found in shallow, marshy sites, in wet mud at the edges of puddles or in shallow, stagnant water. It can survive for several weeks under dry conditions, but when drought is prolonged the snail is mainly found close to springs, broken land drains or in any puddles surrounding water troughs. The snail is not normally present in rivers, streams, large ponds, salt marshes or peat bogs.

Animal Susceptibility

Most cattle infested with liver fluke show no signs of illness. Signs are more common in young cattle, particularly during the first and second grazing seasons. Acute fascioliasis is almost always in young cattle. Signs in maturing or adult animals are rare and when they occur, they often follow calving, stress or bacterial or viral infections.

Fasciola Hepatica Life Cycle

Infestation in Snail

The adult leaf-like parasite is found in the bile ducts of the livers of cattle and sheep. It tends to be about 30 mm (1 in) long by 13 mm (½ in) wide at its widest point (the shoulders) which is anterior. The parasite is supplied with two suckers as well as spines to its cuticle. Its colour is grey or brown. The parasite produces an operculated egg which passes out with the bile into the duodenum and then on to the pasture via the faeces. Development depends on eggs being deposited in water or a marshy environment, as well as the temperature. Optimum development is at around 27°C (80°F) and takes about 10 days. Maturation reduces as the temperature lowers and ceases at about 10°C (50°F). In Britain, development usually requires 4 to 8 weeks, when a ciliated miracidium is produced, which is about 130µ long. Following emergence from the egg, which is stimulated by light, the miracidium usually survives about 24 hours and requires moisture to move in.

The parasite actively swims, seeks and penetrates the fleshy foot of the intermediate snail host. Once inside the snail, the cilia are shed and within 48 hours a rounded sporocyst is produced of about 1 mm length.

Inside the sporocyst, five to eight redia develop and they reach a length of 1 - 3 mm in eight days under optimum conditions. The redia have a collar below the pharynx and on being released actively ingest the liver tissue. Secondary rediae may develop. particularly if the temperature is low. Although the young stages can survive in the intermediate host over winter, the infestation may often die out in the snail during the winter period.

Ultimately the rediae contain cercariae which are small, being 0.25 to 0.35 mm long, but with tails twice that length. They actively migrate out of the snail's pulmonary aperture. In the spring this occurs seven to 12 weeks after the miracidium entered the snail but in summer it can reduce to between four-and-a-half and seven weeks. Once released, the cercariae swim to blades of grass where they become attached just below the water level. Here they lose their tails and encyst. The cysts are able to survive cold and freezing, and thus they can overwinter. The metacercariae can remain viable for up to a year unless subjected to desiccation. Thus, although they can survive for a few weeks on dry hay, they can remain for one year on damp or improperly-dried hay.

Snail Life Cycle

L. truncatula is quite small, about 8 mm (0.33 in) in length and is conical in shape. It is self-fertilising and usually hatches two or three generations per year. The first brood is usually late March or April, with a second batch in July. The snails can live for up to a year and they lay up to 60 eggs per day. In wet seasons the snails increase to considerable numbers and their habitat may increase to extend over much of the wet pasture. A snail which has been infested with the intermediate stages of *F. hepatica* tends to be weakened and will usually die earlier than an uninfested snail. Emergence of the cercariae from the snail can be enhanced by removing snails from a dry habitat and placing them in water. Thus, in nature, temporary flooding makes it favourable for the cercariae to emerge and survive. Sometimes the metacercariae can be transported over long distances and infest animals on farms away from the recognised fluke areas.

Infestation in Definitive Host

Cattle are infested by ingesting the metacercariae. Usually these are in areas of shallow, marshy ground or close to puddles, brackish water or occasionally near streams or rivers. Following ingestion, the cyst wall is digested in the duodenum, allowing the cercaria to escape and burrow through the intestinal wall and then enter the body cavity. Others pass up the bile duct and a few may enter a blood vessel and travel to the liver or they may become aberrant, entering and developing in other organs such as the lungs. Most parasites, however, do enter the peritoneal cavity and migrate to the liver. On the way they attach themselves to various visceral organs to feed on blood. The parasites reach the liver in about five to six days and then actively penetrate this organ. Migration then occurs in the hepatic parenchyma where the young flukes feed and grow. They enter the bile ducts about eight weeks or more after ingestion and then feed and grow until they reach maturity and lay eggs in about 10 to 14 weeks. Infestation in sheep may remain for many years but in cattle it is usually lost after six to nine months.

Overwintering of Infestation

Most overwintering occurs as metacercariae on the pasture although some is as eggs and a small number remain as the early stages in dormant snails.

Morbidity

If following a wet spell there is a brief dry period in summer, then the cattle are driven into areas of high infestation with a large population of snails, and infestation levels may be high, in the region of 50 per cent or more. However, mortality in cattle solely as a result of liver fluke infestation is unusual in Britain.

Acute Fascioliasis

This is occasionally seen in sheep but the condition is very rare in cattle. It depends on a massive ingestion of miracidia with simultaneous invasion of the liver with large numbers of immature liver fluke. In sheep this occurrence results in significant national losses about once every 10 years. However, because of dry summers in recent years, cases even in sheep have been minimal. Cases are usually seen in August or September.

Chronic Fascioliasis

This condition often produces few signs or a reduced production, and is often only diagnosed after death. In the abattoir, levels of infestation seen may well be high. This is partly because any *Fasciola* spp. damage tends to result in permanent thickening of bile ducts and so any previous infestation can be detected. Occasionally activation of dormant infections may occur, e.g. *Clostridium novyi* (*Cl. oedematiens* type B). Most cases are usually clinically seen in November to January.

Signs

Acute

The animal is usually found dead. In some cases a blood-stained discharge is present at the nose, anus and vulva. If the animal is alive it is usually moribund, dull, with pale mucous membranes and there are signs of pain in the liver region.

Chronic

Usually the animals show a reduced growth rate with diarrhoea. The coat appears to be of poor quality and in some cases there are pale mucous membranes.

Necropsy

Acute

The liver is markedly swollen and damaged. The peritoneal cavity will contain some blood-stained fluid and the hepatic surface tends to be covered with subcapsular haemorrhages and penetration marks. The liver parenchyma often shows migratory tracts although the young flukes are small and so difficult to find.

Chronic

The carcase may show a varying degree of emaciation with anaemia. As the infestation persists the liver tends to take on a triangular appearance. The bile ducts become thickened and calcified and are readily apparent on the liver surface. During active infestation the parasites can be found within the bile ducts. The parenchyma tends to become paler and show fibrosis as the condition continues. The bile duct calcification persists after elimination of infestation.

Diagnosis

1. Area - places with habitats suitable for the snail.

2. Faecal examination - presence of one or more operculate *Fasciola* spp. eggs indicates infestation.

3. *Post mortem* findings will usually indicate the presence of liver flukes or at least damage caused by them. In chronic cases the liver becomes triangular in shape. Acute cases show enlarged livers with parasitic tracts, and bloody peritoneal fluid. If a cut piece of liver is taken and washed in water, immature flukes may be seen to come out of the tissue.

4. Anaemia.

5. Bile duct damage is indicated by a raised plasma gamma glutamyl transferase (γGT) level. This is greater than 20 iu/litre.

6. Parenchymal damage can be shown by a raised plasma glutamic dehydrogenase (GDH) level. A level of over 40 iu/litre is indicative of damage.

Differential Diagnosis

Acute

1. Anthrax - always check in cases of sudden death.

2. Clostridial infections including *Cl. novyi*.

3. Ruminal tympany.

4. Lightning strike.

Chronic

1. Parasitic gastroenteritis - check faeces for presence of eggs.

2. Coccidiosis - check faecal sample for oocysts.

3. Copper deficiency - depends on area. Blood copper levels should be low.

4. Cobalt deficiency - usually end of grazing season. Check blood vitamin B_{12} levels.

5. Johne's disease, but usually a herd history. Repeated faecal sampling identifies the acid-fast organism or a positive complement fixation test is obtained.

6. Malnutrition.

Treatment

In the past, carbon tetrachloride, hexachloroethane and hexachlorophene had been used orally as well as carbon tetrachloride intramuscularly. The last tended to cause toxicity in cattle and the others had limited efficacy and then only against adult liver flukes. Subsequently several new compounds have become available and many are currently in use (see Table 1.1). Some of the preparations are only effective against adult flukes whereas others are active against the earlier stages. Where it is likely that the fluke infestation is not all mature then preparations with activity against both the adult and immature stages should be used. Several preparations are available to deal with both parasitic gastroenteritis and liver fluke infestations. It is, however, unusual for cattle to suffer clinical manifestations of both of these problems at the same time and so their use together is often uneconomic. When looking at the cost of the specific fasciolicides, they are always many times less expensive for an animal dose than those for parasitic gastroenteritis, and so the use of combined preparations is extremely costly when just dealing with fluke infestation.

Prevention

Eradication

Eradication of liver fluke problems is possible if the intermediate host can be removed. This is only practicable by destroying all suitable habitats for the snail. It is possible to do this by drainage, either mole drainage or the use of plastic or earthenware pipes. These should allow the free flow of water into drainage ditches or streams, where again water movement must be rapid.

Control

This can be undertaken in two ways, firstly by controlling snail populations and then by controlling infestation in the cattle.

Snail Control

Local drainage of snail habitats can be helpful and fencing of suspect areas can be undertaken although often the cattle will wish to eat the lush grass in these enclosed areas and the snails themselves will be no respecters of such man-made barriers. The use of molluscicides can be helpful. In the past, chemicals such as Frescon or Santobrite have been used but little uptake of them has resulted in their becoming unavailable. Copper sulphate can be used and is effective against the adult snails but not their eggs. In marshy areas, copper sulphate can be mixed with sand and spread at a level of 23 kg/ha (20 lb/acre), or it can be made into a 0.5 per cent solution and sprayed at 1500 litres/ha (135 gallons/acre). Copper sulphate should be used with care because of potential toxicity, especially to sheep. Any molluscicide is best used twice yearly in April and August, although a single application before the snails start multiplying may be sufficient. A possible method of biological control could arise from the observation that snails infested with the lung fluke *Haplometra cylindracea*, xiphidiocercarid stage, were not infested with *F. hepatica* (Whitelaw and Fawcett, 1982).

TABLE 1.1

Anthelmintics for Cattle with Activity against Fascioliasis

Compound	Preparation	Dose Rate		Efficacy		
		mg/kg	mg/lb	Adults 0-12 weeks	Immature 6-10 weeks	Immature Less than 6 weeks
Single Preparations						
Albendazole	Suspension Drench	10	5	+	-	-
Nitroxynil	Solution Injection s.c.	10	5	+	±	-
Oxyclozanide	Suspension Drench Granules in Feed	10	5	+	-	-
Rafoxanide	Suspension Drench	7.5	3.5	+	±	-
	Solution Injection s.c.	3	1.5			
Triclabendazole	Drench	12	6	+	+	+

(cont'd)

TABLE 1.1 (cont'd)

Compound	Preparation	Dose Rate mg/kg	Dose Rate mg/lb	Efficacy: Adults 0-12 weeks	Efficacy: Immature 6-10 weeks	Efficacy: Immature Less than 6 weeks
Combined Preparations - the combination has activity against the adult and larval parasitic gastroenteritis helminths.						
Levamisole +	Suspension	7.5	3.5	-	-	-
Oxyclczanide	Drench	15	7.5	+	-	-
	Granules in Feed					
Oxibendazole +	Suspension	10	5	-	-	-
Oxyclczanide	Drench	12	6	+	-	-
Thiabendazole +	Paste	66	33	-	-	-
Rafoxanide	Suspension	11.25	5	+	±	-
	Drench					

There are various formulations of preparations to allow administration by drench, in the feed or by injection. Most cases of clinical fascioliasis result from other problems such as poor nutrition, etc. It is therefore important to ensure an adequate feeding level and if there are any other underlying disease problems, these should also be dealt with.

Cattle are best not grazed in areas where the mud snail is likely to survive. If this is not possible it is best to graze such pastures as late in the year as possible, i.e. after May, and then only use until early autumn.

Cattle Infestation Control

As adult fluke lay large numbers of eggs, control can be obtained by the use of a routine dosing programme. This should ideally involve the use of a flukicide active against the immature as well as the adult parasites. Dosing cattle twice a year if outside all the time can be helpful, once in December and again in March to May.

The use of combined parasitic gastroenteritis and liver fluke anthelmintics cannot usually be justified as the times when routine drenching for each of these parasites is carried out are usually different. In addition, the cost of the flukicide is many times less than that of the nematicide. However, if the cattle are treated for liver fluke at the time of autumn housing this may be an indication for a combined worming.

Liver Fluke Forecasts

The Ministry of Agriculture each year issues a forecast as to likely infestation levels in different parts of Britain.

References

WHITELAW, A and FAWCETT, A R (1982) Veterinary Record, 110, 500-501.

Dicrocoelium dendriticum Infestation

Lesser liver fluke, Lancet fluke.

Aetiology

An infestation of the bile ducts with the fluke *Dicrocoelium dendriticum*.

Occurrence

The condition is far less common in Britain than *F. hepatica* infestation, being mainly found in the western isles of Scotland. It occurs mainly in sheep although occasionally in cattle, goats, deer, pigs, rabbits and coypu. Man has been reported to have been infested. The fluke is smaller than *F. hepatica*, being 6 to 10 mm long (½ in) and 1.5 to 2.5 mm wide (1/10 in). The cuticle of the parasite is smooth and so less damage is done to bile ducts. Often infestation is associated with black disease (*Cl. novyi* - *Cl. oedematiens* type B) infection.

Life Cycle

The fluke requires two intermediate hosts to complete its life cycle. The eggs in the faeces already contain a miracidium which is not released until it is ingested by a land snail. Several species and genera are suitable, including *Helicella* spp., *Zebrina* spp., etc. The egg shell is digested following ingestion and the miracidium moves in the gut lumen before entering a digestive gland via its duct. It penetrates the gland wall and loses its cilia. In the connective tissue of the gland it produces non-motile sporocysts which in turn form a second generation of sporocysts which are amorphous, elongated and motile. No redia are produced, but cercariae are released from the sporocysts in damp weather and they enter the pulmonary chamber of the snail. They become covered in mucus to produce slime balls often containing 100 to 400 cercariae. These slime balls are periodically ejected by the snail, usually in damp weather following a dry spell. The balls adhere to vegetation and dry out quickly in dry weather, but they can survive up to three weeks at 1 to 5°C (34 to 41°F) and in moist air conditions. Most slime balls are produced in the autumn and some are carried away by the second intermediate host, ants of the genus *Formica*. They eat the slime balls and become infested.

Once in the body, the cercariae tend to be found in the abdominal cavity where they encyst and become metacercariae. The final host is infested by accidentally eating the ants. The cyst wall is dissolved in the small intestine to release the parasites which quickly pass to the liver via the common bile duct. Various ducts and the gall bladder are invaded and in about 7 to 8 weeks after ingestion, the adult starts to lay eggs. The whole life cycle takes from 1 to 5 years.

Signs

Most cases are asymptomatic but occasionally an animal is found dead with black disease and the parasite is found to be the activating factor. Otherwise, in massive infestations, there may be a reduction in weight gain.

Necropsy

A mild cirrhosis may be present with fine fibrous streaks in the connective tissue. In severe cases the liver surface may become lumpy with the bile dicts distended, darkened and containing many *D. dendriticum* adults. Occasionally mixed infestations of *D. dendriticum* and *F. hepatica* occur.

Diagnosis

1. Area - mainly western isles of Scotland.

2. Presence of ova in faeces containing a miracidium.

3. *Post mortem* findings - often signs of black disease with fluke present.

Treatment

Information on the use of anthelmintics in the treatment of *D. dendriticum* is limited and is mainly confined to dosing of sheep. Thus a single dose of albendazole at a rate of 15 mg/kg (7.5 mg/lb) produced a 95 *per cent* reduction of the parasite in sheep. Fenbendazole and thiabendazole at increased dose rates and given singly or in multiple doses have also been used effectively. Praziquantel as a single dose of 50 mg/kg (25 mg/lb) is claimed to be between 92 and 98 *per cent* effective against *D. dendriticum*.

Control

This is usually unnecessary but if undertaken often it will involve snail control. Copper sulphate can be mixed with sand and broadcasted at 23 kg/ha (20 lb/acre) or it can be made into a 0.5 *per cent* solution and used at 1500 litres/ha (135 gallons/acre).

Parasitic Gastroenteritis

Worms, ostertagiasis, nematodiriasis, trichostrongylosis, cooperiasis.

Aetiology

Infestation of the gastrointestinal tract with one or several species of nematodes of the *Ostertagia* spp., *Trichostrongylus* spp., *Nematodirus* spp., and *Cooperia* spp.

Occurrence

Infestation of young cattle is very common with one or more of the nematode species. The most important pathogenic species for cattle is the stomach worm *Ostertagia ostertagi*, although usually mixed infestations are present. *Trichostrongylus axei* can also, on occasion, produce severe clinical signs. Generalising, clinical syndromes tend to be unusual in Britain today because of the presence of many efficacious anthelmintics and the tendency, if anything, to overuse them. Most of the helminths involved are specific to individual species although the same strains of *T. axei* can develop in cattle and sheep.

Distribution of Helminths in Cattle

Abomasum	Small Intestine
Trichostrongylus axei	*Trichostrongylus colubriformis*
Ostertagia ostertagi	*Trichostrongylus longispicularis*
Ostertagia lenticularis?	*Cooperia oncophora*
Ostertagia lyrata?	*Cooperia pectinata*
	Cooperia punctata
	Nematodirus battus
	Nematodirus filicollis
	Nematodirus helvetianus
	Nematodirus spathiger

When infestation occurs it is usually the result of overstocking the land or not providing sufficient supplementary feeding. Most cases occur within six weeks of turnout in the spring or in the period from mid-July until yarding.

Animal Susceptibility

Cattle in their first grazing season are exposed to infestation and are totally susceptible. Subsequent resistance to infestation is mainly due to previous exposure to helminths although age may play a small part in this. Immunity to infestation takes a considerable time to develop, thus cattle in the first grazing season not only become infested but the adult helminths produce large numbers of eggs to contaminate the pasture. During the second grazing season there is some resistance to infestation but some helminths still develop. However, the number of eggs produced by these is reduced. Subsequent grazing seasons result in fewer larvae developing in the gastrointestinal tract and minimal numbers of eggs being found in the faeces. It is possible, by overzealous worming or by keeping cattle indoors and then exposing them to a high level of infestation, to produce clinical parasitic gastroenteritis in adult cattle. Most cases occur in animals aged between three and six months but clinical signs can be seen up to two years old.

Duration of Infestation

The eggs passed out in the faeces require warmth and moisture to develop. This is usually a gradual progressive situation. Development tends to be fast in the summer provided there is moisture. However, when conditions are very dry there is no egg maturation and numbers tend to build up. Once moisture returns there is rapid development, allowing large numbers of infective larvae to be present on the pasture at the same time. Production of infective third stage larvae tends to be slow during the autumn and winter and it usually ceases in the winter. The longer the time interval between an egg being deposited on the pasture in the faeces and the third stage larvae being ingested by cattle, the more likely it is to have died off. Infestation deposited in the summer tends to remain viable up to five months, although eggs deposited prior to the winter may survive seven or eight months. It is unusual for larvae to remain much over a year, but some infestation has been recorded as surviving up to two years.

Route of Infestation

Helminth infestation is acquired orally by the cattle.

Origin of Pasture Infestation

During the early part of the grazing period infestation, which is present, tends to be on a declining plane and consists of eggs which have overwintered and subsequently developed or some third stage infective larvae which have survived. Any of the overwintered infection which has not been ingested by the end of June or beginning of July will have died off. In the second half of the grazing season infestation comprises (i) eggs deposited from infested animals which are allowed to graze the area, or (ii) eggs which are the result of infestation derived from the infective third stage larvae present on that pasture, ingested in the first part of the grazing season, thus becoming adult and starting to produce eggs.

Pasture Infestation

Most commonly, infestation occurs on permanent pastures, often where the ground is overstocked. In the spring, most cases appear on pasture grazed the previous year by infected young stock which produce large numbers of helminth eggs. In the autumn, infestation on the pasture is the result of cattle grazing earlier in the season or entering the area in the second half of the grazing season without being wormed.

Life Cycle

The life cycle in all the genera is simple and is direct with infestation produced in the faeces of one animal being infective to another once larvae are found. The number of eggs produced depends on the resistance of the host and the number of helminths present. Thus in the non-immune animal small numbers of worms will produce large numbers of eggs, whereas when large numbers are present, each worm will produce fewer eggs. Eggs reach the pasture in the faeces where, under suitable conditions of warmth and moisture, they moult twice to produce infective third stage larvae. The embryonated eggs are relatively resistant to drying but once formation of the first or second larval stages is produced they cannot withstand drying although they resist freezing. The third stage larvae are ensheathed in the previous larval coat and are more resistant to environmental exposure. Eggs of *Nematodirus* spp. do not hatch until the third stage infective larva is produced.

Following ingestion by a suitable host they exsheath and then enter the alimentary mucosa. A third moult occurs and under normal conditions the fourth stage returns to the surface of the gut where it undergoes another moult or ecdysis to produce the adult stage. During the autumn many third stage larvae become inactive or hypobiotic and remain in the gut lining until the following spring. After maturation and fertilisation the females lay eggs. The prepatent period for the helminths depends partly on the species and previous exposure of the host to them but it is usually about three weeks. The adult helminths will lay eggs for a variable period but many are ejected after a month or so of adulthood.

Morbidity

When outbreaks of infestation occur and all the animals are of a similar age and with the same history of exposure, then most of the group will be affected.

Signs

Early

Most cases occur in the first season. The signs are usually insidious in onset and there is a reduced feed intake. The animals have a reduced weight gain or lose weight. The faeces become loose and then there is diarrhoea which becomes watery. The faecal colour is variable, but may be dark brown or black, although more often it tends to be a dark green to yellow. The coat becomes staring and tends to be dull and dry with erect hairs. Signs of dehydration can occur and the mucous membranes may become pale.

Late

The heart rate may increase with the progressive dehydration. The animals will become thin, emaciated and dull. There are signs of weakness and then there is recumbency.

Necropsy

Although many helminths may be present, they are difficult to see because of their small size, except for Nematodirus spp. which are 1.0 to 2.5 cm (½ to 1 in) long. The worms are present in the abomasum or small intestine, dependent on species. They can be stained brown with iodine solution or diluted with saline and viewed over a dark surface. The abomasal or intestinal mucosa may be thickened, with mucoid inflammation and some hyperaemia. Chronic cases tend to show a hyperplasia of the abomasum or intestinal wall with increased surface mucus. Carcases show emaciation with a lack of fat, dehydration and in some cases there is anaemia. In the abomasum the mucosa may show hyperplastic nodular changes due to the presence of large numbers of embedded helminths.

Diagnosis

1. Time of year - usually first six weeks of grazing or mid-July on.
2. Type of animals - usually first grazing season or heavy pasture contamination, or not previously exposed to infestation.
3. Grazing history - usually permanent pasture and overstocked.

4. Faecal egg counts - useful in first grazing season.

   Over 1000 eggs per gram (epg) - clinical disease.
   500 - 1000 epg - less severe disease.
   Less than 500 epg - usually no signs.

   Once exposed to infestation then some immunity is present and so egg production is reduced or stopped.

5. Pasture larval counts.

   Levels over 1000 larvae/kg DM herbage result in clinical disease.
   200 - 300 larvae/kg DM result in reduced weight gains.

6. Plasma pepsinogen levels.

   Levels over 1.5 iu/litre in plasma (1 iu = 1000 milli-units of tyrosine/minute) in first grazing season or 3.0 iu/litre subsequently.

7. Low serum protein levels (normal 6 - 8 g/100 ml; 60 - 80 g/litre)

8. Low serum albumin levels.

9. *Post mortem* findings and isolation of helminths.

Differential Diagnosis

1. Coccidiosis but faecal sample shows oocysts.

2. Copper deficiency but blood copper level is usually low and the animals are on a low copper diet or in a deficient area.

3. Cobalt deficiency but usually at the end of the grazing season.

4. Fascioliasis but faecal samples show operculate eggs.

5. Johne's disease but animal usually too young, usually herd history and hopefully acid-fast organisms are shown to be present if repeated faecal samples are taken or positive results found to complement fixation test.

6. Malnutrition.

Treatment

Remove the cattle from the infested pasture and worm with a suitable anthelmintic (see Table 1.2). Do not leave cattle on the same infested pasture otherwise the worm burden will again quickly rise. If no suitable pasture is available house the animals and feed indoors. In all cases where disease has occurred, some supplementary feeding should be given. Most products used for treatment are given orally (by drench or in the feed) or by injection. Recently, novel methods of application include the use of the "pour-on" route and intra-ruminal injection.

Control

Various questions should be asked before an animal is put out to pasture at the start of the grazing season:-

1. Is the animal likely to become infested?

TABLE 1.2

Compound	Preparation	Dose Rate mg/kg	Dose Rate mg/lb	Helminths Adults	Helminths Developing Larvae	Helminths Hypobiotic Larvae
Albendazole	Suspension, drench	7.5	3.5	+	+	+
Febantel	Paste, suspension, powder premix	7.5	3.5	+	+	+
Fenbendazole	Suspension, drench, paste, pellets, granules, powder	7.5	3.5	+	+	+
Ivermectin	Solution, injection s.c.	200 mcg	100 mcg	+	+	+
Levamisole	Solution, drench, injection s.c., solution pour-on, granules	7.5	3.5	+	+	-
Oxfendazole	Suspension, drench, injection, intraruminal	4.5	2.0	+	+	+
Oxibendazole	Paste drench, suspension drench	10	5	+	+	-
Parbendazole	Suspension, powder in feed, pellets	20-32	10-16	+	+	-
Thiabendazole	Paste, powder, wormer pellets, premix, suspension, drench	66	30	+	+	-
Thiophanate	Powder, suspension, drench	60	30	+	+	±

(cont'd)

TABLE 1.2 (cont'd)

Compound	Preparation	Dose Rate mg/kg	Dose Rate mg/lb	Helminths Adults	Helminths Developing Larvae	Helminths Hypobiotic Larvae
Combined Preparations - These have activity against adult liver fluke.						
Levamisole +	Granules in feed,	7.5	3.5	+	+	-
Oxyclozanide	suspension, drench	15	7.5	-	-	-
Oxibendazole +	Suspension, drench	10	5	+	+	-
Oxyclozanide		12	6	-	-	-
Thiabendazole +	Paste, suspension, drench	66	33	+	+	-
Rafoxanide*		11.25	5	-	-	-

*Rafoxanide has activity against immature liver fluke.

2. Is the animal likely to become a major source of infestation for future groups entering that pasture?

Other questions should be asked before animals are wormed:-

1. Why am I worming?

2. Is the animal ill with parasitic gastroenteritis?

3. Is the animal likely to become ill if not treated?

4. Is the animal likely otherwise to become a major source of infection for future groups using the pasture?

5. Is the animal to be moved to a pasture which will be contaminated if the animal is not treated?

Control depends on understanding the relationships between

A. Parasite
B. Animal
C. Pasture.

When these are known, adequate control measures can be calculated.

A. Parasite

1. Eggs laid in faeces are not immediately infective.

2. The longer the period between deposition of the egg on the herbage and the time it is ingested by cattle, the more likely it is that the parasite will have died. (Most larvae die off over winter. In the spring fewer larvae are ingested as they are diluted in large quantities of grass).

3. Eggs require some moisture and development to larvae is affected by warmth (i.e. development is slow in the spring, fast in summer, slow in the autumn and stops in winter).

4. Adult worms remain in cattle for a limited period.

5. Although eggs are laid in the faeces all the year round, most reach the infective stage at the same time (i.e. mid-July onwards).

6. Most worm species in cattle and sheep are different.

B. Cattle

1. Cattle infestations occur only in cattle at pasture or on pasture products.

2. Cattle inside do not have worms unless fed infested pasture products.

3. Resistance to worms is mainly due to previous exposure to helminths.

4. In first grazing season the cattle are susceptible and shed large quantities of helminth eggs.

5. In second grazing season the cattle are less susceptible as there is some immunity, some eggs are present in the faeces but are less in number than in first grazing period.

6. Adult cattle are relatively resistant and have only a few helminths present and they deposit very small numbers of eggs on the pasture.

C. Pasture

The amount of infestation present on a pasture depends on the species which have grazed the pasture, the age of cattle on the pasture, the time since it was grazed and the time of year. Pastures can conveniently be divided into those of spring and those not grazed until mid-July onwards. Grass can be considered "clean" or "safe", i.e. with little or no worm infestation, if:-

Spring

Land not grazed by cattle the previous season, e.g.

(a) New leys (after arable crops, maize, etc).

(b) Grazed by different species previous year, i.e. sheep.

(c) Used for conservation only the previous year.

Mid-July Onwards

Land not grazed by cattle during the first half of the season, e.g.

(a) Hay or silage aftermath if not grazed previously that year.

(b) Grazed by a different species earlier in the year, i.e. sheep.

(c) New leys.

(d) Land not grazed that year until mid-July.

(e) (Clean land grazed by clean cattle.)

The current parasite status of the pasture can be deduced by asking questions such as:-

When was the pasture last grazed?
Was it this year or last year?
If grazed by cattle, what was the likely worm infestation of the cattle?
What time and seasons have elapsed since it was last grazed by cattle?
What have been the weather conditions during the period since the area was last grazed?

One can then decide:

The likely parasite status of the pasture, i.e. clean, little risk or doubtful.

The cattle which should be allowed to graze the pasture during the year.

Grazing Systems

Several grazing systems have been devised to keep worm infestation to a low level and to allow maximum grass utilisation. These include:

One-Third - Two-Thirds System

The available area for grazing and conservation is divided into two, one of one-third the area and the other of two-thirds.

	One-Third	Two-Thirds
Turnout to mid-July	Grazed	Cut for silage or hay
Mid-July	Worm and move	
Mid-July to yarding	Cut for hay or silage	Grazed

The cattle start off on the smaller area while the larger part is used for conservation. By mid-July most infective larvae will have died off on the two-thirds area and the cattle are wormed and then moved. If the cattle are not moved,but wormed,all that happens is a delay of three weeks before eggs are again produced in the faeces from a reinfection with helminths. If the cattle are moved to the new pasture but are not wormed then the safe pasture will become contaminated. The use of the larger area in the second half of the grazing season recognises the fact of the reduced grass growth in the second half of the season as well as the increased appetites of the cattle.

1 - 2 - 3 System

This is a modification of the one-third - two-thirds system. Initially it follows the same system but in early September the whole pasture is used up for grazing. This means that the cattle may become reinfected with larvae previously deposited on the one-third area in the first part of the grazing season. Thus the cattle will require anthelmintic treatment at yarding.

	One-Third	Two-Thirds
Turnout to mid-July	Grazed	Cut for silage or hay
Mid-July	Worm and move	
Mid-July to September	Cut for hay or silage	Grazed
Mid-September to yarding	Grazed	Grazed

Leader/Follower System

This involves dividing the grazing area into a series of paddocks. It has been found to produce better grass utilisation as well as some helminth control. The calves (i.e. first grazing season animals) graze the area first and are followed into the paddock by older cattle (i.e. second year grazing cattle). The calves take up most of the young, tender grass whereas the lower levels, where many of the helminth larvae are present, are eaten by the older cattle. The latter are less susceptible to worms and in addition, any helminths maturing will produce fewer eggs for further pasture contamination. The cattle are moved when the older animals have completed the grazing in their paddock, and they then enter the one occupied by the calves. The calves enter a fresh paddock.

The system allows rotation around the paddocks which should be six to 10 in number. Moving occurs every few days with return to the first paddock in a month or so. The ratio of calves to older cattle should be no greater than 3 : 1 as the followers must have the greater appetite. Extra paddocks may be needed during the mid to late grazing period. If the pasture is not clean or safe in the spring, helminth levels can be kept low by worming the cattle at three-week intervals until July.

Mixed Grazing

This means grazing cattle and sheep or other species in the same system. The animals are not grazed together but in rotation. A two- or three-year rotation is used. The system works because only a few helminths are common to both species and so only *Trichostrongylus axei* and a few other parasites may build up. The three-year system involves a third of the area being kept for conservation and in some cases it may be used to graze lambs or calves in the second half of the grazing season. The third of the area used for conservation the previous year is used by the cattle, and the area vacated by the cattle is grazed that year by the sheep.

Set Stocking

On many farms the only system available is set stocking. This often does not make the best use of available grass. Where used, the liberal application of fertilizers will assist in reducing the worm burden. Contamination of the pasture with eggs can be reduced by worming the cattle every three weeks until July. This usually entails two or three dosings and will keep the animals relatively lightly infested until yarding when they should again be wormed. The repetitive use of anthelmintics is often called the "Poor Man's Grazing System".

Zero Grazing

When cattle are housed and fed cut grass there is little problem from helminths unless the pasture has been grazed by infested cattle. Even then, infestation levels will tend to be low.

Sustained Release Bolus

The complexity of helminth control and grazing systems has led to the production of a bolus given orally and designed to lodge in the reticulo-rumen. The bolus releases anthelmintic (morantel tartrate) over a period of at least 90 days and if given at the start of the grazing season will ensure only a few helminths reach maturity, thereby keeping pasture larval and animal infestation levels low throughout the season. As the anthelmintic is not 100 per cent effective and some helminths mature, the animal develops immunity. At present, the worms have not shown evidence of anthelmintic resistance.

Ostertagia Type II Infestation

"Winter Scours"

Most *Ostertagia* spp. infective larvae become adult within 18 to 21 days of ingestion. However, some of those taken in during the late autumn, winter or early spring are arrested as fourth-stage larvae within the gastric glands of the abomasal wall. These hypobiotic larvae remain quiescent for several months, often four or five. They will then often all develop over a short period, causing considerable damage to the abomasum.

Clinical cases may be seen in cattle from one to three years old so that occurrences can follow the second grazing season (Petrie, Armour and Stevenson, 1984).

Signs

Development usually occurs from February onwards and so animals are often indoors. Usually the animals start to have a reduced appetite, lose weight or stop growing. The cattle may develop a profuse and severe diarrhoea. Usually there is not gross anaemia but the mucous membranes tend to be pale and dry. Submandibular oedema is quite common. As the condition progresses there is dehydration and a taut skin with the eyes becoming sunken. Anthelmintic treatment often does not result in cessation of scouring because of the damage to the abomasal wall.

Necropsy

The adult *Ostertagia* are small and very difficult to detect. They may be present in large numbers - i.e. 100,000 to 200,000. In the inhibited stage the abomasal wall has umbilicated nodules which are said to resemble Morocco leather. Often there is degeneration of the abomasal epithelium with foul-smelling contents due to putrefactive bacteria. The pH of the abomasal contents tends to be high (6 to 7). Histologically, there is marked hyperplasia and a loss of cellular differentiation of the cells lining the abomasal glands.

Diagnosis

1. Time of year.
2. Previous grazing history.
3. *Post mortem* findings - Morocco leather, abomasal pH.
4. Faecal egg count - often not many eggs present.
5. Plasma pepsinogen levels - these tend to be high if larvae are emerging from the abomasal glands. Levels over 3 iu tyrosine/litre are positive.
6. There is a reduced response to anthelmintic therapy.

Differential Diagnosis

1. Coccidiosis.
2. Secondary copper deficiency.
3. Salmonellosis.
4. Fascioliasis.

Treatment

Although most anthelmintics will work against the adult helminths, it is probably best to use compounds effective against the hypobiotic larvae. Otherwise these larvae cause further damage on their emergence. Effective anthelmintics include fenbendazole, albendazole, oxfendazole and ivermectin. Febantel and thiophanate also have some activity against the arrested larvae. Often anthelmintics have variable effects on hypobiotic larvae, either because of the effect of the larvae themselves or the entry of the drug directly into the abomasum via the oesophageal groove closure rather than a slow passage of the compound into the abomasum from the reticulo-rumen. Diarrhoea may continue due to severe abomasal damage. Systemic fluid therapy and blood or plasma transfusions may be helpful. Good quality roughage and concentrates should be liberally provided.

Control

Where young cattle are kept out in the late autumn, they should be treated with an anthelmintic effective against hypobiotic larvae following housing. The types of drugs which are effective are listed under Treatment.

Reference

PETRIE, L, ARMOUR, J and STEVENSON, S H (1984) Veterinary Record 114, 168-170.

Anthelmintic Resistance

Although a potential problem, at present there are no authenticated cases in cattle. However, in recent years some cases of resistance in sheep have been recorded. This is probably due to the tendency for anthelmintics to be used more frequently in sheep than cattle.

Heifer Infestation Levels

Many heifers which are slaughtered tend to have moderate *Ostertagia* infestation levels. One study has shown 60 *per cent* of heifers at slaughter had over 10,000 helminths in the abomasum (Hong, Lancaster and Michel, 1981). Although *Ostertagia ostertagi* are commonly present, other types of helminths included *Trichostrongylus axei*. Almost always small numbers of *O. lyrata* were also present.

Reference

HONG, C, LANCASTER, M B and MICHEL, J F (1981) Veterinary Record 109, 12-14.

Haemonchosis

Aetiology

Infestation of the abomasum with helminths of the *Haemonchus* species.

Occurrence

The condition is less common in cattle than sheep. Two species can be involved, namely *H. placei* and *H. contortus*. The latter infestation occurs more commonly when cattle are grazed with sheep or goats and it is usually less severe. The helminth is commonly called the barber's pole worm because of the ingestion of blood which gives the female a spiral red and white appearance, although the male is uniformly red in colour. Most cases occur following hot spells in summer which are broken by rain.

Cases usually occur in stock grazing in their first or second seasons, although some are seen at three years old. Most cases follow a reduction in grazing. Low levels of protein in the diet are considered a predisposing factor. However, some outbreaks do occur in animals in good condition where there is lush pasture, a hot, humid climate and overcrowding. Subclinical outbreaks can occur when the animals are on a high level of nutrition. The fourth stage larvae and adult parasites feed on large quantities of blood which can result in anaemia and hypoproteinaemia. There tends to be a rise in pH of the abomasum as well as in plasma pepsinogen levels.

Life cycle

Infestation is acquired by cattle grazing pasture contaminated with infective larvae. An adult female *H. contortus* can produce up to 10,000 eggs per day for several months although egg production lasts about 11 to 14 weeks with *H. placei*. Following passage in the faeces, two moults occur to produce third stage infective larvae. The time for such a stage to be reached varies considerably from about five days to several months. Although the first and second stage larvae are susceptible to desiccation, the infective third stage larvae are more resistant. Many larvae die off over winter. Following ingestion, the prepatent period is about 18 to 21 days (*H. contortus*) or 26 days (*H. placei*). Some larvae may become hypobiotic.

Signs

The animals are grazing and can show varying degrees of severity.

Acute

This results in sudden death but is rare in Britain. The mucous membranes tend to be very pale or blanched.

Subacute

Animals tend to be lethargic, graze less and lag behind their group. Diarrhoea is uncommon and there is usually constipation. Often there are signs of anaemia with very pale mucous membranes. Anasarca may be present with submandibular oedema and oedema of the ventral abdomen.

Chronic

Such animals tend to show a marked loss of condition, some lethargy and pale mucous membranes.

Necropsy

There are usually obvious signs of a pale carcase with anasarca particularly in the submandibular area and ventral abdomen. The carcase may show signs of emaciation with gelatinisation of the fat deposits. Usually there are large numbers of Haemonchus spp. helminths in the abomasal contents which tend to be red-brown in colour. The abomasal wall mucosa may be haemorrhagic and hyperaemic.

Diagnosis

1. Clinical signs.
2. History
3. Faecal egg count (eggs are larger than those of other helminths).
4. Anaemia.
5. Raised plasma pepsinogen levels.
6. Helminths easily recognised in abomasum (thick worms 1 - 2.5 cm (½ - 1") long and red or red and white in colour).

Differential diagnosis

Acute

1. Anthrax.
2. Blackleg.
3. Ruminal tympany.
4. Hypomagnesaemia.

Subacute

1. Coccidiosis but oocysts usually in faeces.
2. Sucking lice but usually loss of hair and parasite easy to see.
3. Parasitic gastroenteritis - usually no anaemia.
4. Babesiosis, but has to be a tick area, there is haemoglobinuria and parasite can be shown in stained blood sections.
5. Excessive cold water drinking but haemoglobinuria.
6. Leptospirosis but often pyrexia and usually only one or two animals affected.
7. Kale poisoning but usually later autumn, history and haemoglobinuria.
8. Bacillary haemoglobinuria but usually pyrexia, haemoglobinuria and older cattle.
9. Copper poisoning but haemoglobinuria.
10. Bunostomiasis - rare.
11. Fascioliasis - faecal egg examination.
12. Malnutrition.
13. Coccidiosis - faecal oocyst count.

Chronic

1. Parasitic gastroenteritis.
2. Coccidiosis.

3. Chronic copper deficiency but diarrhoea.
4. Chronic cobalt deficiency.
5. Selenium deficiency.
6. Chronic molybdenum poisoning.

Treatment

All anthelmintics used in treatment of parasitic gastroenteritis are also suitable for haemonchosis. Resistance of *H. contortus* to some anthelmintics is reported in sheep, particularly in Australia, but no problems are currently apparent with *Haemonchus* spp. infestation in cattle. The plane of nutrition of the cattle should be improved if it is poor. In some cases the anaemia should be checked by the use of iron and vitamin B_{12} injections.

Control

Methods used for control of parasitic gastroenteritis are also suitable for haemonchosis. Work on an irradiated larval vaccine against *H. contortus* has not proved practically successful in sheep.

Bunostomiasis

(Hookworm infestation)

Aetiology

Infestation of the small intestine with hookworms, usually Bunostomum phlebotum.

Occurrence

The condition is very rarely diagnosed in Britain and normally occurs during the first year of life. Once exposed to infestation, immunity appears to be good. Most cases are seen during the winter period. Wet conditions in yards, pastures, etc. assist in allowing cutaneous penetration of the host and maintaining the viability of the larvae. Overcrowding of pasture and pens can exacerbate the problem.

Life cycle

Eggs are passed with the faeces and an infective larva can be produced in about a week. The larvae undergo two moults and during the first two stages they are susceptible to drying. The third stage infective larva is more resistant and can enter the host by skin penetration. Following entry to the body, the larvae enter the bloodstream and pass through the heart and lungs. In the lungs the larvae penetrate the alveoli, grow and moult to produce the fourth stage. They they pass via the bronchi and trachea to the pharynx. They are swallowed and go to the small intestine where they spend some time in the intestinal wall before returning to the lumen. The prepatent period is about eight weeks. The immature and adult helminths actively feed on blood and, in levels as low as a hundred, they can produce marked anaemia.

Signs

Acute

Marked signs of anaemia may be present, including pallid mucous membranes, submandibular oedema and in some cases oedema along the ventral abdomen.

Subacute

There may be mild signs of colic, stamping and kicking, and then diarrhoea.

Necropsy

In the first part of the small intestine the intestinal contents may be blood-stained. Often only a few helminths (100 or so) are present. The helminths have to be searched for carefully but are red-brown in colour and 1 - 2.5 cm (½ - 1") long.

Diagnosis

1. Faecal egg count - eggs embryonated, deeply pigmented.
2. Occult blood in faeces.
3. Anaemia.
4. Necropsy (helminths red-brown in colour, 1 - 2.5 cm (½ - 1") long in first part of small intestine).

Differential diagnosis

1. Haemonchosis.
2. Parasitic gastroenteritis.
3. Fascioliasis.
4. Copper deficiency.
5. Cobalt deficiency.
6. Selenium deficiency.
7. Chronic molybdenum poisoning.
8. Malnutrition.
9. Coccidiosis.

Treatment

Most anthelmintics work well against Bunostomum spp. infestation. Those with specific indications include fenbendazole, ivermectin, levamisole, oxfendazole, oxibendazole and thiabendazole.

TABLE 1.3

Anthelmintics Effective against Bunostomum spp. and Oesophagostomum spp. Infestations

Albendazole	Oxibendazole
Fenbendazole	Parbendazole
Ivermectin	Thiabendazole
Levamisole	Thiophanate
Oxfendazole	

The diet should be improved to overcome the protein loss and in severe cases of anaemia iron and vitamin B_{12} injections may be helpful.

Control

Pasture control for parasitic gastroenteritis is also effective for bunostomiasis. Improved drainage of pasture or yards is likely to reduce the viability of the free-living larvae. Cattle pens should be cleaned out regularly and there should not be overcrowding.

Oesophagostomiasis

Nodular worm disease, oesophagostomosis.

Aetiology

It is the result of Oesophagostomum spp. infestation, mainly with Oe. radiatum or Oe. venulosum, of the large intestine.

Occurrence

As a clinical entity, oesophagostomiasis is very rare but often infestation is present with other parasitic problems.

Life cycle

The life cycle is direct with eggs being deposited in the faeces. Larvae hatch from the eggs and after two moults they reach the infective third larval stage. The eggs and larvae are very susceptible to drying or cold but under ideal circumstances the infective stage can be reached in about a week. The calf is infected by ingestion of the larvae which invade the small intestinal wall. They remain in the wall for about five days before they re-enter the intestinal lumen and pass to the large intestine. In the large intestine some develop immediately into adult helminths while others enter the intestinal wall. The prepatent period following first exposure to infestation is about six weeks. However, subsequent infestation tends to result in the infective larvae entering a histotrophic phase. When immunity is good the larvae remain in the intestinal walls forming nodules. These larvae may continue to live for periods of a year or so and should resistance of the host subsequently reduce, the larvae leave the intestinal wall and enter the lumen to become adult. Where past resistance remains high the larvae are destroyed within the intestinal wall. Re-entry of the larvae into the intestines and the activity of adults can result in bleeding and anaemia. Survival of infestation from year to year is mainly by those larvae present in nodules in the intestinal wall as the free-living larvae are usually rapidly reduced by climatic conditions.

Signs

There may be signs of anorexia, debility, with loss of condition and anaemia. Animals often start by showing intermittent bouts of constipation and diarrhoea. Subsequently the diarrhoea becomes continuous with the faeces being foetid, and dark brown in colour.

Necropsy

When large numbers of larvae penetrate the small intestinal wall there is a mild catarrhal enteritis. Once adults are present there is often a catarrhal colitis and helminths may be found in the catarrhal exudate. The worms tend to be relatively easy to see as they are thick and about 0.5 - 2.5 cm (1/4 - 1") long. However they do tend to be present in only small numbers, i.e. 200 or so. When nodules are present, they can be seen at all levels of the small and large intestine. They tend to be about 0.5 cm (1/4") in diameter, with thickening of the wall. The contents of the nodules vary from a green, thick liquid material to dry, semi-calcified material.

Diagnosis

1. Faecal egg count (eggs similar to other strongylid species).
2. Faecal culture - allows identification of the larvae *Oesophagostomum* spp.
3. *Post mortem* (presence of adult helminths, nodules in the intestinal wall).
4. Hypoproteinaemia.
5. Anaemia.

Differential diagnosis

1. Parasitic gastroenteritis.
2. Bunostomiasis.
3. Haemonchosis.
4. Malnutrition.
5. Coccidiosis.

Treatment

Most anthelmintics work well against the adult stages but they are less effective against the larvae present in the intestinal wall nodules. Most of the effective anthelmintics are listed in Table 1.3, p.34.

Control

Usually there is little need to consider pasture control as most larvae die off over winter. As most continuation of infestation is from the larvae in the nodules, drenching in spring, midsummer and late autumn can be helpful. There has been some work on vaccine production, particularly in sheep, but as yet it is of no practicable value.

Parasitic Bronchitis

Hoose, husk, verminous bronchitis.

Aetiology

Infestation with the lungworm *Dictyocaulus viviparus*.

Occurrence

The infestation is common in about 66 *per cent* of unvaccinated herds. Calves which are not vaccinated are often infected with lungworm in their first grazing season, particularly calves which go out late in the season and are mixed with older calves. Yearlings are a very dangerous source of infection. Pastures grazed by adult cattle will only have low larval counts on endemic farms. There is no evidence of age immunity. Thus if *Dictyocaulus* spp. infection enters a new farm, all animals are susceptible. Intensification has led to outbreaks of husk in suckler herd calves, especially those born in the autumn, although a few problems are also seen in spring-born herds. Immunity following exposure to infection is quickly produced and effective.

The larvae build up quickly on pasture in warm and wet periods, particularly between May and September. The duration of infective larvae is not known but it is probable that infection lasts more than a year. The larvae cannot always be found on the herbage early in the year but large numbers of larvae have been present in July and August, despite areas not being grazed by cattle. The fungus *Pilobolus* spp. aids in the spread of larvae by 'fungal gunnery'. Earthworms have also been incriminated in spread. Mechanical transmission of infection can be via tractor tyres, boots, etc. Only small numbers of larvae are required to cause an infestation.

Route of infestation

Infestation is acquired orally via the infective third-stage larvae.

Life history

Following ingestion of the infective larvae, consumed with herbage, the larvae are released through the alimentary canal. Infective larvae penetrate the intestinal mucosa and migrate via lymphatic and blood circulation. The third moult occurs in the mesenteric lymph nodes. The larvae pass to the lungs where, following a fourth moult, the fifth stage is reached. The adults are found in the bronchial tree where embryonated eggs are laid. The eggs are coughed up and swallowed. They hatch during their passage through the alimentary tract to produce first stage larvae in the faeces. The larvae then develop and moult twice to produce third stage infective larvae. The prepatent period is about 21 days.

Signs

Day 1 to 7

No signs normally present.

Day 8 to 25

Usually the first signs are respiratory although a transient episode of diarrhoea may occur but be overlooked. The signs are usually of respiratory distress with abdominal breathing and a rate up to 100 per minute. The heart rate tends to be raised to 100-120 per minute. There is a bronchial cough with, in some cases, slight nasal discharge and a raised rectal temperature (40-40.5°C; 104-105°F). There is an increase in both bronchial and vesicular sounds over the whole lung area. The animal tends to be active and bright and in some cases it will eat. Some animals will be less severely affected with a cough, some increase in respiratory rate and a loss of condition.

Severe

Some sudden onset cases will develop severe dyspnoea with marked respiratory chest movements and a respiratory grunt. There is then cyanosis and recumbency with death, often within 3 to 14 days of the onset of signs. Auscultation of the chest reveals marked bronchial sounds, emphysema crackles over the dorsal two-thirds of the lung with moist rales in the bronchial tree and areas of consolidation.

Patent phase - Day 26 to 55

There is a loss of condition in the animal with paroxysmal coughing and a raised respiratory rate to about 70 per minute. In severe cases there is an inspiratory grunt and prolonged expiration. On auscultation there may be bronchial sounds as well as areas of consolidation.

Post patent phase - Day 56 to 90

In most animals the signs subside. However, some cattle may show dyspnoea, with a raised temperature (40°C; 104°F) and respiratory rate (100 per minute).

Necropsy

Prepatent

The mature and immature parasites are usually found in the smaller bronchi and there is a marked interstitial emphysema. There is an early bronchitis. Histologically there are eosinophils, macrophages and giant cells resulting in an alveolitis, bronchiolitis with the lumina being plugged, and a bronchitis.

Patent

Often there are areas of emphysema and bronchitis, particularly in the diaphragmatic lobes. The adult helminths are present in the lumina of the bronchi often covered in froth. Histologically there is hyperplasia of the epithelium as well as infiltration of the lamina propria by eosinophils and plasma cells. The helminths tend to be surrounded by mucus, plasma cells and eosinophils.

Post patent

Pulmonary interstitial emphysema and oedema may be present. Histologically there is hyaline membrane formation and diffuse alveolar epithelial hyperplasia.

Diagnosis

1. History - the farm and animals grazing. Otherwise, if no previous farm history, animals are on new pasture or some are bought-in. Respiratory signs often occur 7-20 days after entering a new field.
2. Signs - loss of condition, paroxysmal coughing, whole lung field affected on auscultation.
3. Faecal examination - larvae present in patent period.
4. ELISA test for adult or larval *D. viviparus*.

Differential diagnosis

1. Enzootic pneumonia - calves usually indoors.
2. Cuffing pneumonia - calves indoors; single dry cough.
3. Pasteurellosis - pyrexia, usually after a change of environment.
4. IBR - conjunctivitis, pyrexia.
5. Malnutrition.

Treatment

This normally involves the use of anthelmintics (see Table 1.4). If secondary bacterial infection is suspected then broad spectrum antibiotics should be given. It should be remembered that anthelmintics such as thiabendazole, thiophanate, parbendazole and oxibendazole have little activity against lungworm.

When using an anthelmintic there has been some argument as to the most efficacious type in terms of possible effects after use. It has been found that some animals die soon after the use of wormers. It has been suggested that a greater reaction occurred following the death of the helminths (e.g. oxfendazole, fenbandazole and albendazole) than occurred where the worms were paralysed (e.g. levamisole) (Oakley, 1982). It appears that epithelisation is more marked with fenbendazole and obstructive bronchial lesions are more common with levamisole (Jarrett, Urquhart and Bairden, 1980). It would thus appear that a reaction can occur with compounds which paralyse the helminths as much as with those that kill them. The degree of damage depends on the stage of infection and it is always best to treat early.

When an outbreak occurs, the cattle should be removed from the infected pasture until healthy and until immunity has built up. Where this cannot be done, sequential anthelmintic treatment at 14-day intervals may help.

Control

There are at present no methods of control involving pasture management as can be undertaken with parasitic gastroenteritis. Once infection is on a farm, the only satisfactory method of control is the use of lungworm vaccination. The dose of 1,000 irradiated larvae is given orally. Two doses are given, one month apart, and turnout should not occur until two weeks after the second dose, i.e. six weeks after the first dose. The dose is for calves over two months old and this can delay the turnout of certain calves, especially those born in February. There is, however, no reason why, in some conditions, healthy calves should not receive the vaccine when under a month old. Suckler calves are usually drenched before going out to grass but may occasionally be dosed at grass. If any problems are present in the calves, e.g. latent enzootic pneumonia, these may be activated by the use of irradiated lungworm infection. Recently the monthly use of some anthelmintics, particularly ivermectin, has been advocated for control. Caution in their use is necessary as regular labour is required, parasitic drug resistance could result and unless serology is undertaken it will not be known when parasitic treatment can cease.

References

JARRETT, W F H, URQUHART, G M and BAIRDEN, K (1980) Veterinary Record 106, 135.

OAKLEY, G A (1982) Veterinary Record 111, 23-31.

TABLE 1.4

Anthelmintics for the Control of Parasitic Bronchitis

Compound	Preparation	Dose Rate mg/kg	Dose Rate mg/lb
Albendazole	Suspension, drench	7.5	3.8
Diethylcarbamazine citrate	Solution, injection, drench	90	45
Febantel	Suspension, drench	7.5	3.8
Fenbendazole	Suspension, drench	7.5	3.8
Ivermectin	Solution, injection	200 μg	100 μg
Levamisole	Solution, drench, pour-on, injection	7.5	3.8
Oxfendazole	Suspension, drench, injection	4.5	2.0

Coccidiosis

Aetiology

This is normally the result of Eimeria zurnii and E. bovis infestation.

Occurrence

Most cases occur in cattle under six months old, although infestation can be present up to one year or occasionally older. The disease usually results from overcrowding, with large numbers of calves feeding and drinking in small areas, and this allows faecal contamination of feed and water. Some outbreaks are associated with cold conditions. Disease can occur indoors or at grass. Morbidity is variable but usually is under 20 per cent and mortality is often very low, unless there is a sudden exposure to mass infestation.

Life cycle

Infestation with E. zurnii and E. bovis mainly occurs in the last part of the ileum, caecum and colon. Infestive oocysts contain sporocytes which in turn contain sporozoites. These are released by the digestive enzymes of the host and tend to enter the mucosa of the lower ileum. They undergo schizogony (asexual division) to produce merozoites which are contained within schizonts. These tend to enter cells of the caecum and colon and undergo second generation schizogony. This cycle appears to be self-limiting. The merozoites invade other cells and in turn they become male and female gametocytes. It is the production of merozoites and gametocytes which causes rupture and exfoliation of the epithelial cells and this produces the clinical signs. The conjugation of the male and female gametocytes produces the oocysts which are voided in the faeces, and this takes about 20 days from ingestion of E. zurnii oocysts.

Oocysts can sporulate if sufficient oxygen is present and there is a temperature of 12-32°C (54-90°F) and they can survive for up to two years. However, although they can resist freezing to -7 to -8°C (19-18°F) for two months, high or low temperatures and dry conditions are lethal in a few weeks (Marquardt, 1976). Disease only occurs if large numbers of oocysts are ingested and immunity following infestation is usually good.

Source of infestation

From feed or water contaminated by infested or carrier animals.

Entry of infestation

Oral.

Incubation period

16 - 30 days.

Signs

In most cases body temperature is normal but sometimes a mild fever up to 39°C (103°F) is found. Appetite tends to be decreased but anorexia is uncommon, the animals still tend to drink and so dehydration is mild. The duration of signs is about five to six days but often convalescence is long and associated with poor weight gain and appetite.

Acute

This has been reported in very cold weather in Canada and America (Julian, Harrison and Richardson, 1976). Up to 50 per cent of calves can be affected and mortality can be high (up to 90 per cent) with calves dying 24 hours to several days after the onset of signs. Animals tend to have a normal temperature, dysentery and nervous signs which include opisthotonus, medial strabismus, hypersensitivity, tetanic spasms, convulsions and ventral flexion of the neck. Some animals which survive a few days show mild opisthotonus and lateral recumbency. The origin of the nervous signs is debatable as it has not been reproduced experimentally. Prognosis is poor, even with treatment, when nervous signs are present.

Subacute

This is normally the clinical entity which is observed in practice. The animal shows slight depression, the first sign is of malodorous diarrhoea which may contain mucus or blood. The blood may be digested or fresh and there tends to be staining of the tail, buttocks and perineum. Tenesmus is often present and may lead to rectal prolapse.

Mild

In this form calves show poor weight gain or loss of weight and mild diarrhoea.

Chronic

These animals appear slightly ill and have poor weight gains.

Necropsy

Deaths can occur at three different times after infection (Stockdale, 1977). Those which died 18 - 20 days post infection had diarrhoea and dehydration, at 21 - 25 days after infection there was dysentery, dehydration and anaemia and animals dying over 25 days post infection became progressively weaker and debilitated. Lesions occur in the ileum, caecum, colon and rectum. There is congestion and haemorrhagic enteritis with blood-stained faeces in the large intestine and, in severe cases, sloughing of the mucosa is seen. Thickening of the mucosa occurs which results in ridging. Histologically there is desquamation of the epithelial cells, haemorrhage and various stages of coccidial development are seen in some of the remaining epithelial cells.

Diagnosis

1. There is a history of overcrowding or faecal contamination of the feed and water.
2. Diarrhoea is present, usually with evidence of blood and tenesmus.
3. Usually the outbreak involves only a few animals.
4. Faecal samples reveal more than 5,000 oocysts per gram of faeces.
5. Very occasionally nervous signs may be present but there is normal eyesight.

Differential diagnosis

1. Salmonellosis, but the animal is generally more ill.
2. Parasitic gastroenteritis but faecal egg count helps.
3. Haemonchosis but faecal egg count helps.

4. Bunostomiasis but faecal egg count helps.
5. Oesophagostomiasis - again faecal egg count.
6. Copper deficiency but area helps and blood sampling.
7. Cobalt deficiency but usually end of grazing season and blood vitamin B_{12} level helps.

Therapy

Therapy should be oral unless there are nervous signs or the presence or possibility of secondary bacterial infections of the alimentary or respiratory systems. Methods of treatment are given in Table 1.5. Sulphonamides work well, e.g. sulphadimidine or triple sulphonamides, as do other drugs such as amprolium and di-iodohydroxyquinoline. Response to therapy is variable, mainly because later stages of the life cycle (i.e. after days 13 - 15) are not susceptible to therapy.

TABLE 1.5

Treatment of Clinical Coccidiosis

Therapeutic Agent	Dose per kg/lb Body Weight		Duration
Amprolium	10 mg/kg	5 mg/lb	4-5 days
Di-iodohydroxyquinoline	22 mg/kg	11 mg/lb	2-3 days
Furazolidone	20 mg/kg	10 mg/lb	7 days
Sulphadimidine - initial dose	140 mg/kg	70 mg/lb	
- continuation dose	70 mg/kg	35 mg/lb	3-4 days
Triple sulphonamide			
- initial dose	140 mg/kg	70 mg/lb	
- continuation dose	70 mg/kg	35 mg/lb	4-7 days
(sulphadiazine, sulphamerazine, sulphapyridine)			

Control

Management

This can best be achieved by ensuring that overcrowding does not occur. Make sure that adequate bedding is provided and there is good drainage, whether the animals are inside or outside, and this particularly applies around feed and water areas. Troughs for feed and water should be high enough off the ground to prevent contamination. Feeding from the ground should be discouraged.

Chemotherapy

Preventive use of drugs should only be considered for in-contact animals during the course of an outbreak. It cannot be justified economically at other times and the results of treatment are variable depending on the stage of the life cycle present. Drugs are probably best used at the same level of dosage and duration as for treatment in the assumption that most calves will be infected at the time of the outbreak. Subsequent clinical cases are then treated individually. Various preventive therapy routines have been suggested and these are shown in Table 1.6 .

TABLE 1.6

Preventive Therapy for Coccidiosis

Therapeutic Agent (all in feed)	Dose per kg/lb Body Weight		Duration
Amprolium	5 mg/kg	2.5 mg/lb	21 days
Chlortetracycline and sulphadimidine	350 mg each drug per animal		35 days
Furazolidone	22 mg/kg	11 mg/lb	14 days
Monensin sodium	1 mg/kg	0.5 mg/lb	33 days
Sulphadimidine	35 mg/kg	17.5 mg/lb	15 days

(After Blood, Radostits and Henderson, 1983)

References

BLOOD, D C, RADOSTITS, O M and HENDERSON, J A (1983) 'Veterinary Medicine' 6th edition, Bailliere Tindall, London. p. 879-885.

JULIAN, R J, HARRISON, K B and RICHARDSON, J A (1976) Modern Veterinary Practice, 57, 711-719.

MARQUARDT, W C (1976) Journal of Protozoology, 23, 287-290.

STOCKDALE, P M G (1977) Canadian Journal of Comparative Medicine, 41, 338-344.

Tapeworm Infestation

Aetiology

Infestation of the small intestine with *Moniezia benedeni*.

Occurrence

Infestation can occur quite frequently but usually there are no clinical signs. Extremely heavy infestations are required before disease occurs in young cattle. When signs occur, they are usually due to the poor nutritional status of the young cattle as well as the large numbers of tapeworms present. Most cases of disease occur in animals under six months old.

Life cycle

The eggs are passed in the faeces either in proglottids or singly. The life cycle is indirect with the intermediate hosts being mites of the family *Oribatidae*. The mites are free-living and found in moist pastures where the herbage is long. They can survive about 14 months. The tapeworm egg is eaten by the mite and hatches in the intestine. The six-hooked embryo migrates into the body cavity of the host and becomes a cysticercoid in 3 to 5 months. The mites are accidentally ingested by the cattle. The tapeworms become fixed by the scolex to the intestinal wall and then remove nutrients from the gut as well as producing some toxic excretory products and altering the motility of the gut.

Signs

The most common sign is of proglottids in the faeces without any other signs. Most cases where infestation causes problems result in poor growth, and a dull, staring coat. Digestive signs are variable, usually with diarrhoea or constipation. However, occasionally there is dysentery and anaemia. Prolonged infestation can lead to the animal becoming pot-bellied and stunted.

Necropsy

In most cases the tapeworms are found in the small intestine, with an ulcer present at point of attachment of the scolex to the intestinal wall. In severely affected animals there is emaciation and anaemia.

Diagnosis

1. Proglottids (tapeworm segments) in the faeces.
2. Thick-walled embryonated egg present in faeces on microscopy.

Differential diagnosis

1. Parasitic gastroenteritis.
2. Coccidiosis.
3. Malnutrition.
4. Copper deficiency.
5. Cobalt deficiency.
6. Selenium deficiency.

Treatment

Several methods of treatment are available. Niclosamide at a dose rate of 75 mg/kg BW can be effective. In the past, dichlorophen at 500 mg/kg BW has been effective, as well as lead arsenate (0.5 - 1.5 g for growing cattle). Oxfendazole is specifically stated to be effective against Moniezia spp. in cattle, although other benzimidazoles such as albendazole and fenbendazole state their efficacy for sheep infestations. Levamisole removes tapeworm segments but not the scolices and so is of limited value in treatment.

Control

Control would require removal of the intermediate host, which is impracticable. However, improvement of pasture will tend to reduce suitable mite habitats.

Coenuriasis

(Gid, Sturdy, Coenurosis)

Aetiology

Infestation with Coenurus cerebralis, the intermediate stage of the tapeworm Taenia multiceps, involving the brain or spinal cord.

Occurrence

The condition is uncommon and is seen much less frequently than in sheep. Most cases in Britain occur in the South West and Wales. Very occasionally prenatally-acquired infestation has occurred in newborn calves.

Life cycle

The life cycle is indirect and ruminants act as the intermediate host. The final host for T. multiceps is usually the dog. Eggs are passed in the dog's faeces. Once ingested by cattle, the eggs hatch in the small intestine and then they pass into the bloodstream. Only embryos which lodge in the central nervous system continue to survive and grow into the coenurid stage. The coenurus is usually about 5 cm (2") in diameter when full size and it may take six to eight months to reach this.

Signs

These are very variable.

Migratory phase

A few affected cattle may show convulsions and signs of frenzy. Occasionally there may be sudden death.

Pressure phase - Brain

With increased pressure on the nervous tissue there may be head pressing, dullness, incomplete mastication and occasional epileptiform convulsions. There may be unilateral blindness, head deviation and circling. Papilloedema may be present. In young cattle there may be local softening of the cranium which may allow the cyst to be lost. Death occurs after several months.

Pressure phase - Spinal cord

Developing cysts cause a progressive paresis and eventually the animal cannot rise.

Necropsy

Brain

The fluid-filled C. cerebralis cyst can occur anywhere on the brain surface and there is pressure atrophy of the nervous tissue and in some cases the bone. The most common areas of the brain to be affected are the cerebral hemispheres.

Spinal cord

The cyst is most commonly in the lumbar region but a few cases involve the cervical area. There is often local pressure atrophy of the cord.

Diagnosis

1. Area of Britain.
2. Signs of progressive lesions.
3. Haemagglutination test.
4. Skin allergy test.

Differential diagnosis

1. Encephalitis.
2. Brain abscess.
3. Brain tumour.
4. Brain haemorrhage.

Treatment

The animal can usually be slaughtered. Others can have the cyst removed or drained.

Control

This depends on the routine worming of all dogs likely to come into contact with cattle or sheep. Suitable drugs include bunamidine hydrochloride, fenbendazole, niclosamide, nitroscanate, praziquantel. Usually quarterly worming is advocated. Dogs should not be given uncooked offal.

Cysticercosis

(*Cysticercus bovis*)

Aetiology

The intermediate stage of the human tapeworm *Taenia saginata*.

Occurrence

The condition is only occasionally seen in cattle. Reports have also sometimes involved sheep and goats. However, small outbreaks have occurred following the use of treated human sludge on grazing land, as well as where fields adjoin camping sites, caravan camps, road lay-bys, etc. Following infestation, a strong immunity tends to develop in cattle. The condition is only of importance in trying to break the life cycle for human infestation. The worm inhabits the small intestine of man, where it can be 4 to 15 metres in length (12 to 45 feet). The gravid segments are 16 to 20 mm long and 4 to 7 mm wide but they each contain about 100,000 eggs.

Life cycle

The gravid segments are passed in the faeces and the proglottid wall may disintegrate, allowing release of the eggs. The eggs can remain viable about five months on pasture, a month in river water, two months in liquid sludge and half a month in concentrate sludge. Once ingested by cattle, the hexacanth embryo hatches in the small intestine and penetrates the gut wall to enter the bloodstream. It is then carried to various parts of the body. Embryos which lodge in the muscle and, in some cases, other organs, develop into opalescent, milk-white cysticercie, *C. bovis*. The bladder worm is oval or round and 7.5 to 9 mm long by 5.5 mm wide, and it is usually found in the connective tissue capsule of muscle. About 18 weeks are required for complete development in cattle, although it can be infective to humans somewhat earlier than this. The infestation in cattle is known as "beef measles" and can usually be detected six weeks after infestation. Any muscles can be infested but often the cysticerci are present in the mandibular and heart muscles, and in some cases the diaphragm and shoulder. The oesophageal muscles are a favourite site. In some cases the intermediate stage may be present in the fat. The cysticerci die about a year after their development, become calcified and eventually disappear.

Signs

No signs are present in cattle. It is, however, of zoonotic importance.

Necropsy

C. bovis is detected in one or more muscles of the animal.

Diagnosis

Post mortem findings.

Treatment

At present there is no effective method of diagnosis in the live animal and so treatment is not feasible.

Prevention

Ensure that cattle do not graze in areas likely to have been contaminated by human sludge. Badly infested carcases are condemned at meat inspection. However, if only a few cysts are present, suggesting that the infestation is localised, then the carcase can be refridgerated at a temperature not more than -6.5°C (20°F) for three weeks or not more than -10°C (14°F) for two weeks and then released for consumption.

Cysticercus tenuicollis Infestation

Aetiology

The intermediate stage of *Taenia hydatigena*.

Occurrence

This condition is very uncommon in cattle but it occurs more frequently in sheep and goats. The final stage is found in the small intestine of dogs, pine martens, stoats, weasels, polecats and other wild carnivora. The adult worm is 75 to 500 cm (30 to 200 in) long, with the gravid segments being 10 to 14 mm long and 4.7 mm wide.

Life cycle

The proglottids are passed in the faeces and the gravid segment walls then often disintegrate. The hexocanth embryos hatch in the small intestine, pass through the gut wall and then enter the bloodstream. They reach the liver and break out of the portal vessels. Some embryos pass into the posterior vena vaca and they may be transported to other organs. In the liver the embryos burrow through the hepatic parenchyma, reaching the liver surface in three to four weeks. At that time, the embryos are 8.5 mm long by 5 mm wide and they then enter the peritoneal cavity. The scolex at this time is not completely developed but once in the peritoneal cavity, the invaginated head matures within a vesicle of 5 cm (2 in) diameter, containing a watery fluid. *C. tenuicollis* can be found anywhere within the abdominal cavity. The cysticercus is then ingested by the final host.

Signs

In cattle there are no signs. It is of some public health importance.

Necropsy

The liver, during the embryo passage, tends to develop dark red foci and streaks in the hepatic parenchyma. In some cases the liver surface is uneven. In others, the liver is fragile and immature embryos are present in the organ. In the abdomen, the characteristic *C. tenuicollis* may be found.

Diagnosis

Post mortem signs.

Treatment

There is no treatment for cattle, but dogs can be given appropriate therapy (see Table 1.7).

Prevention

Ensure all infested parts of offal are condemned and that dogs only receive cooked offal.

TABLE 1.7

Some Anthelmintics Effective against *Taenia hydatigena* in the Dog

Bunamidine	Niclosamide
Dichlorophen	Nitroscanate
Fenbendazole	Praziquantel
Mebendazole	

Hydatid Disease

Aetiology

This is caused by a minute (2-5 mm) worm whose eggs are found in the faeces of dogs. The worm is known as *Echinococcus granulosus* and there are two strains, a horse strain, *Echinococcus granulosus equinus*, and a sheep strain, *Echinococcus granulosus granulosus*.

Occurrence

The worm is particularly found in dogs in mid-Wales (i.e. Dyfed and Powys) where the prevalence is 25 *per cent* of farm dogs. It is also present in farm dogs in other parts of Wales, the Lake and Peak Districts and parts of Western Scotland. It is not found in farm dogs on the eastern side of England and rarely is it seen in dogs living in cities.

Life cycle

The dog is the main host. Although foxes can be infected, there are usually only a few worms present. Eggs passed in the faeces of dogs are eaten by cattle or sheep. The hydatid cysts tend to form in the liver or lungs. Consumption of the infested offal by dogs completes the life cycle.

Sheep strain

The Ministry of Agriculture, Fisheries and Food obtains returns of partial and total condemnations of meat and offal at meat inspection. At present hydatid disease is the most common cause of condemnation of sheep. It occasionally occurs in cattle.

TABLE 1.8

Condemnation Rates for Hydatid Disease (Sheep)

Year	No. of Offals Condemned	Percentage
1969	39,385	3.32
1970	41,171	3.39
1971	39,126	2.95
1972	33,957	2.58
1973	30,274	2.26
1974	32,585	2.37
1975	50,113	3.28
1976	39,997	2.83
1977	34,003	2.41
1978	44,640	3.56

A special study of the condemnation returns for one quarter in 1978 involving eight Welsh abattoirs gave an overall percentage of 3.68 and individual variation of 0 - 11.66 *per cent*. In a similar period, no hydatid cysts were found in nine abattoirs in Eastern Europe.

Signs

These are usually nil in the live animal. Infestation is detected at slaughter.

Human Infestations

These are hard to quantify but a few cases are confirmed annually. Some years ago in Scotland 17 children within a small area had hydatid cysts. About 50 years ago, one in five Icelanders was affected but today human disease is virtually unknown. In humans, the hydatid cyst bladder may rupture into the peritoneal cavity, producing daughter cysts up to 50 in number and containing many litres of fluid. This may result in a distended abdomen. Treatment is surgical or by therapy.

Control

It is not possible to treat the hydatid cyst in cattle or sheep satisfactorily at present. Control is by adequate worming of dogs with appropriate wormers, and the detection of hydatid cysts at slaughter with their subsequent condemnation and destruction. Suitable preparations for dogs include bunamidine hydrochloride, nitroscanate, mebendazole and praziquantel.

CHAPTER 2

ALIMENTARY CONDITIONS

Abomasal Erosion and Ulceration

Aetiology

The cause of these conditions is not understood, except in specific disease conditions such as mucosal disease and bovine malignant catarrh.

Occurrence

Abomasal erosions and ulcers are relatively common, but there are no clinical signs with erosions and most ulcers are not diagnosed. Cases can occur at any age but reach their peak at two to four months old. They are often seen in calves around the time of weaning but they are common in veal calves, particularly those which have had access to roughage. In some ulcers there is often an association with the presence of hair balls, or calves which have pica. Acute cases have been seen in two to four-month old suckler calves with their dams at grass in the summer (Blood *et al*, 1983). In most cases, however, when the condition occurs around weaning, it is possibly associated with the provision of poor quality roughage or too-rapid weaning of a calf which is not eating enough solid feed, or to nutritional or digestive deficiencies. Ulcers have been related to infection in other organs with *Corynebacterium pyogenes*, *Fusiformis necrophorus* or *Pasteurella multocida*. In some ulcers, fungal mycelia are present.

Signs

Peracute

There is sudden death following perforation of a haemorrhagic ulcer.

Acute

In these cases there is usually haemorrhage which results in a dull animal with a fast heart rate (100-plus beats per minute) and pale mucous membranes. Abdominal pain is usually evident with an arched back, and there is usually melaena present. Animals with severe haemorrhage may die in 24 hours.

Subacute

The signs are less marked, but there is usually some dullness, and increased pulse, pale mucous membranes and loud heart sounds. Melaena is usually present. In this case, although the animal may die, many recover.

Chronic

There are few signs present except perhaps mild irritance after eating, particularly if still on a milk substitute diet. The faeces may be slightly darker than usual, but in others they are normal. There may be occult blood present in the stool. This syndrome merges with:-

Subclinical

Where no signs are present, but an ulcer is incidentally found after slaughter. This would appear to be the most common form of the condition.

Necropsy

The ulcers can be very small or up to 7.5 cm (3 in) in length and they are usually in the ventral fundic region of the abomasum. The ulceration is generally well-defined and, in severe cases, there may be a very thickened abomasal wall. The surface of the ulcer may be covered with blood or a necrotic membrane. In some cases fungal hyphae are found in the ulcer. If perforation has occurred, adhesions with the surrounding viscera may be apparent and, in cases of haemorrhage, an eroded blood vessel may be seen.

Diagnosis

1. If malaena is present then this is almost pathognomonic.
2. Signs of abdominal pain and loss of condition are helpful.
3. Occult blood should be tested for in the faeces.
4. If there has been perforation then there is normally a leucocytosis.
5. In some cases a neutrophilia and shift to the left are present.

Differential diagnosis

The main problem is diagnosis in the animal which is not growing well, but is not showing any other marked signs.

1. Chronic diarrhoea, but this should be obvious from the history.
2. Chronic respiratory disease should again be obvious.
3. Selenium/vitamin E deficiency but in such cases the area of the country where seen will be helpful, plus the determination of blood glutathione peroxidase and vitamin E levels.
4. Cobalt deficiency.
5. Copper deficiency.

Treatment

In bad cases the use of coagulants such as oxalic or malonic acids may assist. Blood transfusions can be helpful. Treatment is otherwise conservative and consists of the use of gastric sedatives and antacids. The use of kaolin and pectin at 1 ml/kg BW may be helpful, as also might up to 16g (½ oz) of magnesium trisilicate or 1-2 mg/kg BW of magnesium oxide, or up to 16g (½ oz) magnesium carbonate.

Control

As the aetiology is uncertain, no firm guidance on control can be offered. However, as the condition often occurs clinically around weaning, it could possibly be of use to ensure that all milk substitutes are of good quality and contain adequate amounts of all nutritional constituents so as to prevent any deficiencies. All roughages must be of good quality and sufficient in quantity. The calf should not be weaned until sufficient concentrate is being consumed.

Reference

BLOOD, D C, RADOSTITS, O M and HENDERSON, J A (1983) 'Veterinary Medicine' 6th edition, Bailliere Tindall, London. pp. 257-259.

Actinobacillosis

Also known as wooden tongue as this is the organ most commonly infected.

Aetiology

Infection with the bacterium *Actinobacillus lignierisi* (small Gram-negative rods).

Occurrence

The condition is not uncommon but there is a distinct impression that infection with the organism has reduced during the last few years. *A. lignierisi* is an aerobic organism but it grows best in the presence of 10 *per cent* carbon dioxide. The bacterium is killed by sunlight, disinfectants, etc. It can survive several days on hay or straw. Infection is by the ingestion of the organism in contaminated feed or pasture. The organism can quite often be isolated from the skin or mucous membranes of healthy animals. *A. lignierisi* can infect man, sheep and other animals. Although infection can occur in the calf, it is seen most commonly in the older animal. Infection involves an inflammation with production of a granulomatous lesion containing necrosis and suppuration. There is often spread to the regional lymph nodes.

Signs

The signs depend on the location of the infection.

Lingual - Acute

Most cases involve the tongue and the organism causes it to become swollen, hard and painful. This in turn interferes with prehension and leads to a loss of appetite with excess salivation. Some cattle show chewing movements and manipulation of the tongue is resented. The tongue is particularly hard towards its base and the side of it often shows an ulcer or nodule.

Lingual - Chronic

Following the acute stage the tongue becomes shrunken, contains fibrous tissue and loses its mobility. Thick pus may exude from sinuses on the sides of the tongue.

Lymph Node

Enlargement of the lymph nodes may be related to tongue infection or be independent. In cases involving lingual infection, the parotid and submaxillary lymph nodes may become enlarged and firm. Sometimes the lymph nodes rupture discharging a thin pus. The retropharyngeal lymph nodes may become infected, resulting in a snoring respiration and making swallowing difficult.

Skin

Large cutaneous lesions can occur on the sides of the face, limbs, thorax and abdomen. They are thick and granulomatous and they may discharge pus. Swelling of the lymph ducts and nodes may also be present.

Mouth

Lesions can occur in the mouth without affecting the tongue and these can be associated with skin infection.

Viscera

Occasionally there is infection of the oesophageal groove, or the caudal part of the oesophagus or cranial wall of the reticulum. This may lead to intermittent bloat, indigestion and intermittent diarrhoea.

Necropsy

There are usually indurated granulomas of variable size in one or more sites such as the tongue, skin, oesophagus or reticulum. The surface of the lesions may be ulcerated and contain a sinus tract discharging green-yellow pus. The mandibular, parotid, suprapharyngeal or anterior cervical lymph nodes may be involved.

Diagnosis

1. Usually the tongue is involved, causing salivation, anorexia, chewing movements.
2. There may be enlarged lymph nodes.
3. One or more nodules may discharge pus which contains A. lignierisi.

Differential diagnosis

1. Tuberculosis but usually history will help plus tuberculin test.
2. Sporadic bovine leukosis but a needle puncture of lymph node reveals pus.
3. Enzootic bovine leukosis but again a needle puncture should help, then maybe a lymphocytosis and agar gel immunodiffusion test will help.
4. Foot-and-mouth disease but many vesicles in mouth, the tongue is not hard and a marked pyrexia is present.
5. Foreign body in mouth but then no lesion on tongue and the object should be visible if mouth properly examined.
6. Calf diphtheria but usually the ulcerative lesions greater and the animal younger.

Treatment

Often penicillin (5,000-10,000 units/kg; 2,500-5,000 units/lb BW) or streptomycin (5 g daily for three days) parenterally or sulphonamide (1 g/7 kg (15 lb) BW for 4 to 5 days) orally are useful. Potassium iodide has been used in the past and still may be helpful in recalcitrant cases. Potassium iodide can be given orally at a daily dose of 6 to 10 g for seven days. Sodium iodide may be used intravenously at 1 g/12 kg (25 lb) BW once or repeated after 10 to 14 days. Iodine toxicity can result and should this occur, iodine therapy should be stopped. The signs are described on page 272. The cutaneous form of the disease is often resistant to treatment. When successful therapy has been undertaken there is always the possibility of a relapse and so affected animals should be slaughtered at a convenient time.

Prevention

Any infected animal should be isolated. Always treat such cattle adequately and then slaughter once recovered.

Actinomycosis

This infection is also known as lumpy jaw.

Aetiology

Infection with Actinomyces bovis (Gram-positive bacteria of various shapes including coccoid rods, filaments, branching forms, club-shaped forms and spiral elements).

Occurrence

The condition is not uncommon but is rarer than actinobacillosis and again appears to have decreased in frequency over the last few years. Act.bovis can produce osteomyelitis in man as well as disease in pigs and horses. The condition occurs most frequently between one and two years old but it can occur in younger or older animals. Infection is said to occur more frequently in Guernsey bulls. Act. bovis occurs as a natural inhabitant of cattle mouths. Infection often follows feeding abrasive, fibrous feeds, sharp objects or it can occur when temporary teeth are lost and the permanent teeth erupt. Most infection involves the maxilla, mandible or other bones of the head but it can infect soft tissues such as the reticulum, testicles, penis, brain and lung. There is no spread of infection to involve the local lymph nodes.

Route of Entry

Abrasions or wounds in the mouth, erupting teeth.

Signs

Bone

Most cases involve a unilateral immobile enlargement of the bone which is initially painless but later it is painful. The swelling normally involves the mandible in the mid-molar regions although the maxillae may be the site of infection. The swelling is usually discrete but it can be diffuse and sometimes involves the ventral edge of the mandible, thereby greatly reducing the intermandibular space. One or more sinuses may appear and discharge a sticky, honey-like pus containing yellow-white sulphur granules. The skin around the sinuses loses its hair. Teeth present in the affected area may be lost or become malaligned and this can lead to a painful mouth and difficulty in mastication. When the maxilla is involved it can impinge on the nasal cavities causing dyspnoea. In some cases of bone infection there is a spread to other soft tissues.

Soft Tissues

Infection can involve the oesophageal groove, caudal part of the oesophagus and wall of the reticulum. This can lead to chronic bloat and diarrhoea. Other organs have occasionally been infected, including the lungs, brain and testicles.

Necropsy

The dimensions of infected bones increase with bone rarefaction, with the presence of cavities and intercommunicating sinuses containing thick fibrous tissue and pus. Lesions may occur in the oesophagus, the caudal part of the oesophagus and wall of the reticulum and they tend to be granulomatous with pockets of pus present. There may be local areas of peritonitis.

Diagnosis

1. Signs, with a hard, immobile swelling of the bone.
2. If sinus present and pus discharging there are "sulphur granules" in it.
3. Bacteriology of smears reveals Gram-positive filaments.

Differential diagnosis

1. Cheek abscesses etc. are moveable and can be punctured with a needle to reveal pus.
2. Impaction of feed between the cheek teeth and the cheek.

Treatment

Injection with penicillin at a dose of 5,000 - 10,000 units/kg (2,500 - 5,000 units/lb) BW or streptomycin at 5 g per day for three days can be helpful. Sulphanilamide can be given orally for 4 to 5 days at a dose of 1 g per 7 kg (15 lb) BW.

Prevention

Infected cattle should be isolated from the herd until clear of the infection. In many cases it is best to consider subsequent slaughter of the animal as there is a possibility of relapse.

Antibiotic Contamination of Feed

Aetiology

One of several antibiotics or other antibacterial agents entering the feed and resulting in illness.

Occurrence

Several reports have been made of this condition during the last few years. Often it follows the use in the feed of lincomycin which is a common additive for pig feeds. Dimetridazole and tylosin have also been incriminated in a few cases. A carry-over rate of five per cent of a mixture of chlortetracycline, sulphadimidine and procaine penicillin has not been shown to upset cattle. Most problems have arisen in dairy cows which appear to be very sensitive to small quantities of the included contaminant. It is much less likely that any signs will appear in growing cattle and if they do occur, they tend to be less severe than in the adult cow.

Signs

There is usually dullness with a loss of appetite and ruminal stasis in a large number of animals at one time. The faeces tend to become sour in smell with a grey-green or brown-black diarrhoea. In milking cows a ketosis often develops.

Diagnosis

1. Sudden onset of the condition in many animals.
2. Presence of antibacterial agent in the feed.

Differential diagnosis

1. Salmonellosis.
2. Winter dysentery.
3. Mucosal disease.
4. Lead poisoning.
5. Arsenic poisoning.
6. Other poisonings.

Treatment

Remove the offending feed and place cattle on a bulk diet, preferably hay or straw, for 24 - 48 hours. Introduce concentrate feeding again slowly.

Prevention

Ensure thorough cleaning out of mills between batches of feed for different species.

Indigestion

Aetiology

There are many different causes, but frequent changes of feed can lead to the problem.

Occurrence

Indigestion is very common. It can result from overfeeding. Dietary content can also cause problems such as low protein intake, indigestible roughage (e.g. straw), mouldy feeds and sudden changes in the type of grain. Prolonged use of oral antibiotics or sulphonamides can reduce the ruminal flora and thereby cause indigestion. The reason for ruminal atony is hard to explain in many cases.

Signs

There is a reduced appetite or complete anorexia, with a mild depression. Ruminal movements stop or are decreased in number and amplitude and there is usually constipation. There can be moderate tympany. The temperature, pulse and respiratory rates are normal. No painful areas are found in the abdomen.

Necropsy

The condition is not fatal.

Diagnosis

1. History - a change in feed or unsatisfactory feeding.
2. Signs - digestive signs but no painful focus or pyrexia.

Differential diagnosis

1. Acidosis but history should help and heart rate increased.
2. Traumatic reticulitis but pyrexia.
3. Acetonaemia but usually in a recently-calved cow.

Treatment

Various stimulants can be used including mixtures of ginger, gentian, nux vomica, ammonium bicarbonate. Magnesium hydroxide can be used at the rate of 400 g (13 oz)/ 450 kg (1000 lb) cow. Epsom salts can be effective at 0.5 - 1 kg (1 - 2 lb) per cow and act as a mild purgative. Multi-vitamin injections and vitamin B_{12} have been used. Practitioners often use menbutone at 5 - 10 gm/kg BW (2.5 - 5 mg/lb BW) to act as a stimulant for secretory gland function.

Control

Ensure good quality feed is offered and all feeding changes are made slowly.

Liver Abscesses

Aetiology

The condition usually follows a rumenitis which in turn allows the entry of bacteria, usually *Fusiformis necrophorus*, to the liver.

Occurrence

The condition is very common in cereal beef cattle or others on a high cereal diet but usually no signs are apparent and the lesions are only seen at slaughter. Most cases follow a rumenitis which can result from a rapid change from a roughage to a high concentrate diet. The condition may be exacerbated if the cattle do not have roughage with a long fibre length. The ruminal epithelium becomes smooth and inflamed, allowing penetration by foreign bodies including hairs. This allows entry into the bloodstream of organisms, usually involving the anaerobic, Gram-negative rod, *F. necrophorus* (*Sphaerophorus necrophorus*), although sometimes *Corynebacterium pyogenes* are present and these enter the liver. A repeatedly low pH in the rumen tends to result in mucosal changes, parakeratosis and hyperkeratosis. The mucous membranes of the rumen and reticulum become thickened and hardened, particularly in the anterior ventral sac of the rumen. Organisms then penetrate via wounds and abrasions resulting from plant fibres, hairs and foreign bodies.

Morbidity

This may be up to 20 to 25 *per cent* of the cattle.

Signs

Acute

This is an unusual form and there is dullness, usually with abdominal pain, pyrexia - 105°F (40.5°C), anorexia, depression and weakness. The animal has an arched back and is usually reluctant to walk or lie down. The liver may be swollen and palpable in the right sublumbar fossa. There is often pain on percussion of the posterior right ribs. These signs may then pass into a chronic phase with wasting, a reduction in appetite, and intermittent digestive disturbances resulting in periods of constipation or diarrhoea. A few cases may die.

Chronic

Most cattle liver abscesses are of this type and there are no clinical signs although lesions are detected at slaughter.

Necropsy

There may be local or diffuse lesions of the anterior ventral part of the reticulo-rumen with thickening of the wall, depigmentation, ulceration, loss of papillae and the possible presence of granulation tissue. The liver abscesses are variable. There are usually several, although occasionally one large one is seen.

Diagnosis

1. In the live animal this is extremely difficult unless acute signs are present.

2. Signs - liver palpable, pain in right posterior rib region.
3. Haematology - leucocytosis, neutrophilia.
4. Liver function tests may be of use in those animals showing signs.

Differential diagnosis

1. Traumatic reticulitis but usually there is no ruminal stasis with an abscess and the site of pain is different.
2. Traumatic hepatitis unusual - history will help, but may require an exploratory laparotomy to confirm.

Treatment

If an acute case is detected, a sustained course of antibacterials may be useful, such as oxytetracycline, 2-5 mg/kg BW (1-3 mg/lb BW) for 3 to 5 days, sulphadimidine, either orally (1 g/7 kg BW; 0.25 oz/100 lb) or by injection 15-30 ml/50 kg BW (15-30 ml/110 lb BW) of a 33.3 per cent solution, sulphamethoxypyridazine 22 mg/kg BW (10 mg/lb BW) daily or sulphapyrazole 30 - 60 mg/kg BW (15 - 30 mg/lb BW).

Control

The condition occurs because of a lack of long fibre roughage. Provision of at least 1 kg (2 lb) hay or straw daily should overcome the problem or if it is not possible to feed from racks, etc. then 2 kg (4½ lb) of straw bedding, preferably barley straw, should be used daily.

Malignant Catarrhal Fever

(Bovine Malignant Catarrh)

Aetiology

The cause is probably a herpes virus which is very fragile and difficult to isolate.

Occurrence

The condition is very uncommon but occasionally cases occur in cattle. Usually individual animals are affected but recently a possible outbreak has been described (Foster, 1983). Sheep and wildebeeste have inapparent infection and deer are also affected. Usually the cattle have been associated with sheep or deer. The virus is very labile but can survive a few days in citrated blood at 5°C (40°F) and so it is perhaps possible to transmit infection by blood. Lymph node suspensions lose infection quickly at -20°C (-4°F) but when preserved in serum and glycerol at -7°C (20°F) then infections survives for 15 months. Culture of the virus is extremely difficult, making definite diagnosis hard. The virus can initially be cultured in calf thyroid glands and it will then grow in other calf cells producing a cytopathic effect of syncytia with eosinophilic intranuclear inclusions. As the virus is cell-associated, initial passages are with intact cells.

Following infection there is an eclipse phase of 9 to 17 days before the virus is in the blood and viraemia continues until death. After a further 3 to 15 days clinical signs develop. Death occurs 5 to 10 days after illness starts. The disease in cattle is not apparently contagious for other cattle.

Portal of entry

Inhalation or possibly blood transfusions.

Incubation period

34 to 38 days.

Signs

Cases are sporadic. Animals are very ill with anorexia, pyrexia - 40.5 - 41.5°C (105 - 107°F), extreme depression and marked loss of condition. An early pathognomonic sign is an intense scleral congestion with keratitis starting at the edge of the sclera which spreads and mainly involves the whole cornea of both eyes, causing blindness. Early lesions also involve the buccal mucosa. There is reddening of the lips, gingivae and muzzle. Erosions develop, including necrosis of the tips of the labial papillae at the corners of the mouth and on the hard palate.

Other signs vary but they can include nervous signs such as excitement, muscle tremors and hyperaesthesia. The superficial lymph nodes are grossly enlarged. Often the head and eyes are involved with keratitis and hypopyon. There is profuse mucopurulent ocular nasal discharge, which tends to accumulate and encrust around the nostrils and eyes. There is often excessive salivation and this is followed by dyspnoea and stertor due to accumulation of exudates. There tends to be a considerable variation in the faeces between profuse diarrhoea and soft, scanty faeces.

At later stages more prominent nervous signs may be present such as incoordination, leg weakness and nystagmus followed finally, in some cases, by head pressing, convulsions or paralysis.

Necropsy

Lesions occur in many parts of the body including the upper respiratory tract, nares, oropharynx, vocal cords, trachea; the alimentary tract, muzzle, oesophagus, fore stomach and gastrointestinal tract, as well as the kidney, pelvis, ureter or bladder. There are lesions including varying degrees of haemorrhage, hyperaemia or erythema and discrete or extensive erosions. The eye shows scleral congestion and keratitis. The lymph nodes show marked superficial enlargement. The skin around the coronets may show lesions. Histologically the epidermis shows extensive hydropic degeneration and vesicle formation with rupture. The dermis shows vasculitis with proliferation and necrosis and marked lymphoid cuffing.

Diagnosis

1. History - contact with sheep or deer, usually single animals.
2. Signs - nervous signs, lymph node enlargement, scleral congestion, corneal opacity, diffuse mucosal erosion.
3. Necropsy - histological vasculitis.
4. Haematology - leucopaenia.
5. Serology - serum neutralisation test may be of use.
6. Viral isolation - take blood and transfer to other cattle.

Differential diagnosis

1. Mucosal disease - ocular lesions not severe, no lymph node enlargement or encephalitis.
2. Rinderpest - herd problem, no severe ocular lesions, no lymph node enlargement or encephalitis. Diarrhoea and dysentery not often main signs.
3. IBR - usually several animals affected, mainly respiratory signs.
4. Foot-and-mouth disease - herd problem.
5. Calf diphtheria - no ocular involvement or lesions of buccal mucosa other than a necrotic local area.

Treatment

None.

Control

Separate infected animals from others. Cattle should not be grazed with sheep, particularly at the time of lambing. Where farms buy-in sheep, they should not be from areas where disease has occurred.

Reference

FOSTER, P D (1983) Veterinary Record, 113, 477.

Mucosal Disease

Aetiology

This is also known as bovine viral diarrhoea (BVD) and is caused by a togavirus of the genus Pestivirus, which is related to the border disease virus of sheep and the swine fever virus.

Occurrence

Clinical disease is not common although the virus is widespread in Britain with about 60 per cent of cattle having serological evidence of past infection. Originally BVD and mucosal disease were thought to be separate entities. Thus BVD had a high morbidity and low mortality and was described initially in the USA, whereas mucosal disease had a low morbidity but a high mortality. However, these differences are really epidemiological and clinical and the aetiological agent appears the same.

Mucosal disease is often considered to be the result of immunotolerance usually established as a result of intrauterine infection. The infection can cross the placental barrier and infect the conceptus. Acute disease is normally seen between six and 18 months but it can occur in calves as well as adult cattle. Sporadic chronic cases are seen in animals from one to several years old. The virus tends to be immunosuppressant. Calves which become infected are born to dams which are immunologically unresponsive or immunosuppressed. However, most cows pass on sufficient antibody in their colostrum to last 3½ to 7½ months. Occasionally levels will persist for 13 months. Thus usually individual animals become susceptible to infection at varying ages, they are then exposed to natural infection and develop immunity without showing clinical signs. Recently it has been hypothesised that induction of mucosal disease infection follows superinfection with cytopathic virus of animals which have previously become persistently infected with non-cytopathic virus following *in utero* infection (Brownlie, Clarke and Howard, 1984). These cattle can become potent sources of infection. The majority of infection in the animals is subclinical. However, if an animal is pregnant then transplacental infection occurs easily. Congenital infection occurs in foetuses up to 80 days' gestation and mortality in persistently infected foetuses and calves is high, but some survive. Persistent infection becomes less common after 100 days' gestation but can still be found after 125 days of pregnancy. Foetuses infected in early pregnancy are immunotolerant whereas those affected in mid-gestation show an immune response.

Although cases occur in housed animals and those at pasture, there is a higher incidence in the winter. Occasionally outbreaks occur in closed herds with up to a quarter of the calves and other cattle showing signs. Usually only one age group of animals is affected and often a similar situation develops every three or more years. In dairy herds where cattle are often bought-in or in beef herds, then only sporadic cases occur. In beef suckler calves disease often occurs at about six to 10 months and a few weeks after weaning. Morbidity is usually low at about five per cent but occasionally, if infection enters unexposed herds, it can reach 90 per cent. Mortality tends to be high in cattle showing acute signs (90-100 per cent) but overall infection is subclinical and mortality is very low.

Incubation period

This varies from one to three weeks.

Portal of entry

It is usually the mouth, but intrauterine infection can occur from semen.

Source of infection

Introduction to a herd is usually by buying-in a persistently infected animal or a cow pregnant with an infected foetus. Other ruminants can also become persistently infected. Infection can be transferred by hypodermic needle, removal of foremilk, in the semen and by ovum transplantation of infected ova.

Once present in a herd, the source of infection can be contaminated faeces but occasionally nasal exudate or urine spread infection. Corticosteroid injections may cause the onset of signs in a carrier animal. Herd infection can be the result of a persistently infected cow or a carrier animal.

Signs

Acute

Experimentally the infection produces a biphasic temperature rise. However, the initial rise to 40°C (104°F) is often missed and there is a depression of the leucocyte count by 50 per cent. The second rise is usually the first to be detected with a rectal temperature of 40.5-41°C (105-106°F), with anorexia, marked depression and wetting of the lips and muzzle due to saliva retained in the mouth, possibly because swallowing causes discomfort. Diarrhoea often occurs which is watery, foul-smelling, profuse and may occasionally contain blood or mucus. Mouth lesions vary but may be diffuse, involving any part of the oropharynx. Vesicles are not seen but the mucosa shows diffuse hyperaemia with small, irregularly-shaped weals appearing. Those present on the tongue tend to be arranged transversely and they may be deeper than those elsewhere with a well-defined border. Handling of the tongue is resented. Ulcers elsewhere often coalesce and become covered by a thin, pale-yellow or grey covering.

Signs in the respiratory system tend to be few but often the nostrils have a purulent or mucopurulent discharge. Ulcerations may develop in the rhinarium or nares. There is usually a keratoconjunctivitis with mucopurulent ocular discharge. In some cases there is ulceration of the skin of the interdigital cleft causing lameness. The hoof horn is occasionally underrun and there can be laminitis. Long-standing cases may show a thickening of the coronary band and hoof ridging, suggesting an association with laminitis.

Subacute

Some cases survive but do not completely recover. They then tend to develop periodic bouts of inappetance, diarrhoea, progressive emaciation, and a dry and rough coat. Chronic erosions may be present in the mouth and on the skin and occasionally intermittent bloat occurs. Erosions can occur in other parts of the body such as the interdigital cleft, heels, close to the dew claws, skin-horn junction, perineum, scrotum, prepucial orifice and vulva. Often secondary infection occurs, resulting in pneumonia or other serious complications.

Chronic

These cases may show a thickening of the coronary band and hoof ridging from previous laminitis. There is often recurrent diarrhoea and a slowly progressive loss of condition with a poor coat. Many of these cattle ultimately die although surviving for long periods, often over a year, with anaemia, neutropaenia, leucopaenia and lymphopaenia, i.e. pancytopaenia.

Congenital deformities

Pregnant cows can show a variety of disorders in their calves. Infection at about one-third of the gestation period results in about a third of cows aborting or having stillbirths, and two-thirds producing live calves with growth retardation plus, in some cases, other abnormalities (Done, Terlecki, Richardson, Harkness, Sands, Patterson, Sweasey, Shaw, Winkler and Duffell, 1980). Defects include cerebellar agenesis, ocular agenesis, brachygnathism, musculo-skeletal deformities, etc. In advanced pregnancy there is much less likelihood of persistent infection of the progeny. Persistently-infected cows can often subsequently produce persistently-infected calves.

Abortion

Up to a third of pregnant cows may abort and mucosal disease is a common cause of diagnosed abortions.

Necropsy

Acute

Ulcers may be present in the mouth and rhinarium and interdigital cleft. Any part of the alimentary tract may be involved, but brown, longitudinally-arranged shallow ulcers of the oesophagus are characteristic. If bloat has occurred, often there are some irregularly-shaped ulcers in the rumen. Multiple, haemorrhagic peptic ulcers of the abomasum occur frequently with oedema. Erythema, haemorrhages and oedema occur to a lesser extent in the small intestine. In the large intestine there is often superficial ulceration with mucous membrane desquamation.

Histologically there is a micro-vesicle resulting in erosions. The vesicles rupture to form an irregular, shallow ulcer. The area is colonised by polymorphonuclear leucocytes and occasionally bacteria. There is remarkably little inflammatory response around local lesions.

Subacute

These animals may only show a few ulcers or erosions in the mouth and oesophagus.

Chronic

Necrotic epithelium may persist as slightly raised, friable plaques. Often these plaques occur between the villi of the tongue and rumen.

Congenital

There may be cerebellar hypoplasia or agenesis, ocular agenesis, cataracts, retinal degeneration, optic nerve neuritis or hypoplasia. Most nervous system lesions are due to dysmyelination.

Diagnosis

Often typical lesions are not present and in such cases diagnosis is very hard to make.

1. History - age of animals - six to 24 months, sporadic unless a closed herd.
2. Lesions - erosions of the mucosa, diarrhoea, congenital deformities.
3. Necropsy - erosions in one or more parts of the alimentary tract.
4. Presence of viral antigen by immunofluorescent staining of antigen cells in nasopharynx. (Use a brush swab and transport in 5 ml of Eagle's minimal essential medium supplemented at 10 *per cent* BVD-MD virus - and antibody-free foetal calf serum and antibiotics (Roeder and Drew, 1984).
5. Presence of virus in faeces (should be kept on ice during transport as some strains heat-labile).
6. Presence of virus in blood (as a long viraemia - transport on ice).
7. Leucopaenia often present with a depression by about 50 *per cent*.

8. Serology - various tests undertaken including serum neutralisation (test most commonly performed), agar gel, complement fixation, immunofluorescence test (this gives a quick answer). However, as the virus tends to be immunosuppressive, paired samples are required at least 3 to 4 weeks apart with the first collection taken early in the disease. All the serological tests have advantages and disadvantages and at present no one test gives definitive results in all cases.

9. Necropsy - helpful but often the classic picture is not seen. Lesions of the mucous membranes of the intestinal tract, mesenteric lymph nodes, pancreas or other tissue can be subjected to fluorescent antibody or agar gel diffusion testing.

10. The histological signs with micro-vesicles, ulcers and little inflammatory response are indicative but not pathognomonic.

Differential diagnosis

1. Rinderpest - widespread alimentary disturbance of all age groups. Not present in Britain.

2. Malignant catarrhal fever, usually association with sheep or deer. Usually only one animal affected. Signs tend to be more severe with an erosive stomatitis, loss of labial papillae, erosive gastroenteritis, severe hyperaemia, corneal opacity, lymph node enlargement and sometimes nervous signs.

3. Foot-and-mouth disease - more animals of different ages affected. Salivation is greater.

4. Winter dysentery - usually older animals.

5. Salmonellosis - faecal culture.

6. Johne's disease - usually older animals and a herd history.

7. Copper deficiency - farm history, animals usually grazing, blood sampling helps.

8. Parasitic gastroenteritis - faecal egg count, and plasma pepsinogen levels help.

9. Molybdenum poisoning - again area and low blood copper levels.

10. Arsenic poisoning - history, signs of abdominal pain, arsenic in urine in live animals.

Treatment

Infected cattle are best isolated. There is no specific therapy but supportive treatment with alimentary astringents may assist, such as chalk, kaolin or chlorodyne. Parenteral injections of electrolytes can also help. Recently intravenous injections of whole blood from recovered animals have appeared to help some animals to recover and in young cattle this can be supplemented with colostrum orally. Otherwise, in cases with profuse, watery diarrhoea, slaughter is best. Chronic cases should be destroyed.

Control

Once infection occurs, all in-contacts should be checked for oral or foot lesions or diarrhoea. In a closed herd without mucosal disease present in it, introduction of cattle should be discouraged. If animals must be introduced they should be checked for the presence of virus in nasopharyngeal swabs. Only cattle with a negative result and which are negative on serology should be introduced. Such cattle should perhaps be injected with a corticosteroid and rechecked before entry to the farm. Once on the farm the animals should be retested for virus and by serology. In herds with infection present, problems can arise from buying-in non-exposed infected cattle. These are usually seronegative and so only animals with a positive titre to mucosal disease should be introduced to the herd.

Vaccination is used in many parts of the world. The only vaccine available in Britain is an inactivated combined vaccine for BVD, bovine parainfluenza II virus, bovine adenovirus 3, bovine reovirus 1, and infectious bovine rhinotracheitis virus. The vaccine is given intramuscularly twice with an interval of two to four weeks. Its use in outbreaks of disease in young stock is probably limited but it has been claimed to help in herds where the disease causes abortion.

References

BROWNLIE, J, CLARKE, M C and HOWARD, C J (1984) Veterinary Record, 114, 535-536.

DONE, J T, TERLECKI, S, RICHARDSON, C, HARKNESS, J W, SANDS, J J, PATTERSON, D S P, SWEASEY, D, SHAW, I G, WINKLER, C E and DUFFELL, S J (1980) Veterinary Record, 106, 473-479.

ROEDER, P L and DREW, T W (1984) Veterinary Record 114, 309-313.

Oral Necrobacillosis

This condition is also known as calf diphtheria.

Aetiology

A localised infection which involves the mouth or larynx and is caused by Fusiformis necrophorus (Gram-negative filaments, anaerobe).

Occurrence

The condition is relatively common. Most cases occur sporadically, but with bad hygiene, disease outbreaks can occur. Animals which have an intercurrent infection, nutritional deficiency or erupting their cheek teeth are more susceptible. The oral form is seen in calves up to about three months old, but the laryngeal form usually occurs in older calves or yearlings. F. necrophorus is ubiquitous in habitat so that cases can occur in suckler calves at pasture although most cases are in housed, bucket-fed animals.

Origin of infection

Contamination of feeding buckets, etc., and poor hygiene.

Portal of entry

Infection probably enters through abrasions.

Incubation period

This is not known because the disease is hard to reproduce experimentally, but it has been recorded in calves as early as four days old.

Signs

Laryngeal form

This is uncommon and usually only one animal is affected. The cow shows marked respiratory signs and it will usually die if left untreated. There is pyrexia 40.5°C (105°F), depression and inappetance leading to anorexia. There is stertor (an audible, snoring inspiratory sound) and respirations are dyspnoeic (laboured). The laryngeal region is very painful and this leads to pain on palpation. Saliva is held in the mouth to prevent it being swallowed which causes pain, and there is a moist, painful cough. The breath may be foul-smelling. In some cases infection spreads to the lungs and a pneumonia results. Death can be very sudden and is due to complete respiratory obstruction.

Necropsy

The mucous membrane of the affected area is sharply circumscribed, thickened due to oedema and necrotic with a dirty white colour, and is often firmly adherent to the underlying tissue. If the necrotic membrane sloughs, an ulcer is left. In the laryngeal form, besides the mucous membrane being affected, the cartilage may become involved. If there are lung lesions, they are dry or purulent necrotic areas surrounded by catarrhal pneumonia.

Diagnosis

The oral form is easy to diagnose but the laryngeal form is more difficult.

1. Site of lesions.
2. The presence of a smell.
3. A swab of the lesion should be taken for bacteriology.

Differential diagnosis

1. IBR.
2. Laryngeal oedema.
3. Laryngitis.
4. Vocal cord paralysis.

Therapy

Isolate the affected animal. In most cases therapy will be parenteral and suitable drugs include streptomycin, oxytetracycline, sulphadimidine orally or parenterally, chlortetracycline orally, or penicillin parenterally. If there is inappetance, oral or parenteral fluids may need to be administered. In the laryngeal form a tracheotomy may be required to assist respirations. Ensure in all cases of oral necrobacillosis that the feed is of good quality as intake may be reduced. Poor quality feed may initiate or exacerbate the lesions.

Prevention

The disease occurs as a problem in conditions of poor husbandry or where very coarse feeds are given. Improvement in the standard of hygiene will usually overcome the problem. Good quality roughage and concentrates only should be offered. Occasionally prophylactic oral feeding of oxytetracycline or chlortetracycline is required, but this is an admission of defeat on the part of the veterinary surgeon and farmer concerned.

Pancreatic Calcillosis

(Pancreolithiasis)

Aetiology

The cause is unknown.

Occurrence

The condition is very uncommon and sporadic cases are diagnosed in the slaughterhouse or at *post mortem* examination. Most calculi consist of 90.5 *per cent* calcium carbonate, 5.2 *per cent* calcium phosphate, traces of magnesium carbonate, fat and proteins two *per cent* (Jensen and Mackey, 1971).

Signs

The signs associated retrospectively with the condition are vague and variable.

Necropsy

The pancreatic duct and its branches may contain up to 1,500 white stones. They vary from 1 to 10 mm in diameter and may be circular or angular. Occasionally there is rupture of the pancreatic duct with necrosis of the adipose tissue.

Diagnosis

Made at necropsy.

Treatment

None can be suggested as the condition's aetiology is unknown.

Reference

JENSEN, R and MACKEY, D R (1971) Bovine Pancreolithiasis in "Diseases of Feedlot Cattle", 2nd edition. Lea and Febiger, Philadelphia, p.299.

Ruminal Acidosis

(Overeating, rumen overload, barley poisoning, lactic acidosis, rumenitis, toxic indigestion, engorgement toxaemia)

Aetiology

The sudden overeating of large quantities of cereal or other easily-digested carbohydrate resulting in excess lactic acid production.

Occurrence

The problem is a common feeding fault where cattle are either suddenly provided with access to cereals or they have gained entry to a cereal store or a cereal crop. Cases occur more frequently on barley, wheat or maize and more especially when the grain is ground, milled or processed rather than fed whole. Most cases involving groups of animals are caused at the time of introducing the concentrate or where there is a sudden increase in the amount of cereal offered, or the cereal has run out for 12 - 24 hours and then the cattle receive the same quantities as previously. Individual cases normally result from animals being greedy, or finding access to extra feed. Where access to a feed store occurs, then group or individual cases may occur.

There is considerable variation in the susceptibility of individual animals to the condition of cereal overeating. This partly depends on the previous exposure of the cattle to cereals. The greater the amount fed before, the more is required before signs occur.

On a highly digestible roughage diet the rumen fluid of animals tends to have molar percentages of 70 *per cent* acetic acid, 20 *per cent* proprionic acid, eight *per cent* butyric acid and two *per cent* miscellaneous acids (formic, valeric and succinic acids). The pH of the rumen is about 6.5, that of blood 7.45 and the packed cell volume is about 35 *per cent*. Lactic acid levels in the rumen tend to be low at about two *per cent* or less.

As more cereal is fed the ruminal acidity increases and a pH change from 6.5 to 5.5 can occur due to an increase in miscellaneous acids, formic, valeric and succinic. This causes in the rumen:

Decrease in protozoa.
Decrease in normal Gram-negative bacteria.
Increase in Gram-positive bacteria (*Streptococcus bovis*).

Extra cereal will cause a further decrease in pH from 5.5 to 4.5. This results in rumen changes:

Decrease in normal Gram-negative bacteria.
Decrease in *Strep. bovis*.
Protozoa are minimal.
Increase in lactic acid formation.
Increase in lactobacilli (Gram-positive rods).
Increase in coliform organisms.
Increase in *Clostridium perfringens* organisms.
Reduction in intraruminal bicarbonate.
Increase in lactobacilli in caecum.
Increase in *Cl. perfringens* in caecum.
Blood pH 7.3.

TABLE 2.1

Changes in Lactic Acidosis

Diet	Low cereal High roughage	66% cereal 33% roughage	90% cereal 10% roughage
Rumen pH	6.5	5.5	<4.0
Bicarbonate buffer	Adequate	Adequate	Inadequate
Ruminal fatty acid contents (molar percentages)			
Acetic	70%	55%	0-10%
Proprionic	20%	25%	25-35%
Butyric	8%	15%	0-10%
Others (lactic, formic, succinic)	2%	5%	50-90%
Rumen protein	Normal	Normal	Histamine Thyramine
Ruminal osmotic pressure	Normal	Slight Increase	Extreme Increase
Blood pH	7.45	7.3	<7.1
PCV	35%	40%	>50%
Urine pH	8.0	7.5	<6.0
Butterfat	4.3%	3.8%	3.0%
Ruminal motility	3 every 2 minutes	Same	Ruminal Stasis
Rumen epithelium	Normal Rough	Red	Smooth Inflamed
Abomasum	Normal	Normal	Abomasitis
Liver	Normal	Some fatty change	Fatty Infiltration Hepatic Abscesses Peritonitis
Feet	Normal	Normal	Laminitis

(After J L Howard, 1981)

Extra concentrates will further decrease the ruminal pH from 4.5 to below 4.0. This causes:

Cessation of ruminal movements.
Increase in ruminal fluid osmotic pressure.
Ruminal fluid volume decreases.
Body tissue fluids decrease.
Dehydration.
Packed cell volume over 50 per cent.
Blood pH 7.1.

When the pH of the rumen falls to below 4.0 and that of the blood to below 7.2, there is an uncompensated metabolic acidosis. This may result in a further lowering of the blood pH to below 7.0 and this in turn will cause death if it continues for any length of time. Those animals which survive tend to develop ruminal stasis. This usually results in an increase in the intraruminal levels of histamine as well as causing endotoxin formation, giving rise to a severe chemical rumenitis with increased absorption of bacteria and toxins. The rumenitis tends to include ulceration and necrosis of the ruminal epithelium, thereby again leading to an increase in absorption of toxins (leading to toxaemia and death), bacteria, especially *Fusiformis necrophorus* (leading to infection of other organs and particularly causing liver abscesses) or fungi, especially of the Mucoraceae spp. (*Mucor* spp., *Rhizopus* spp. and *Absida* spp.), leading to an extensive rumenitis and possible death.

As lactic acid builds up, various changes occur, some of which are to compensate for the problem (see Figures 2.1, 2.2).

The ruminal wall undergoes marked changes with the mucosa becoming reddened and then smooth and inflamed. The abomasum shows signs of abomasitis as ruminal pH reaches 4.0. The liver shows a change first to fatty infiltration and then to abscess formation and possible peritonitis. As ruminal pH lowers, there is also the possibility of laminitis.

Lactic acid in the bowel is buffered by plasma bicarbonate. In the lungs compensation for the acidosis is by removal of carbon dioxide. If the rate of lactic acid going into the blood is not too great, the animal can compensate. Occasionally in acidosis, overcompensation can occur, resulting in alkalosis. However, in severe cases the plasma bicarbonate is reduced and the blood pH falls, leading to a fall in blood pressure. This in turn leads to a decrease in blood perfusion to peripheral tissues, thereby resulting in anaerobic oxidation which will cause a further build-up of lactic acid. Blood flow to the kidneys is reduced, thus allowing a decrease in glomerular filtration rate and later anuria, shock and death.

Morbidity

This depends on the cause of the overeating but it can be up to 90 per cent if large amounts of cereal are eaten by animals not accustomed to it, and no treatment is given. In those treated, morbidity in severe cases may still be 30 to 40 per cent. When only small amounts of cereal are consumed, many cattle will recover spontaneously.

Early signs

In the early stages after ingestion signs are few and can often give a false sense of security to the stockman. The animals may be bright and alert although a little inappetant and they may exhibit mild colic and kick at their bellies.

FIGURE 2.1

The Course of Changes following the Feeding of Excessive Highly Fermentable Feeds

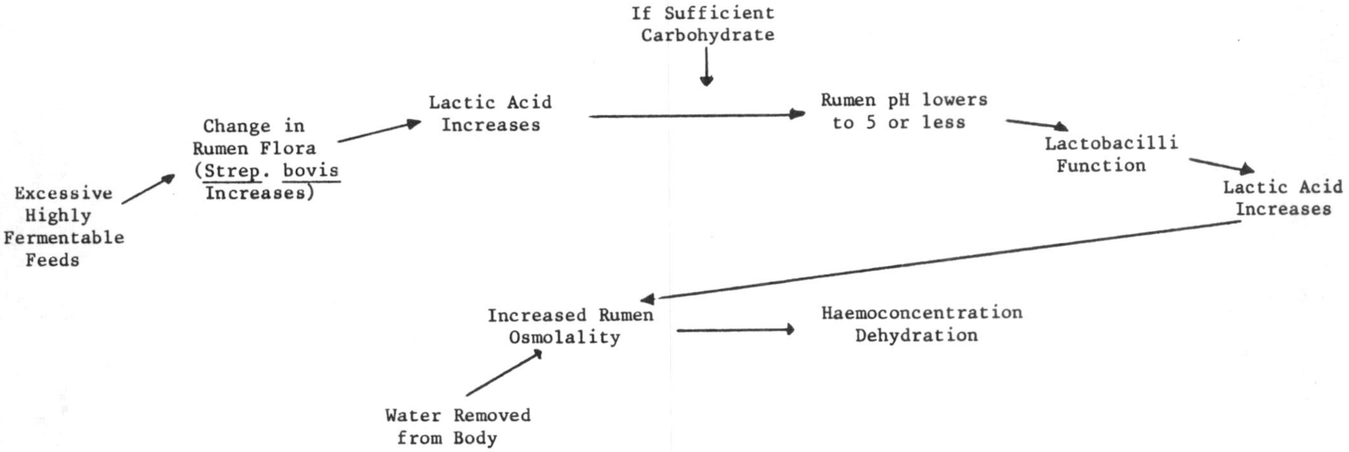

FIGURE 2.2

Compensatory Mechanisms of Cattle following a Rise in Lactic Acid Concentrations in Rumen

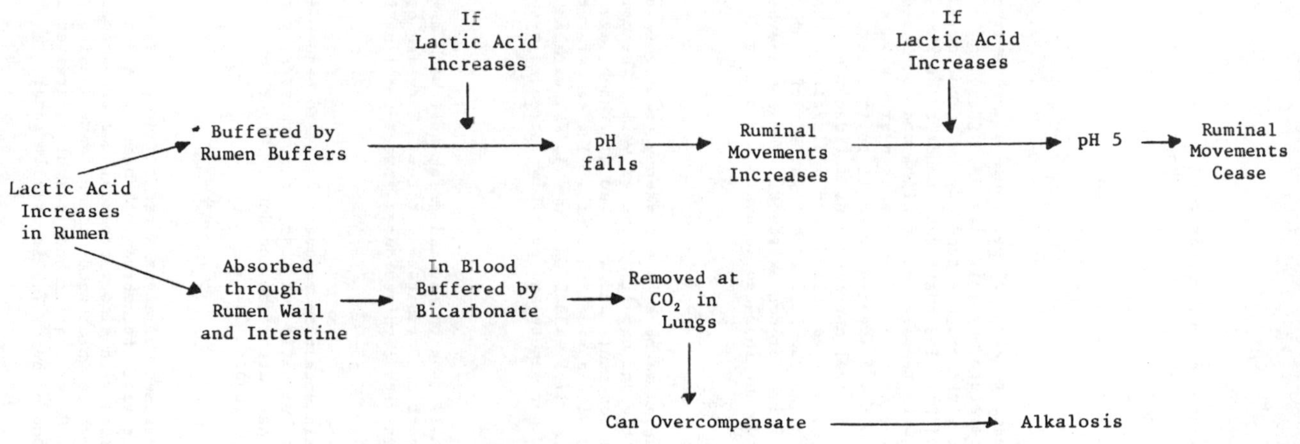

Signs

Peracute

Death in 12 to 24 hours after feed ingestion. Those not dead will be recumbent or have a staggering gait. Most will stand by themselves and will be disinclined to eat or drink. However, a few animals tend to habitually drink water. There is often anuria and in a few cases there will be death before any signs of diarrhoea. Usually, however, examination will reveal severe loose or watery diarrhoea.

Acute

Of these cattle, about 25 per cent will show signs of bloat or colic. The rectal temperature may initially be high, 40 - 41°C (103 - 106°F) but in most cases the temperature tends to be normal or subnormal, 36.5 - 38.5°C (98 - 101°F). The heart rate tends to be increased and may be up to 140 per minute with respirations shallow and increased to 60 to 90 per minute. In these animals, diarrhoea is nearly always present and it tends to be yellow and has a sweet-sour smell to it. Cereal grains may be present in the faeces. Central nervous signs include muscle tremors and a staggering gait. Some animals appear blind with a sluggish or non-existent palpebral eye reflex, although the pupillary light reflex is normal. Ruminal movements are minimal or non-existent. The most severely affected animals will become recumbent in 24 to 48 hours and die in 24 to 72 hours, following coma.

Subacute

In these animals there is a tendency to slight lethargy but they will still eat a little and usually drink as well. The main signs are of reduced ruminal movements and a marked diarrhoea, again usually yellow or light in colour with a sweetish smell. The temperature is normal or just slightly low i.e. 37.5 - 38.5°C (100 - 101°F) with an increased heart rate up to about 100 per minute and possibly increased respiratory rate to 40 per minute.

Mild

These animals tend to eat and drink well with a normal rectal temperature, heart and respiratory rates. They are bright and alert but have a diarrhoea with light-coloured, sweet-smelling faeces.

Relapses

Some animals appear to recover , only to become ill again in 2 to 3 days due to a fungal rum nitis and also, in some cases, peritonitis. Some cattle abort 10 to 14 days after the incident. Others only make a slow recovery or never seem to respond fully.

Prognosis

Rapid development of signs after eating the excess cereals is a bad sign, as also is rapid recumbency. A heart rate over 120 per minute is usually associated with a poor prognosis as are animals which do not pass faeces. A diarrhoea which tends to be foamy is also considered to be bad. Dehydration of 12 per cent of body weight or greater is liable to lead to death and a blood pH below 7.0 is usually fatal.

Signs of recovery

Improvement can be gauged by a decrease in the heart rate, a rectal temperature returning to normal, ruminal contractions becoming normal in intensity and frequency and a return of appetite.

Necropsy

Peracute

The contents of the reticulo-rumen tend to be pasty with an odour of fermentation. The epithelium tends to be soft and easily removed, revealing a dark, haemorrhagic surface underneath. The abomasum may contain grain and be inflamed. Enteritis is often present. The blood tends to be dark and thick.

Acute

Cattle surviving 72 to 96 hours often have a reticulo-ruminal wall which is covered by a soft, black, raised area of gangrene. The wall is thickened, friable and gelatinous. There is, on histology, infiltration with fungal mycelia and a haemorrhagic necrosis. There is a terminal ischaemic necrosis. There may be a secondary enteritis. In cases examined early, ruminal pH is a useful indicator but this tends to fall after death.

Diagnosis

1. History - access to excess grain, management change.
2. Signs - pale-coloured, sweet-smelling, pasty diarrhoea, reduced ruminal movements, dullness, apparent blindness, staggering gait.
3. Ruminal pH - tends to be below 5.5.
4. Blood pH - below normal of 7.45.
5. Haematocrit value - tends to be raised, usually about 35 per cent.
6. Urine pH - tends to be low.
7. Microscopic examination of ruminal flora:
   Low power - absence of protozoa.
   Gram stain - mainly Gram-positive organisms rather than Gram-negative organisms.
8. Haematology - normal or a neutrophilic leucocytosis if ruminitis, abomasitis.
9. Blood glucose levels - often hyperglycaemia.
10. Serum glutamic oxalacetic transaminase (SGOT) levels may be raised if rumenitis or abomasitis (normal 50u/l; 50 iu/l).
11. Lactic dehydrogenase (LDH) levels occasionally high.
12. Blood pyruvate levels high (usually < 2.0 mg/100 ml).

Differential diagnosis

1. Peracute coliform mastitis but individual animal, usually freshly calved.
2. Acute diffuse peritonitis but usually greater pain, arched back, persistent standing, shuffling gait.
3. Enterotoxaemia but usually there is not an outbreak.

4. CCN but usually nervous signs are more obvious, ruminal movements are normal and there is unlikely to be diarrhoea.
5. Haemophilus somnus septicaemia but a pyrexia and signs of lung involvement.
6. Parturient paresis - usually only a few cattle and it is associated with the calving period.
7. Acute hepatic insufficiency but this is rare and there is jaundice.

Treatment

Peracute

In cases with a severe prognosis, emergency slaughter is often the best course if undertaken soon after the cereal has been ingested. Otherwise a rumenotomy can be performed to remove rumen contents or a rumen lavage undertaken. The latter involves the use of a large bore tube. Warm water is pumped into the rumen until there is distension of the left lumbar fossa. The rumen is then allowed to empty by gravity. The procedure is continued until the rumen is empty. The rumen should then be reinoculated with 15 to 20 litres of fresh rumen contents. Intravenous sodium bicarbonate can be used (five litres of five per cent i.v. over 30 minutes, then 1.3 per cent sodium bicarbonate, 150 ml/kg body weight is used every 6 to 12 hours). Calcium borogluconate has been found to be helpful in some cases. Thiamine hydrochloride at the rate of 5 to 10 mg/kg body weight may be useful and often other B-complex vitamins are administered. When feeding starts, provide only good quality hay.

Acute

Again perhaps consider emergency slaughter or rumen lavage, or rumenotomy. The rumen could just be flushed with 20 to 40 litres of water orally to dilute the acidity and reduce the osmotic pressure. Sodium bicarbonate can be used intravenously as for peracute cases and calcium borogluconate may be helpful. Thiamine hydrochloride and B-complex vitamins may be useful. The oral administration of antacids or mild cathartics can be helpful. Magnesium oxide is the most effective antacid, followed by magnesium hydroxide, but both can cause alkalosis if used to excess, and so they should not be given to animals without acidosis (Gartley, Ogilvie and Butler, 1981). Magnesium sulphate or sodium sulphate are the most effective saline cathartics. Magnesium carbonate can also be used. The dose of the antacid is 1g per kg body weight (1½ oz per cwt), followed by a quarter to half the dose every 6 to 12 hours. The antacid is best dissolved in 8 to 12 litres of warm water to ensure adequate rumen dispersal.

Oral use of antibiotics can result in lowered volatile fatty acid production, particularly that of lactic acid. The most effective antibiotics are bacitracin, methylene disalicylate, capremycin disulphate, novobiocin and oxamycin (Howard, 1981) although erythromycin, hygromycin B and tylosin tartrate are moderately useful. Hay should also be given. The use of oral thiabendazole may help control the development of secondary mycotic ruminitis.

Subacute

In these cases antacids can be given orally and usually about 500g (16 oz) of magnesium oxide or magnesium hydroxide can be given to an animal of 450 kg (1000 lb). A few cases may require isotonic sodium bicarbonate or saline intravenously. Again hay should be given.

Mild

These cattle should receive hay and they should be kept under observation for at least 48 hours to ensure there is no inappetance.

Prevention

Make sure introduction to a new feed or changes in feed are made gradually. In yearling cattle not used to concentrates, give 1 kg (2 lb) per day, and provided there are no digestive disturbances, increase by ½ to 1 kg (1 to 2 lb) every 3 to 4 days until the required daily amount is being fed. If cattle are used to cereal feeding the consumption can be increased more quickly. It is essential to ensure that adequate coarse roughage is eaten when cattle are introduced to cereal diets. It must be remembered that finely-ground cereals are more likely to cause problems than those which are rolled or bruised. The ideal concentrate to roughage ratio for cereal beef production is 88:12. The addition of fat, such as tallow, to the diet, appears to lower the production of lactic acid and may help control ruminal acidosis.

References

HOWARD, J L (1981) Bovine Practitioner, No. 12, 44-53.

GARTLEY, C, OGILVIE, T H and BUTLER, D G (1981) Proceedings of 13th Annual Convention of the American Association of Bovine Practitioners, November 19th-22nd, 1980, Toronto. p. 17-19.

Ruminal Parakeratosis

Also known as hyperkeratosis of the rumen.

Aetiology

The condition normally occurs on diets of high concentrate pellets subjected to heat treatment. Finely-ground feeds are also thought to contribute to the condition.

Occurrence

In the affected rumen the papillae tend to be enlarged, leathery, brown in colour and clumped together. The condition probably reduces the efficacy of feed utilisation. It is thought some cases may be the result of vitamin A deficiency and diarrhoea in the calf. It is probable that the condition mainly occurs in intensively-fed cattle and the incidence can be up to 40 *per cent* although nine *per cent* is a more usual level.

Signs

Almost all cases show no signs, they are found following slaughter.

Necropsy

The lesions tend to be most severe on the dorsal surface of the rumen above the level of the ruminal contents. The papillae affected are enlarged, hardened, brown, leathery and usually clumped. Individual papillae may be completely or partially hyperkeratinised and in the latter case, the dorsal half or the tip tends to be hard and rough. In the non-papillated mucosa, especially along the dorsal curvature of the rumen, there are often several areas of hyperkeratosis, seen as firm brown scales, adherent to the mucosa. Histologically, hyperkeratosis is depicted as an increase in the thickness of the cornified portion of the ruminal epithelium with the presence of nuclei in the cornified cells. Feed particles and clumps of bacteria may be present on the surface, or possibly in deeper layers.

Diagnosis

This is not made during life.

1. *Post mortem* findings indicate the condition.
2. Histological examination confirms the problem.

Control

Ensure that the animals receive a daily supply of long fibre roughage.

Ruminal Tympany

Bloat.

Aetiology

The distension of the reticulo-rumen with either free gas or gas trapped within bubbles; in each case the gas is the product of rumen fermentation.

Occurrence

Bloat is a relatively common condition, particularly under certain circumstances. Ruminal tympany is often conveniently divided into frothy bloat or gaseous bloat.

Frothy Bloat

This is also known as foamy bloat, pasture bloat, legume bloat and primary bloat. In this condition the gas of fermentation becomes entrapped in millions of tiny bubbles. These bubbles increase and do not break down so there is no eructation and intraruminal pressure increases.

Plant factors

The primary cause of frothy bloat is introduction to a diet containing bloat-producing plants, but it is exacerbated by other factors. The plants most likely to cause problems are lush young pastures, particularly if they contain a high amount of clover, but it can occur on young grass, cereal crops, rape, kale and cabbages.

There are two types of soluble protein in the plants:-

Fraction 1 - A homogeneous protein of molecular weight 500,000 in plant chloroplasts identified as ribulose diphosphate carboxylase.

Fraction 2 - A mixture of proteins between molecular weights 10,000 and 200,000 and it includes all soluble leaf proteins other than those of Fraction 1.

Both fractions foam at a pH of 5.4 to 6.0 and in the case of Fraction 1, maximum foam is produced at 5.8.

Saponins - These were at one time thought to be a major cause of bloat but they are no longer so considered.

Pectins - These are not primary foaming agents but they help to stabilise the foam in bloat.

Tannins - These are polyphenolic compounds with a molecular weight of 500 to 3,000 which can combine with and precipitate proteins. The most effective compounds are the polymeric flavanols or flavolans.

Lipids - Particularly those of the chloroplasts appear to act as anti-foaming materials.

Animal factors

Although not as important as the plant factors, they still influence the individual animal's susceptibility to bloat.

Individual variation - There appears to be considerable variation in susceptibility.

Breed differences - may occur.

Inherited differences - Some sires produce progeny which are predisposed to bloat.

Saliva - Daily secretion varies considerably from 25 to 190 litres (5 to 40 gallons) in adults and it consists of two phases:-

(a) Serous, which is thin and high in bicarbonate and it is strongly buffered and contains little protein. Although secreted continuously the amount depends on whether the animal is eating, ruminating or resting.

(b) Mucous, which is thicker and contains much protein, including mucin and is mainly secreted during feeding. Mucin is an anti-foaming agent but other proteins in the saliva may stabilise the foam.

Ruminal organisms

Bacteria - With ruminal changes, the production of more mucinolytic bacteria might accelerate foam stabilising material from mucoprotein.

Protozoa - Holotrich ciliates burst following excess starch storage if substrate is in excess. The starch storage grains in the ciliates are released, producing potent stabilisers or rumen foam.

Environment

More bloat occurs in the afternoon and evening than in the morning.

Gaseous Bloat

This is also known as secondary bloat, and some forms are known as feedlot bloat or cereal bloat. Many cases result from the obstruction to eructation which can be the result of a foreign body such as a potato or turnip in the oesophagus, but occasionally carcinoma and papillomata of the oesophageal groove and reticulum can occur, or due to stenosis of the oesophagus or enlargements outside the oesophagus such as the thymus, or enlarged mediastinal or bronchial lymph nodes. Obstruction of the cardia can also occur. Oesophageal groove function can be interfered with by vagal indigestion or diaphragmatic hernia. Tetanus can occur because of oesophageal musculature spasm. Anaphylaxis can result in bloat due to muscle atony. If sudden changes of acidity and alkalinity occur then there can be ruminal atony, but usually it is of a minor type. Occasionally mucosal disease results in bloat, as also does Haemophilus somnus infection.

Cases of bloat on high cereal feeds are not uncommon. The cause of these is often not known but can be the result of oesophagitis, acidosis, rumenitis and failure of ruminal movement. Many of these cases are relieved by the stomach tube and do not recur. However, some animals become persistent offenders.

Semi-frothy

Some bloats consist of froth plus a relatively large volume of free gas.

Management factors

Often bloat occurs following management changes such as:

1. Sudden access to highly fermentable feed.
2. A failure of water supply.
3. Troughs for *ad libitum* feed becoming empty and then filled so the animals eat excessively.
4. Barley not being rolled.
5. The texture of the feed - the use of finely-ground or milled feed even when pelleted.

Most cases of pasture or feedlot bloat do not show ruminal atony. Frothy bloat causes a physical obstruction of the cardia and then inhibits eructation. When death occurs in bloat the cause is obscure as in many cases the distension is not sufficient to completely depress the respiratory or cardiovascular systems. However, there is considerable individual variation in susceptibility.

Morbidity

This can be very variable but it can be up to 60 to 80 *per cent* of cattle in pasture bloat and the same with management problems in gaseous bloat.

Mortality

This again is very variable but it can be high, particularly if treatment is not readily to hand.

Signs

Peracute

The animal is found dead. More deaths occur in beef animals than dairy cattle as the former are observed less frequently. Most deaths are found first thing in the morning.

Acute

Pasture bloat normally occurs one to two days after placing on the offending pasture. There is a distension of the left side with the whole of the abdomen expanding. Percussion produces a tympanitic note. The animals show discomfort and they may kick at their bellies or roll. There is usually marked salivation, dyspnoea with the head extended and the tongue protruding. The respiratory rate may increase to 60 per minute and the heart rate may rise to 100 per minute. In the early stages there are increased ruminal movements but later they tend to become few or absent. As the condition worsens, the animal becomes recumbent. Death usually occurs at least three or four hours after first signs and is without a struggle. If the case is one of gassy bloat, passage of a stomach tube relieves the problem but in cases of frothy bloat, only small amounts of gas are released.

Subacute

When a group of animals is affected, some will only show mild distension with some abdominal discomfort. They tend to reduce their grazing time.

Chronic

Some animals, particularly those on high cereal diets, will show irregular distension of the rumen. Often this is only slight but it can become a nuisance because occasionally such animals will suddenly develop severe bloat.

Necropsy

Usually there is marked congestion and distension of the blood vessels in the head and neck. Congestion also occurs in the epicardium and upper respiratory tract. The cervical oesophagus is congested whereas the thoracic part tends to be blanched. The lungs are compressed. The rumen will be distended with gas but in frothy bloat this tends to subside following death. There is erythema of the ruminal mucosa, particularly ventrally. The liver tends to be pale. In animals which have been dead for several hours there will be little froth in the rumen, exfoliation of the cornified ruminal mucosa, congestion of the submucosal tissues and subcutaneous emphysema.

Diagnosis

1. History.
2. Signs.
3. Passage of a stomach tube.

Differential diagnosis

Acute

1. Tetanus but signs of muscular rigidity.
2. Vagal indigestion but usually chronic with ruminal movements and there is distension of the left sublumbar fossa and right ventral abdomen.
3. Diaphragmatic hernia - again normally more chronic and a moderate tympany. There is no obstruction to passage of the stomach tube but the animal may vomit.

Peracute, or following death, diagnosis may be difficult.

1. Anthrax, but may be bleeding from orifices.
2. Blackleg but emphysema of affected area.
3. Hypomagnesaemia but there may be signs of a struggle.
4. Lightning strike but history plus position and scorch marks may detect.

Treatment

Frothy bloat

The use of synthetic surfactants is the treatment of choice and poloxalene is very useful. In other countries, alcohol ethoxylates are used. Silicones have been used but are less effective than poloxalene. Almost any non-toxic oil is useful. Mineral oils are probably best. In some cases it is best to administer the medicament via stomach tube. In cases of extreme distension and imminent death a trochar and cannula might be used to relieve the pressure and then an antifoaming agent applied.

Gaseous bloat

This is best tackled by the introduction of a stomach tube. Less severely affected animals can be relieved by walking them about, and then the cattle will normally belch. In animals which are down, emergency treatment may mean opening the left sublumbar fossa with a sharp knife. Otherwise a trochar and cannula can be used. The standard size cannula is too narrow in diameter, and it is better to use a larger bore instrument 2.5 cm (1 in) in diameter. The use of 150 - 200 g sodium bicarbonate in 1 litre (5 - 7 oz in 2 pints) of water can assist, or a non-toxic oil may be administered.

Chronic cases

These should be removed to a less intensive system. However, if close to finishing, the cattle can have a permanent fistula made in their rumen.

Control

Frothy bloat

Management can help such as turnout in the spring for short periods. Ensure the cattle receive and eat roughage before they are turned out. The cattle could otherwise be strip-grazed. All cattle on suspect pasture should be watched carefully when first turned out. Poloxalene can be provided in water or in the feed. Oil can be provided daily and can include mineral oils, vegetable oils and emulsified tallow. In other countries alcohol ethoxylate detergents have been used and sustained release capsules are of use, releasing an antifoaming agent over two weeks.

Gaseous bloat

The cattle should be introduced to cereal gradually. Adequate roughage should be provided. The cereal should not be ground or milled, but rolled or bruised. Poloxalene has been used with variable results in cereal bloat. Oral antibiotics have also been used, with mixed success.

Traumatic Reticulitis

Aetiology

Most cases result from ingestion of foreign material, usually metal, such as nails, wire, etc. Hence the common name of "wire".

Occurrence

When hay was commonly baled with wire the condition was common. It is now only irregularly seen. Cases occur less frequently in beef animals and heifers than dairy cows. Almost all cases occur in animals over two years old. Cattle are not selective in their feeding and so often ingest foreign material which usually passes to the reticulum. The foreign material may cause no problems but it can be caught up in the honeycomb lining of the reticulum and if the object is sharp, the regular reticulo-ruminal contractions can cause puncture of the wall. Most penetrations occur in the ventral part of the anterior ruminal wall. If the full depth of the wall is not penetrated no signs occur, but when penetration is complete there are signs of acute focal peritonitis with pain and ruminal atony. The foreign body may subsequently return to the reticular lumen because of necrosis around the area of penetration and this can lead to spontaneous recovery.

In some cases the peritoneal sac, diaphragm and pericardial sac are penetrated which may lead to acute local peritonitis, diaphragmatic abscess, pericarditis, pleurisy, pneumonia and mediastinal abscess. It does seem that puncture progresses further in cattle which are heavily pregnant. In some cases the foreign body does not pass forward but goes medially into the liver or laterally into the spleen. This can lead to liver abscess, splenic abscess. Infection can enter the bloodstream from the peritoneum, leading to pulmonary abscesses, nephritis and arthritis.

Signs

There is usually pyrexia of 39.5 - 40°C (103 - 104°F), with anorexia. The animal often has an arched back and is reluctant to walk. Rumination is reduced and the abdominal wall is held tight to produce a tucked-up appearance. Grunting is common and bloat may occur. There is constipation and both urination and defaecation are painful to accomplish. Palpation or pressure of the left anterio-ventral abdomen causes pain, discomfort and muscle rigidity. Pinching the withers results in the animal bracing itself rather than depressing its back. Pain can be detected by raising a bar under the abdomen. Pain or uneasiness at the time of primary ruminal movement is a useful sign.

Necropsy

On necropsy a metal fragment may be found. Most penetrations occur in the anterior ventral part of the reticulum. Adhesion may occur between the serosal surfaces. If peritonitis is present there is a fibrinous or suppurative inflammation.

Diagnosis

1. Signs - sudden anorexia, pyrexia and pain in the left anterio-ventral region.
2. There is a leucocytosis.
3. Often there is neutrophilia with a left shift.

4. Metal detectors can be useful but may give false positive results.
5. Rumenotomy.

Differential diagnosis

1. Other causes of peritonitis.
2. Abomasal ulceration.
3. Ketosis.
4. Indigestion.
5. Displacement of the abomasum.
6. Pyelonephritis.

Treatment

Conservative

The animal is kept on its own and supplied with wholesome feed. The roughage level should be reduced to half. In some cases the animal is tied up with its front feet raised above its back ones. Sulphamethazine at the rate of 150 mg/kg BW (75 mg/lb BW) can be given orally for 3 to 5 days. Antibiotic injections can be used for the same period and combined penicillin and streptomycin can be useful. Magnets have been administered to try to remove the embedded foreign body back into the rumen.

Surgical

Removal of the foreign body may be undertaken by a rumenotomy operation.

Control

The provision of magnets in the reticulum has been used successfully but is little practised in Britain. Care should be taken to ensure feeds are not contaminated with metal.

Salmonellosis

Under the Zoonosis Order 1975, salmonellosis became a reportable disease. It requires the reporting of all cases of disease caused by the genus *Salmonella* in food-producing species and allows the Ministry of Agriculture, Fisheries and Food (MAFF) veterinary inspectors to investigate and apply movement restrictions to any kind of animal (except man), birds, carcases and their products. Not all outbreaks of disease are investigated. Reporting of isolates is only required in the case of the usual meat-producing mammals and birds, e.g. cattle, sheep, goats, pigs, rabbits, fowls, turkeys, geese, ducks, guinea-fowls, pheasants, partridges and quails. Although there is no obligation to report in other species, if the presence of infection became known in a non-designated species and was considered to have public health implications, it would be possible to investigate and, if necessary, apply restrictions.

Aetiology

There are many different serotypes in the *Salmonella* genus and they are Gram-negative, non-lactose-fermenting bacteria. The two most important serotypes are *S. dublin* and *S. typhimurium* (see Table 2.2) but there are numerous other serotypes found in salmonella outbreaks including *S. amsterdam*, *S. newport* and *S. agona*.

TABLE 2.2

Number and Percentage of Salmonella Incidents in Cattle

		S. typhimurium	S. dublin	Others	Total
1976	Number	802	683	302	1787
	%	44.9	38.2	16.9	
1977	Number	458	507	199	1164
	%	39.3	43.6	17.1	
1978	Number	684	560	184	1428
	%	47.9	39.2	12.9	
1979	Number	731	566	138	1435
	%	50.9	39.4	9.7	
1980	Number	708	498	168	1374
	%	51.5	36.2	12.2	
1981	Number	845	435	204	1484
	%	56.9	29.3	13.7	
1982	Number	877	556	185	1618
	%	54.2	34.4	11.4	
1983	Number	1215	586	161	1962
	%	61.9	29.9	8.2	
1984	Number	1174	424	165	1763
	%	66.6	24.0	9.4	

(After Animal Salmonellosis Statutory Summaries, 1976-84)

Epidemiology

More salmonella isolations are made from calves than adults (see Table 2.3). S. dublin was the main cause of disease in calves up to 1975; subsequently it has been superseded by S. typhimurium. Salmonella spp. excretory rates vary and in a 1970 survey of known salmonella-infected dairy farms by the Bristol Veterinary School, isolation rates varied between 1.6 and 47 per cent. In calf-rearing units the level of infection varied between 0.12 and 12.4 per cent and it was influenced by the husbandry system.

TABLE 2.3

Proportion of Salmonella dublin and S. typhimurium Isolates from Adults and Calves

		Adult	%	Foetus	%	Calf	%	Total
1976	S. typhimurium	190	23.7	6	0.7	606	75.6	802
	S. dublin	221	32.4	42	6.1	420	61.5	683
1977	S. typhimurium	135	29.5	4	0.9	319	69.6	458
	S. dublin	180	35.5	40	7.9	287	56.6	507
1978	S. typhimurium	151	22.1			533	77.9	684
	S. dublin	215	38.4			345	61.6	560
1979	S. typhimurium	156	21.3			575	78.7	731
	S. dublin	186	32.9			380	67.1	566
1980	S. typhimurium	235	33.2			473	66.8	708
	S. dublin	227	45.6			271	54.4	498
1981	S. typhimurium	242	28.6			603	71.4	845
	S. dublin	196	45.1			239	54.9	435
1982	S. typhimurium	197	33.9			580	66.1	777
	S. dublin	265	47.7			291	52.3	556
1983	S. typhimurium	368	30.3			847	69.7	1215
	S. dublin	290	49.5			296	50.5	586
1984	S. typhimurium	327	27.9			847	72.1	1174
	S. dublin	191	45.0			233	55.0	424

(After Animal Salmonellosis Statutory Summaries, 1976-84)

S. dublin is relatively species-specific to cattle. Normally carrier dams infect the calf at the time of calving by contamination of the teats or infected milk. S. dublin has a tendency to produce latent carriers and so often there is a persistent problem on the farm. Latent carriers under stresses such as calving or intercurrent disease can become active carriers, thereby allowing infection of their own calves or other cattle. Infected calves do not normally become carriers. Infection is most often contained in the faeces, but the tonsils of calves are often infected, so the saliva can contain organisms. In carrier animals, S. dublin is often identifiable post mortem from the gall bladder.

S. typhimurium has a wider host range and it includes man. In many cases infection is the result of contamination of feed or water. The origin is often animal faeces or human sludge. Infection can then be transferred by rodents, birds (especially seagulls and starlings) feeding from feed troughs, etc.

Other serotypes of salmonella are usually similar in origin to S. typhimurium with infection arising from rodents, birds, contaminated feed or water. When infection is by animal serotypes, human beings are most commonly infected with S. typhimurium or other exotic serotypes, rather than S. dublin.

The salmonella organisms vary in their viability outside the host according to the environment. Although S. typhimurium can remain viable for up to seven months, in soil, stagnant water, faeces or pasture, it is quickly killed off by sunlight or drying. Water in ponds and other drinking places may remain infected with Salmonella spp. for up to nine months. Infection is just as possible in animals at pasture as with those housed.

Source of Infection

Faeces or contaminated placentae (S. dublin), contaminated feed, water, etc. (S. typhimurium and others).

Portal of Entry

Usually by mouth.

Signs

Acute enteritis

This is a common form in the growing animal. The temperature is high 40 - 41°C (104 - 106°F), the animal is dull and there is a varying degree of inappetance. Mucous membranes are usually reddened and often there is mucopurulent oculo-nasal discharge. Respiratory rate is often rapid and shallow, the pulse tends to be rapid and in many cases there is evidence of cough and lung sounds. There is evidence of diarrhoea, it is usually malodorous and it may be putty-coloured or watery and contain blood, or mucosal wall. In some cases there are marked signs of colic with moaning, abdominal kicking and general discomfort. Dehydration and toxaemia follow and in untreated animals up to 75 per cent may die in about three to five days.

Chronic enteritis

This is common in some outbreaks. The temperature rise is slight, 39.5°C(103°F), and intermittent. The other clinical signs are all mild and include persistent loose faeces, variable appetite, tucked-in flanks and, if untreated, emaciation occurs.

Abortion

Cases of S. dublin infection can result in abortion in the absence of all other clinical signs. In cases of other salmonella serotypes, the pyrexia and other signs of acute enteritis may later be followed by abortion.

Necropsy

Acute enteritis

The liver has a pale red colour and necrotic foci are sometimes present in the liver and kidney. Particularly in S. dublin infection the gall bladder may be enlarged and thickened. There are varying amounts of subserous petechiation but there is always petechiation under the epicardium. The main signs usually involve the small and large intestines where inflammation ranges from a muco-enteritis with slight submucosal petechiation to a diffuse haemorrhagic enteritis with loss of the mucosal lining in some cases. Lesions may also be seen in the abomasum, particularly in S. dublin. The mesenteric lymph nodes are enlarged, and, on sectioning, reveal oedema and blood. Culture of swabs of the intestinal contents, the intestinal wall, relevant mesenteric lymph nodes, gall bladder, blood and spleen and possibly also the abomasum and joints may reveal salmonella serotypes.

Chronic enteritis

Lesions are normally confined to the caecum and colon walls and are discrete areas of necrosis. Culture of swabs from lesions, the relevant mesenteric lymph nodes and gall bladder should be undertaken. It should be remembered that isolation of salmonella does not necessarily mean that the disease is the cause of any signs present in the animal.

Diagnosis

1. History of feed contamination by birds or rodents.
2. Signs, i.e. pyrexia, diarrhoea possibly with blood or epithelial casts, dehydration.
3. Faecal and possibly tonsillar swabs for bacteriology and culture. However, often swabs are negative and it is best to take them on three consecutive days. Conversely, isolation of the organisms does not always mean to say they are the cause of the problem.
4. Antibiotic sensitivity tests should be undertaken.
5. Post mortem findings and culture of relevant tissues, particularly intestinal wall and contents, mesenteric lymph nodes and gall bladder.
6. Serology can be undertaken (serum agglutination and complement fixation tests can be helpful).
7. A skin allergy test is available.

Differential diagnosis

1. Nutritional scours - but the animal is not ill in this case.
2. Mucosal disease, but virus present.
3. Coccidiosis.
4. Winter dysentery, but animals are not very ill.

5. Inadvertent antibiotic feeding but often many animals ill at exactly the same time.
6. Bracken poisoning but access to plants necessary.
7. Arsenic poisoning but often nervous signs.
8. Lead poisoning but blindness and other signs.
9. Other poisonings.

Therapy

If treatment is to be successful it must be early (see Table 2.4). There are also problems over the use of antibiotic therapy because of the possibility of treatment producing carriers of S. dublin infections. Therapy should include oral and parenteral fluid replacement, synthetic chemotherapeutic agents, antibiotics, ancillaries, management and dietary control. The main forms of antibacterial therapy are given in Table 2.4. In most cases oral therapy is confined to use in the calf. Chloramphenicol should only be used if antibiotic sensitivity demonstrates that this is the only antibacterial agent of use. It does have the property of becoming concentrated in the bile and excreted into the intestine following parenteral use.

Nursing is essential with the animals kept in a warm environment if the weather is cold, with a good, generous supply of bedding. Oral fluids may be required including isotonic saline, glucose saline and sodium bicarbonate intravenously. Electrolyte solutions can be administered at a level of 5 - 10 litres (1 - 2 galls) three to four times daily.

TABLE 2.4

Antibacterial Therapy for Salmonella Infections

Drug	Dosage per kg/lb bodyweight			
	Oral		Parenteral	
Amoxycillin	2-10mg/kg	1-5mg/lb	7mg/kg	3.5mg/lb
Ampicillin	4-12mg/kg	2-6mg/lb	2-7mg/kg	1-3.5mg/lb
Chloramphenicol	10mg/kg	5mg/lb	4-10mg/kg	2-5mg/lb
Framycetin	10mg/kg	5mg/lb	10mg/kg	5mg/lb
Furazolidone	20mg/kg	10mg/lb	-	-
Neomycin	5-10mg/kg	2.5-5mg/lb	5-10mg/kg	2.5-5mg/lb
Spectinomycin	15-25mg/kg	7.5-12.5mg/lb	20-30mg/kg	10-15mg/lb
Trimethoprim and Sulphadiazine	30mg/kg	15mg/lb	15mg/kg	7.5mg/lb

Prevention

In all cases an attempt to ascertain the origin of infection should be made. In some cases investigations will also be undertaken by the

State Veterinary Service. S. dublin infection is usually from the carrier dam or spread between calves, whereas with other salmonella serotypes the source may be a bought-in animal or contaminated feed or water, or infection from other farm animal species, rodents, birds or humans. Unless the source is ascertained, the outbreak cannot be completely contained with certainty. Although carriers occur with serotypes other than S. dublin, they are normally of short duration and so culling is usually unnecessary.

In a closed herd with S. dublin infection, an attempt should be made to identify the carrier cattle. These should preferably be culled, or otherwise they can be isolated and treated, but successful removal of carrier status is difficult. All cows in the herd should be isolated at calving. Identification of carriers is difficult but can best be done by faecal swabbing the whole herd at least three times at seven to 14-day intervals. This can be assisted by the taking of serum for agglutination tests. In addition, faecal and vaginal samples should be taken from cows and rectal swabs from calves at calving. This will help to identify carriers previously missed and they should be culled. The calving boxes should be disinfected between calvings and all infected material disposed of, preferably by burning. The growing cattle should also be swabbed.

When cattle are bought-in, they should be from a salmonella-free source. If an animal is subsequently found to have salmonella, identify the farm and do not use the source again. When the source appears to be due to contamination, try to ensure all feed stores are made vermin-proof and feed hoppers are made bird and vermin-proof. Ensure that all feed offered in fields is in troughs and is eaten quickly.

Vaccination

There are several dead vaccines or sero-vaccines available. These contain killed strains of S. dublin and S. typhimurium and they require two injections for effective immunity. Both calves and cows can be vaccinated. There is also available a live, avirulent S. dublin vaccine which appears to give some cross-immunity to S. typhimurium. The vaccine is best given before moving calves. Otherwise, if this is not possible, inject about two or three days after entry to allow the animal time to settle in. As the vaccine is live, only a single injection is required to induce immunity but the use of systemic antibiotics can kill off the vaccine and prevent immunity developing. Thus in the case of diarrhoea occurring in calves after vaccination, oral drugs may be used which are not absorbed from the gut, e.g. streptomycin, neomycin, framomycetin, gut-active sulphonamides. A local reaction can occur at the site of injection and occasionally hypersensitivity reactions occur, especially if the animal is carrying S. dublin. In such cases, 1 ml of 1 in 1,000 adrenaline should be given s.c. Immunity with the live vaccine will occur more quickly than with the dead types, particularly as only one injection is required. It is probable that new vaccines will soon become available.

National Preventive Measures

Mention has already been made of the Zoonosis Order. In addition, two other major new Orders should affect the situation, namely the Diseases of Animals (Protein Processing) Order 1981 and the Importation of Processed Animal Protein Order 1981. Both these Orders will allow samples to be taken from processed animal protein for direct use or to be incorporated into feedingstuffs for livestock or poultry from processing plants. The samples must comply with the bacteriological standard of being free from salmonellae and, if the standard is not reached, then an order can be served requiring the owner to take action to ensure future production complies with the standard. Consignments of imported processed animal meal will be licensed and sampling undertaken to see they meet the required bacteriological standard. If positive for salmonella, the importer and the country are notified and they will be asked to adopt measures to prevent contamination in future.

References

MINISTRY OF AGRICULTURE, FISHERIES AND FOOD/WELSH OFFICE AGRICULTURAL DEPARTMENT/DEPARTMENT OF AGRICULTURE AND FISHERIES FOR SCOTLAND (1976) Animal Salmonellosis Annual Summary, p. 1-19.

MINISTRY OF AGRICULTURE, FISHERIES AND FOOD/WELSH OFFICE AGRICULTURAL DEPARTMENT/DEPARTMENT OF AGRICULTURE AND FISHERIES FOR SCOTLAND (1977) Animal Salmonellosis Annual Summary, p. 1-27.

MINISTRY OF AGRICULTURE, FISHERIES AND FOOD/WELSH OFFICE AGRICULTURAL DEPARTMENT/DEPARTMENT OF AGRICULTURE AND FISHERIES FOR SCOTLAND (1978) Animal Salmonellosis Annual Summary, p. 1-24.

MINISTRY OF AGRICULTURE, FISHERIES AND FOOD/WELSH OFFICE AGRICULTURAL DEPARTMENT/DEPARTMENT OF AGRICULTURE AND FISHERIES FOR SCOTLAND (1979) Animal Salmonellosis Annual Summary, p. 1-24.

MINISTRY OF AGRICULTURE, FISHERIES AND FOOD/WELSH OFFICE AGRICULTURAL DEPARTMENT/DEPARTMENT OF AGRICULTURE AND FISHERIES FOR SCOTLAND (1980-81) Animal Salmonellosis Annual Summaries, p. 1-58.

MINISTRY OF AGRICULTURE, FISHERIES AND FOOD/WELSH OFFICE AGRICULTURAL DEPARTMENT/DEPARTMENT OF AGRICULTURE AND FISHERIES FOR SCOTLAND (1982) Animal Salmonellosis Annual Summary, p. 1-38.

MINISTRY OF AGRICULTURE, FISHERIES AND FOOD/WELSH OFFICE AGRICULTURAL DEPARTMENT/DEPARTMENT OF AGRICULTURE AND FISHERIES FOR SCOTLAND (1983) Animal Salmonellosis Annual Summary, p. 1-69.

Telangiectasis

"Sawdust" liver.

Aetiology

It may be the result of a too-rapid rate of fattening cattle.

Occurrence

Usually no signs of the condition are seen but cases are noted at slaughter. Most cases occur between six months and two years old. The condition is thought to arise by the rapid deposition of extracellular glycogen between the hepatic cells and the membrane lining the sinusoid. As more glycogen is deposited the sinusoid membrane is broken down, allowing blood to pass through and connect with other sinusoids. The subsequent increase in pressure and blood volume distorts sinusoids, causing trapping and stagnation of blood. In some cases the blood haemolyses and there is necrosis of hepatic cells with leucocytic infiltration into the area creating a "sawdust" liver. Both telangiectasis and "sawdust" liver can resolve. Livers with a large number of lesions are condemned at meat inspection.

Signs

No specific signs are present in life.

Necropsy

In telangiectasis there are one or more red-brown, spherical foci measuring 1 to 20 mm in diameter. These may be on the surface or in the depth of the liver. "Sawdust" liver contains one or more grey foci.

Diagnosis

Lesions at *post mortem* inspection.

Treatment

As there are no specific signs, therapy is not undertaken.

Control

Reduce the rate of fattening but, as the problem is usually minor, such advice is not worth offering.

Winter Dysentery

Also known as winter scours, vibrionic scours.

Aetiology

It was thought to be caused by a Gram-negative organism, Campylobacter (vibrio) fetus subspecies jejuni. However, the aetiology has been the subject of controversy and recently a coronavirus has been suggested as being implicated.

Occurrence

The condition is quite common in some areas such as south-west England. It is particularly seen when animals are housed and in the autumn or winter. The disease is considered to be highly contagious and is possibly transported mechanically from farm to farm. The condition is mild in young stock but tends to be more severe in dairy cows. Mortality is virtually nil although in severe outbreaks up to 100 per cent of the animals may be affected.

Source of infection

Infected faeces of clinical cases or carriers.

Portal of entry

The mouth.

Spread of infection

By carriers or contamination of inert objects e.g. footwear, tyres, etc.

Incubation period

Three to seven days.

Signs

There is usually an outbreak of diarrhoea which tends to be thin, watery and with a black or dark green colour to it. There is no mucus or epithelial threads present in it. The animals otherwise may show a transient anorexia, and slight pyrexia. Usually the faeces return to normal in two or three days.

Necropsy

If animals are slaughtered there is usually hyperaemia of the abomasal, caecal and colonic mucosae. The small intestines tend to show mild catarrhal inflammation.

Diagnosis

1. History - area of country, time of year.
2. Signs - many cattle affected with a diarrhoea with few systemic signs. No epithelial threads in diarrhoea.
3. Presence of C. fetus subspecies jejuni.

Differential diagnosis

1. Salmonellosis but usually there is more systemic illness.
2. Mucosal disease but usually oral lesions.

Treatment

This is of dubious value as the condition is usually self-limiting. However, in severe or protracted cases it may be worth using oral sulphadimidine at 1g/7 kg (1 oz/450 lb) BW or copper sulphate solution (30 ml of a five *per cent* solution).

Prevention

It is extremely difficult to stop infection passing from farm to farm within an area. During an outbreak visitors to the farm should be discouraged, boots should be disinfected and protective clothing worn. Vehicles should also be discouraged and their wheels disinfected.

CHAPTER 3

RESPIRATORY CONDITIONS

Acute Exudative Pneumonia

Aetiology

This is thought in many cases to be a primary bacterial condition from which *Corynebacterium pyogenes* (Gram-positive rods) can usually be isolated or in some cases *Pasteurella haemolytica* and *P. multocida* (Gram-negative short rods) (Pirie, 1979).

Occurrence

This condition is not uncommon and is usually seen as respiratory disease in individual animals. It can be seen in cattle of any age, particularly when there has been chronic pneumonia in the housing period. It can occur in dairy-bred cattle as well as in suckler calves both indoors and at grass. Individual cases may occur but outbreaks can follow some form of stress. The condition is one of sudden onset.

Signs

The animal suddenly goes off its feed and is dull. There is an oculo-nasal discharge which may be mucoid or muco-purulent. The temperature is usually 40-41°C (104-107°F), respiratory rate is between 20 and 60 per minute, usually with hyperpnoea. There is often some coughing but this is not pronounced. On auscultation there are usually squeaks, humming and wheezing often at inspiration, particularly the latter. Cranioventrally there may be moist sounds and there may be pleuritic rub (sandpaper-like) sounds in a few cases.

Necropsy

There are dark areas of consolidation in the ventral parts of the apical and cardiac, and in some cases the cardiac lobes. The areas of pneumonia may be small and scattered, but in more severe cases there are large areas of consolidation and, in some animals, abscess formation. Microscopically there is exudation and vascular congestion with the bronchioles and alveoli showing infiltration with neutrophils and macrophages (Pirie, 1979).

Diagnosis

1. A single animal is usually involved.
2. Pyrexia and respiratory signs are normally evident.

Differential diagnosis

1. Chronic pneumonia; normally less ill and several are affected.
2. Inhalation pneumonia; usually results in a very dull animal and also there is a history of drenching.

Treatment

Isolate the affected animal. Antibiotic therapy with oxytetracycline, penicillin and streptomycin, ampicillin, amoxycillin, sulphadimidine,

Treatment

Isolate the affected animal. Antibiotic therapy with oxytetracycline, penicillin and streptomycin, ampicillin, amoxycillin, sulphadimidine, trimethoprim and sulphadiazine for three to five days is usually successful. Most cases respond well to therapy, but a few relapse and some ultimately develop chronic suppurative pneumonia. Flunixin meglumine may help reduce inflammation.

Prevention

Try to ensure adequate ventilation in housing.

Reference

PIRIE, H M (1979) Respiratory Diseases of Animals. Notes for a post-graduate course. Edited by Pirie, H M, Glasgow University, Glasgow. p. 41-42.

Aspiration Pneumonia

This is also known as inhalation pneumonia.

Aetiology

Although not a common condition, it still occurs too frequently. Obtaining an adequate history is important and often the stockman may realise what has happened, but will be reluctant to admit it or even that he has drenched the animal. Obstruction or paralysis of the larynx, pharynx or oesophagus may produce the problem as can the rupture of a pharyngeal abscess or the products of laryngeal diphtheria. The signs will depend on the nature of the fluid introduced, the quantity and the bacteria introduced. If a large quantity is administered into the lungs, then instantaneous death may occur. If the substance given is soluble, then absorption into the body is rapid because of the highly vascular nature of the lungs and few, if any, signs will occur. Less soluble products will result in a varying degree of toxaemia and respiratory signs which are often fatal after between one and three days.

Signs

Peracute

Death occurs rapidly after drenching.

Acute

Usually only one animal is affected and there is a history of drenching. Signs develop rapidly and include a varying degree of dullness and inappetance, a cough and tachypnoea. The temperature is usually elevated to about 40°C (104°F) and on auscultation there are areas of dullness present normally in the the cranio-ventral parts of the lungs and moist bubbling and crackles may be heard in the area. There is often also a pruritic rub sound and some degree of thoracic pain. If the condition progresses, the signs of dullness and anorexia become more pronounced, and there may be a foetid odour to the breath.

Subacute

In such cases there are few signs present except for episodes of coughing and tachypnoea following the introduction of the fluid.

Chronic

Some animals will survive the immediate episode, but will show ill-thrift and intermittent bouts of respiratory problems.

Necropsy

There is often an acute exudative or gangrenous pneumonia of the ventral parts of the apical, cardiac and usually also the diaphragmatic lobes. In some animals there is extensive suppurative necrosis.

Diagnosis

1. A true history is indicative that the condition is present.
2. Usually only a single animal is affected.
3. The signs are of sudden onset.
4. The respiratory signs are severe.

5. There is a leucopenia.
6. A neutrophilia is present.

Differential diagnosis

1. Septicaemia.
2. Enteritis but then there is diarrhoea present.
3. Acute exudative pneumonia, but in this case there is no history of drenching and usually the animal is less dull.

Treatment

If there is to be a hope of effective therapy, it must be administered as soon as possible after the drenching incident. The use of antibiotics or a sulphonamide is indicated and it is best to give the first dose intravenously. Thus oxytetracycline, amoxycillin, ampicillin, sulphadimidine, sulphamethoxypyridazine or sulphapyrazole can be used. In exceptional circumstances chloramphenicol might be indicated. Therapy should be continued in most cases for about five days. In addition, fluid therapy may be required. The animal should be encouraged to eat and drink. It should be kept on its own in a well-bedded, airy pen.

Prevention

Ensure that all drenching is undertaken slowly, allowing the animal time to swallow.

Avian Tuberculosis

Aetiology

Infection with Mycobacterium avium (Gram-positive, acid-fast rods).

Occurrence

This causes little clinical problem in cattle but it does interfere with interpretation of the tuberculin test. Most cases arise on a herd basis where poultry are kept with cattle. The use of the comparative tuberculin test helps to reduce interpretation problems. Sensitivity to the test usually decreases rapidly after removal of the cattle from the birds. Deer can become infected and act as a source for birds.

Signs

Occasionally there are signs of a cough and a loss of condition. If the uterus is involved there may be abortion and if the udder is infected there is induration.

Necropsy

Lesions may be found in the mesenteric lymph nodes, the udder and meninges.

Diagnosis

1. History; presence of poultry or other birds.
2. Avian tuberculin reaction.
3. Comparative tuberculin test.

Differential diagnosis

1. Bovine tuberculosis.

Control

Keep poultry away from cattle.

Bovine Nasal Granuloma

Also known as atopic rhinitis, summer catarrh, summer sniffles, Jersey catarrh and chronic granulorhinitis.

Aetiology

The condition appears to be due to repeated immediate (Type 1) hypersensitivity reactions.

Occurrence

The condition is uncommon. It is more prevalent in the Channel Island breeds and occurs at the end of the summer. Most cases occur when the animals are outside and subside once housing occurs. Animals first show signs at one to two years old and then become affected each year and the signs become more severe (Wiseman, Gibbs and McGregor, 1982). In a herd there is often some relationship between affected animals, e.g. same sire.

Signs

The animals are bright, alert, and do not usually possess a cough. Initially there is a profuse serous nasal discharge and a serous ocular discharge. The nasal discharge turns yellow and the cattle sneeze. Most animals develop a degree of tachypnoea (30 - 40 respirations/minute), some hyperpnoea and a swollen face. Nasal pruritus often occurs. The nasal mucous membranes often become swollen with ulceration, and the nasal discharge may become streaked with blood. Often the nose is rubbed on the grass or on hedges.

Necropsy

In the nasal mucosa there are often small white nodules which are firm to touch.

Diagnosis

1. The condition does not spread.
2. The same cattle tend to be affected annually.
3. The condition often worsens during each season.
4. Usually signs disappear during the autumn.
5. There is no pyrexia or cough.
6. The nasal mucus contains many eosinophils.

Differential diagnosis

1. IBR but there is pyrexia and a cough in this disease.
2. Dusty feed rhinotracheitis.

Treatment

The animals can be housed as this often helps the condition. Antihistamines or corticosteroid injections can be used but only give temporary relief.

Control

Check the breeding of the cattle. If a link is found in breeding, discontinue the type of mating resulting in the problem.

Reference

WISEMAN, A, GIBBS, H A and McGREGOR, A B (1982) Veterinary Record, 110, 420-421.

Chronic Suppurative Pneumonia

Aetiology

Various initial causes may result in one or more pathological conditions such as bronchopneumonia, bronchiectasis and pulmonary abscesses.

Occurrence

Most cases occur in adult cattle rather than those still growing. It is, however, a very common cause of respiratory signs in the individual animal. Often there has been an outbreak of acute pneumonia in the history. Although most cases appear to progress slowly over a period of weeks or months, the odd case will appear to be of sudden onset due to a rapid exacerbation of a suppurative area in the chest.

Signs

Severe

There is a sudden marked loss of condition with marked dullness, obvious thoracic pain, pyrexia (40.5°C - 105°F). In some animals there is halitosis due to a necrotising bronchopneumonia and pleurisy. Death in these animals often occurs within a few days.

Usual

Usually the animal becomes progressively duller and thinner with a fall in milk yield and intermittent pyrexia, up to 40°C (104°F). A cough is usually present with the production of mucus and there is a variable degree of tachypnoea. Thoracic pain may be obvious by an abduction of the elbows and reluctance to move but in other cases it is only discernible on ballotment. On auscultation there are usually whistles, squeaks and wheezing sounds in the cranio-ventral part of the chest and there are often areas of dullness.

Necropsy

If the main lesion is bronchopneumonia there is usually marked consolidation of the cranio-ventral parts of the lung with exudate filling the bronchi and bronchioles. On histological examination, inflammatory cells pass the alveoli and bronchi. When the main problem is a bronchiectasis often bronchi in the cranial and middle lobes with dilated air passageways contain mucus and fibrous tissue. In severe cases the histological sections show complete destruction of the alveolar tissue. When lung abscesses are the main feature these are usually found in the ventral lung border. Necrotic tissues and pus-containing structures are found within a fibrous capsular wall.

Diagnosis

1. History of a chronic loss of condition with respiratory disease in a single animal.

2. Signs such as pyrexia, thoracic pain, cough.

Differential diagnosis

1. Cuffing pneumonia but this is normally a group problem.
2. Acute pneumonia may be a single animal or several animals.

3. Salmonellosis but at this age there is usually diarrhoea.
4. IBR infection usually results in a marked conjunctivitis.
5. Inhalation pneumonia has a specific history.
6. Tuberculosis will probably have a history of herd infection.
7. Calf diphtheria.
8. Malignant catarrhal fever.

Treatment

Often therapy is of limited use. Any treatment may need to be prolonged for ten days to two weeks or more. Antibiotic therapy with oxytetracycline, penicillin and streptomycin, ampicillin, amoxycillin, sulphadimidine, trimethoprim and sulphadiazine may be helpful. Most cases which respond are likely to break down again and so such animals should be slaughtered.

Control

Cull animals which have had previous bouts of respiratory disease. Ensure all cases are treated early and thoroughly.

Dusty Feed Rhinotracheitis

Aetiology

Particles of varying size meet varying fates following inspiration, see Table 3.1 below.

TABLE 3.1

The Fate of Various-Sized Particles entering the Respiratory System

Particle Size	Fate
Greater than 10.0 μ	Removed in nasal passages.
10.0 to 2.0 μ	Deposited at varying levels in the respiratory tract, but above the alveoli. The smaller the particle the further down the respiratory airways it is deposited. They are removed by muco-ciliary action.
2.0 to 1.0 μ	Deposited in alveoli.
1.0 to 0.5 μ	Exhaled with air.
Below 0.5 μ	Deposited in alveoli due to diffusion forces.

Most of the particles will be in the nasal passages or the trachea, bronchi and bronchioles. The condition results from the introduction of dry, fine-particled feed or very dusty bedding.

Occurrence

The introduction of a dusty, dry feed to animals indoors causes the problem. The signs occur most frequently in the hour or two following feeding. Removal of the feed causes recovery in a few days. The condition occurs most commonly when the relative humidity is low.

Signs

There is the sudden onset of coughing. The cough tends to be dry and can be single or paroxysmal. Several cattle are normally affected. The animals are otherwise bright and alert. They eat well and there are no abnormal lower respiratory sounds. Respirations are normal in rate and extent and temperature is normal. There is conjunctivitis and usually a copious ocular and nasal discharge which is mucoid, but sometimes it is slightly purulent.

Therapy

Replace the feed or bedding used. Otherwise dampen down the feed before giving it or molasses can be added to it. In the case of bedding, the bales should be opened up outside before the cattle are bedded.

Prevention

Dusty hay should not be fed. If the feed is found to be dusty then five *per cent* molasses should be added to it. Dusty bedding should not be used. As the particles affecting the animals can affect humans, it is advisable for workers to wear face masks.

Fog Fever

This is a form of atypical interstitial pneumonia.

Aetiology

Although not fully authenticated, the condition is considered to be a toxicosis following the ingestion of large quantities of L-tryptophan.

Occurrence

The condition is seen in cattle over two years old, particularly those in suckler herds and affects several cattle to a varying degree at the same time. Often the cattle have been receiving little nutrition and are put onto a more lush pasture in the autumn (September to November). The field may have been top-dressed with nitrogenous fertiliser. The condition is normally seen within two weeks of entry to the new pasture. The Hereford and Hereford-cross breeds seem to be particularly susceptible.

It is thought that L-tryptophan in the grass is ingested and metabolised in the rumen to indole acetic acid (IAA). IAA is decarboxylated by *Lactobacillus* spp. to produce 3-methyl indole (3MI). This metabolite can enter the blood and is usually acted upon by the mixed function oxidase system to produce indoles and other metabolites in the urine. 3MI can cause the destruction of pulmonary cells such as type 1 pneumocytes and monociliated bronchiolar secretory cells, resulting in various pathological changes. Mortality in severely affected animals can be high (up to 75 *per cent*) but usually only a small number are so involved (5 *per cent*).

Signs

Several animals will show signs but the degree will vary widely and often the farmer only notices one to be ill at the start. The cattle tend to be much quieter and more approachable than normal and they tend to have a sleepy or tranquil expression. The respiratory signs are usually of distress but vary in degree. Coughing is normally little heard.

Severe

There is the sudden onset of dyspnoea with a loud respiratory grunt, mouth-breathing and often the animal froths at the mouth. Auscultation often reveals little considering the severity of illness in the animals, but it may produce soft, moist sounds and a few crackles. Death can occur as the result of excitement.

Less Severe

There is tachypnoea (rate 50 - 80 per minute) with hyperpnoea and usually there is no dyspnoea. The rectal temperature tends to be normal and the animal is again quiet and tranquil. Coughing is only heard occasionally and in some recovering animals there may develop a subcutaneous emphysema. Auscultation may reveal harsh sounds.

Necropsy

Dead animals have haemorrhages in the larynx, tracheal and bronchial mucosae. The lungs tend to be swollen, heavy and dark red in colour. The cut surface tends to glisten, is smooth and has a red appearance.

Emphysema may be present in the interlobular septa and pleura. Histological examination reveals severe congestion and oedema of the pulmonary tissue, hyaline membrane formation, severe interstitial emphysema and moderate epithelial hyperplasia of type 2 pneumocytes.

Cattle slaughtered in the later stages do not usually show haemorrhages of the respiratory mucosa. There is an overall pale pink colour with variable amounts of interstitial emphysema.

Diagnosis

1. History of group condition, mainly suckler animals moved to a lush pasture in autumn.
2. Signs include acute respiratory signs with little to hear on auscultation, no cough and the animals are more tranquil.
3. Post mortem findings, with pulmonary oedema and emphysema.

Differential diagnosis

1. Husk, but cough present and no vaccination history.
2. Pneumonic pasteurellosis but no pyrexia and usually a mucopurulent discharge.
3. Nitrate poisoning but the blood tends to be brownish and the urine contains methaemoglobin.
4. Infectious bovine rhinotracheitis but usually pyrexia and loud, explosive cough.
5. Thrombosis of the caudal vena cava but a single animal and eventual haemoptysis.

Treatment

Remove the cattle from the incriminated pasture. Most other treatment tends to be empirical. Interference with a severely distressed animal may result in its death. Atropine at 1 g per 450 kg (990 lb) BW intravenously acts as a bronchodilator and corticosteroids may be useful.

Control

If animals are hungry when they enter a new pasture in the autumn, restricted feed them by only grazing for short periods during the first two weeks. This should be for about two hours on the first day, increasing by an hour a day so that the cattle can be left out for the whole day after about 12 days. Otherwise the area can be grazed by strip grazing or initially graze with a less susceptible species such as sheep. If monensin sodium is given at the rate of 200 g/head/day before entering the pasture, this can stop problems.

Infectious Bovine Rhinotracheitis

In America this is often referred to as "red nose".

Aetiology

The disease is due to a specific herpes virus known as Bovine Herpes Virus 1. There appear to be more than one strain of the virus. The disease is seen as different syndromes of varying severity.

Occurrence

The disease was reported in the early 1960's as a mild respiratory syndrome with conjunctivitis, nasal discharge and occasional coughing. A second mild syndrome involved the genital tract of the female (infectious bovine vulvovaginitis - IPV) and male (infectious pustular balanoposthitis - IPB). In the early 1970's between five and 10 per cent of cattle in Great Britain had serum antibody levels to the condition. However, since 1977 a more severe form of the disease has been encountered and more animals have been affected (see Tables 3.2, 3.3), and it has been speculated that it is due to the introduction of a more virulent strain with Holstein cattle imported from Canada. The disease has been reported in other countries to naturally infect goats, pigs and some species of deer.

TABLE 3.2

Number of Outbreaks of IBR diagnosed in the late 1970's

	Moredun, Edinburgh	Weybridge, Surrey	
	% Outbreaks Investigated Positive	Number Positive by Virus Isolation	Number Positive by Serology
1975	2.7	-	-
1976	3.0	-	-
1977	9.5	5	12
1978	20.2	36	53
1979 (first quarter)	39.7	28	30

(Source: Veterinary Record 1979)

Spread of infection

In most cases the disease is of a respiratory nature and so the main source of infection is from nasal exudate and the coughing up of infected droplets. The virus can be found in semen and so venereal spread may be possible. At present most outbreaks in Britain follow the introduction of a new animal to the farm although as the disease becomes more endemic it is likely many cases will arise from carrier animals resident on the farm. Most cases occur in animals during the autumn and winter months, probably as the result of housing and therefore increasing the exposure risk. However, the disease can occur at any time of the year and also at grass. When signs are in a herd, the number affected is usually at its greatest about two to three weeks after onset. Signs are normally mildest in older animals, but the severest form tends to be in rearing animals.

TABLE 3.3

IBR Blood Tests on Export Animals

Year	Number Tested	% Positive
1972	517	0.98
1973	862	1.3
1974	656	2.9
1975	830	5.1
1976	1,288	4.0
1977	1,472	8.4
1978	7,254	6.5
1979	12,746	9.7
1980	8,892	8.9
1981	4,754	9.9

(Source: British Friesian Journal, 1982)

The main problem with IBR infection is that it can produce carrier animals which may remain latent virtually all their lives. Experimentally infection has been shown to persist for up to 17 months (Snowdon, 1975) and it can be activated by the injection of large doses of corticosteroids (Darcel and Dorward, 1975). Morbidity can vary between about five per cent and over 90 per cent. At present in Britain many outbreaks have a high morbidity (Wiseman, Msolla, Selman, Allen and Pirie, 1980) but as more of the national herd becomes exposed to infection, morbidity in individual outbreaks is likely to reduce to 20 or 30 per cent and also the signs will become less severe. Mortality is usually low but varies between nil and 80 per cent. Most deaths are due to secondary infections and occur in the convalescent period.

Route of entry

Usually by inhalation but it could be venereal.

Incubation period

This is normally between about three and eight days, but in some outbreaks it can be up to three weeks.

Abortion rate

It can be up to 25 to 50 per cent.

Signs

There are four main forms of the disease, namely alimentary, nervous, reproductive and respiratory. The alimentary form is seen in new-born calves and is not applicable to this book. The reproductive form occurs in a mild and a more severe form. The nervous form has been reported recently.

Nervous

This is usually seen in animals under six months old. Morbidity is low, but mortality of the affected animals is high. There is an encephalitis with pyrexia 40.5°C (105°F), anorexia, incoordination and intermittent periods of excitement and depression. The heart rate is usually increased.

Respiratory

This is more common in cattle over six months old, but the disease is often seen in young animals. Those cattle which first show signs are usually the most ill (Pirie, 1979). The signs in an outbreak and between outbreaks are very variable. In older cattle, signs usually last one to five days, but recovery can take 10 to 14 days.

Peracute

Animals show signs of pyrexia up to 42°C (108°F) with oculo-nasal discharge, respiratory distress when exercised and a cough. The animal dies after about 24 hours due to obstructive bronchitis.

Acute

Pyrexia is evident, often with a temperature of 41°C (106°F), there is dullness and a reduction in feed intake. Often there is a selective reduction in feed intake with roughage being refused, but concentrates eaten (Wiseman et al, 1980). There is usually a copious serous conjunctival discharge with a conjunctivitis and a similar nasal discharge is usually apparent. Later one or both of the ocular and nasal discharges may become mucoid or purulent. The nasal mucosa may be hyperaemic with small ulcers, whereas in more severely affected animals there are petechial nasal haemorrhages and diphtheritic plaques in the nasal cavities and consequent malodour and stertor. Most animals show tachypnoea and hyperpnoea. There is often an explosive cough and palpation of the larynx is resented. In thoracic auscultation there are increased referred tracheal noises (Wiseman et al, 1980). In all but the severely affected, recovery occurs in about a week.

Subacute

A slightly raised temperature of 40°C (104°F), inappetance with usually profuse serous ocular and possibly nasal discharge. There is some congestion, hyperpnoea and tachypnoea. Recovery is usually rapid.

Mild

No signs are evident except perhaps the odd cough or serous ocular discharge.

Reproductive

Abortion

This is a very common cause of abortion in USA cattle and is often recorded in Britain. Abortion often occurs several weeks after respiratory signs in a herd. Most cases occur at six to eight months of pregnancy. Retention of the placenta is a common finding.

Infectious Bovine Vulvovaginitis (IPV)

This was reported in Britain during the 1970's. It usually occurred following service. Pain is often evident, with frequent micturition and brushing of the tail. There may be pustules and oedema of the vulval mucosa, and erythema. There is a purulent vaginal discharge, often copious, and remaining for several weeks. Often poor conception rates and short oestrous cycles may occur. Each lesion only lasts a few days.

Infectious Bovine Penoposthitis (Infectious Pustular Balanoposthitis, IPB)

This involves the penis and prepuce and may be localised or generalised with roughened papular areas on the penis. There are distinct red spots and frank haemorrhages with yellow necrotic centres. Pustular lesions are infrequent. In severe cases there is a generalised purulent discharge with ulceration and denudation of the epithelium. Some cases show blood or pus at the prepucial orifice.

Necropsy

Nervous

A non-suppurative encephalitis occurs particularly affecting the cerebral cortex and internal capsule.

Respiratory

In uncomplicated cases, lesions are restricted to the upper respiratory tract terminating at the upper bronchi. Inflammation of the muzzle and the nasal cavities varies from some congestion and petechiation, with mucoid exudate, to a fibrino-purulent exudate with necrosis of the nasal mucous membranes. The submandibular and retropharyngeal lymph nodes tend to be swollen and oedematous. There is a laryngotracheobronchitis which varies from a mild congestion of the mucous membranes with a mucoid discharge to large areas being covered by a necrotic layer of exudate (Pirie, 1979). In some cases there is pulmonary emphysema and secondary exudative bronchopneumonia which may be purulent or necrotising. Histologically, the mucous membranes show acute catarrhal inflammation and in some cases the epithelium becomes necrotic and is lost. The lamina propria of the bronchi, trachea and larynx tends to be infiltrated with neutrophils, lymphocytes, plasma cells and macrophages. In naturally-occurring infections, inclusion bodies appear to be absent.

Reproductive

Abortion

The foetus usually shows autolysis and focal necrotic hepatitis.

IPV

There are pustules and oedema of the vulval mucosa.

IPB

There are focal necrotic and haemorrhagic areas with ulceration and loss of epithelium.

Diagnosis

Nervous

1. The herd is infected with IBR.
2. The encephalitis is non-suppurative.

Respiratory

1. There has been the introduction of a new animal.
2. The disease is a group problem.
3. Often there is a marked conjunctivitis and copious serous ocular discharge.
4. There may be necrosis of the nasal mucosa, but not in the mouth.
5. There is often marked pyrexia.
6. Confirmation can be by virus isolation with fluorescent antibody staining of the ocular and nasal discharges within the first two weeks of infection.
7. Paired blood samples will show a rise in the serum neutralisation test. Other tests used include indirect haemagglutination test, complement fixation test, virus neutralisation test and, recently, a micro-enzyme linked immunosorbent assay has been introduced.

Reproductive

Abortion

1. Respiratory disease in herd.
2. Often more than one case.
3. Fluorescent antibody to detect virus in impressions from cotyledons or foetal tissues.
4. Paired blood samples.

IPV

1. Virus detected in vulval lesions.
2. Paired blood samples. Often antibody titres are low and short-lived.

IPB

1. Virus detection in lesions.
2. Paired blood samples often show little or no antibody rise.

Differential diagnosis

Respiratory

1. Acute pneumonia.
2. Chronic pneumonia.
3. Calf diphtheria, but in this case only a few animals are affected and the lesions are in the mouth or the pharynx.
4. Bovine viral diarrhoea but there are then erosions in the mouth and diarrhoea.

5. Bovine malignant catarrh normally affects single animals, there are erosions in the mouth, and keratitis.

6. Infectious bovine keratoconjunctivitis but in this disease there is keratitis and corneal ulceration.

7. Pasteurellosis but toxaemia and lung involvement occur.

8. Bovine nasal granuloma with sneezing and wheezing.

Reproduction

Abortion

1. Vibriosis.

2. Mucosal disease.

3. Leptospirosis.

IPV

1. Granular vulvovaginitis.

Therapy

There is a considerable divergence of opinion as to whether or not to use antibiotic treatment in the respiratory form. If the disease appears to be uncomplicated, and this is unusual, then there would seem to be little point in therapy. If however, as in most cases, there is secondary lung involvement, then therapy is justified. At the start of an outbreak all cases should be isolated as soon as possible because although it may not stop spread of the disease, the first animals are often clinically the worst affected. If antimicrobial agents are to be used, all ill animals should be treated for three to five days with any one of a number of drugs (see Table 3.4), including penicillin and streptomycin, oxytetracycline, ampicillin, amoxycillin, trimethoprim and sulphadiazine, sulphadimidine, sulphamethoxypyridazine and sulphapyrazole. The animal should be given good wholesome feed and it should be encouraged to eat and drink. Some farmers have vaccinated their cattle with live vaccine after the start of an outbreak, with good results, but to be successful, infection must not have become established. It should, however, be remembered that for effective protection, vaccines should be introduced before the onset of infection. Several compounds have been found which are active against herpes viruses in man. Many are, however, toxic, but one drug, acyclovir, has been shown to be safe and may in the future be tried in animals.

TABLE 3.4

Some of the Antimicrobial Compounds used in Pneumonia Therapy

Antimicrobial Compounds	Bactericidal (C) or Bacteriostatic (S)	Route of Administration				Dosage	
						mg/kg	mg/lb
Amoxycillin	C	IV	SC	IM	Oral	7	3.5
Ampicillin	C	IV	SC	IM	Oral	2-7	1-3.5
Chloramphenicol	S	IV	SC	IM	Oral	4-10	2-5
Erythromycin	S	-	-	IM	-	2.5-5	1.25-2.5
Oxytetracycline	S	IV	SC	IM	Oral	10	5
Penicillin plus streptomycin	C	-	SC	IM	-	10-20 10-15	5-10 5-7.5
Spectinomycin	C	IV	-	IM	Oral	12.5-30	6.25-15
Spiramycin	S	-	-	IM	Oral	20	10
Sulphadimidine	S	initial					
		IV	SC	-	Oral	200	100
		maintenance					
		IV	SC	-	Oral	100	50
Sulphamethoxy-pyridazine	S	IV	SC	IM	-	22	11
Sulphapyrazole	S	IV	SC	IM	-	30-100	15-50
Trimethoprim and sulphadiazine	C	-	-	IM	Oral	15-22.5	7.5-12
Trimethoprim and sulphadoxine	C	IV	-	IM	-	15	7.5
Tylosin	S	-	-	IM	Oral	4-10	2-5

Prevention

Management

It is best to keep a closed herd. However in America, and also in Britain, infection has been found in closed herds. Any new animal entering a known uninfected herd should be blood-tested prior to entry. If the test is negative the animal should be isolated for a month and then retested. If the test is again negative the animal can be allowed to enter the herd. The risks then of the introduction of infection are small. If the animal suffers a respiratory problem while in isolation the second test should not be until two or three weeks after the end of the episode. Some farmers may need to go to these lengths to keep their pedigree herds free from disease, because many European countries will not accept exports from Britain unless they are shown to have a negative titre for IBR. The same conditions at present govern the entry of bulls to British artificial insemination centres.

Vaccination

Until the autumn of 1979, the only vaccine available in Britain was an inactivated multicomponent vaccine. The vaccine could be given as doses two to four weeks apart with a third injection at 10 to 12 weeks old. Subsequently, two live IBR vaccines have become available. Both are given by intranasal inoculation and should be administered 24 to 48 hours after entry to the farm (Ismay, 1980). One vaccine is temperature-sensitive and so only replicates in the upper parts of the respiratory tract. However, the vaccine can still produce circulating antibody levels in some cattle which will preclude their export or their sale to AI centres. The other vaccine does replicate in organs other than the lungs and produces a good systemic immunity. The vaccines provide effective immunity (Frerichs, Woods, Lucas and Sands, 1982) but they do allow the replication and re-excretion of the IBR virus which can thus spread infection to non-vaccinated animals (Nettleton and Sharp, 1980).

References

BLOOD, D C, RADOSTITS, O M and HENDERSON, J A (1983) 'Veterinary Medicine' 6th edition. Bailliere Tindall, London. p. 798-804.

BRITISH FRIESIAN JOURNAL (1982) Infectious bovine rhinotracheitis. 64, No. 3, p. 222.

DARCEL, C I R Q and DORWARD, W J (1975) Canadian Veterinary Journal, 16, 87-88.

FRERICHS, G N, WOODS, S B, LUCAS, M H and SANDS, J J (1982) Veterinary Record, 111, 116-122.

ISMAY, W S (1980) Veterinary Record, 107, 511-512.

NETTLETON, P F and SHARP, J M (1980) Veterinary Record, 107, 379.

PIRIE, H M (1979) Respiratory Diseases of Animals. Notes for a post-graduate course. Edited by Pirie, H M. Glasgow University, Glasgow, p. 71-74.

SNOWDON, W A (1975) Australian Veterinary Journal, 41, 135-141.

VETERINARY RECORD (1979) 105, 3-4.

WISEMAN, A, MSOLLA, P M, SELMAN, I E, ALLAN, E M and PIRIE, H M (1980) Veterinary Record, 107, 436-441.

Mycoplasma Bovis Infection

Aetiology

Infection with *Mycoplasma bovis*, also known as *M. agalactiae* subspecies *bovis* and *M. bovimastitidis*.

Occurrence

The organism was first isolated in America during 1962 and was subsequently identified in Britain in 1975. *M. bovis* can survive several weeks in faeces and several days on impermeable surfaces. The signs are variable but there are respiratory, arthritic and vulvovaginitis forms in the grazing animal as well as mastitis in the cow. Mortality, when the organism first enters a herd, can be up to 25 *per cent*.

Spread of infection

By contact, inhalation or venereally.

Signs

Respiratory

There is a pyrexia up to 41°C (106°F) with dyspnoea, apathy, anorexia with widespread coughing.

Arthritis

There is lameness and polyarthritis with one or more joints of the limbs involved.

Vulvovaginitis

There can be a temporary infertility and failure to conceive.

Necropsy

Respiratory

The lungs are consolidated with emphysema. Histologically there is an acute bronchopneumonia with a fibrous exudate and alveolar macrophages filling the air spaces, and bronchitis.

Arthritis

There is a polyarthritis with the joint capsule containing a turbid, straw-coloured fluid.

Vulvovaginitis

There can be a salpingitis and endometritis.

Diagnosis

The signs are very similar to those of other diseases.

1. Isolation of the organism.
2. Serological testing.

Treatment

The use of antibiotics, particularly tylosin, may be of some help.

Control

Good hygiene helps to reduce infection spread. Some American herds have managed to remove infection by separation and culling of infected cows.

Shipping Fever

Transit fever, pasteurellosis.

Aetiology

There has been considerable debate over the aetiology of this condition although it is often associated with *Pasteurella haemolytica* and *P. multocida* (Gram-negative coccobacilli). It is possible that other organisms can be involved, including Bedsonia, mycoplasmas, adenoviruses, parainfluenza III and *Dictyocaulus viviparus*.

Occurrence

The condition is common but less so than enzootic pneumonia. It is almost always a group problem although initially only one or two cattle may be affected. Most cases occur in yearlings, particularly steers, following their removal from suckler herds to other farms for further rearing or finishing. The condition often follows the passage of cattle through the autumn sales or markets as well as following transport. Most cases are seen from October to December. Most infection occurs in Scotland. Cases usually occur 1 to 3 weeks after movement and when the animals have been stressed by weaning, a change of diet, housing, mixed groups from various farms under the same roof, etc. Outbreaks of disease may last 2 to 3 weeks in a unit and there may be further problems as other cattle are brought in or groups are mixed. Often single cases occur in the first week which then allow spread to others in the same group before the second and third weeks, followed by passage to other groups.

Age susceptibility

Most cases occur between six months and two years.

Method of spread

Aerogenous.

Signs

Peracute

Sudden death with no premonitory signs.

Acute

The animals are dull and inactive with excessive oculo-nasal discharges which may be mucopurulent. There is usually anorexia although the cattle still drink, and a marked fever 40 - 41°C (104 - 106°F). There is rapid (40 per minute plus) shallow breathing and a soft, productive cough which tends to increase with exercise. On auscultation there are bronchial sounds over the anterior and ventral parts of the lungs which become louder as the condition continues. In some cases squeaks and high-pitched sounds are heard, together with a pleuritic rub. Later signs can include dyspnoea with marked abdominal breathing and an expiratory grunt. Diarrhoea occurs in a few animals. There is usually a favourable response to therapy.

Necropsy

Death is usually the result of anoxia and toxaemia although occasionally in young cattle there is septicaemia. Usually over a third of the lung shows marked consolidation and the ventral parts of the apical and cardiac lobes are most involved. Initially there is congestion and then hepatisation with exudate and, in some animals, emphysema. Bronchitis and bronchiolitis are usually catarrhal, often with serofibrinous pleurisy and a fibrinous pericarditis. There is usually much pleural effusion.

Diagnosis

1. History - recent move, housing, age 6 to 24 months.
2. Signs - severe respiratory signs involving particularly antero-ventral parts of lung. Pyrexia.
3. Necropsy - lung consolidation, pleurisy.
4. Bacteriology - isolation of P. haemolytica or P. multocida from nasal swabs in live animals or lungs post mortem. Antibiotic sensitivity.
5. Impression smears show bipolar staining organisms with methylene blue.
6. Haematology - little value as variable; sometimes neutrophilia, sometimes neutropaenia.

Differential diagnosis

1. Enzootic pneumonia - usually younger calves.
2. IBR - the signs usually involve the upper respiratory area.
3. Fog fever - cattle are usually too young for this and occurs on lush grass.
4. Husk - usually less pyrexia and toxaemia - larvae present in faeces.
5. Acute bronchopneumonia due to Fusiformis necrophorus, Streptococcus spp. or Klebsiella pneumoniae. These have almost identical signs to shipping fever.

Treatment

Most cattle will usually show some improvement within 1 to 3 days of initiating treatment. Complete recovery may take 4 to 7 days. Antimicrobial drugs can be used and a selection are shown in Table 3.5. Where severe outbreaks occur it may occasionally be necessary to use mass medication as most ill cattle still drink well.

Control

The problem arises because of changes in husbandry and the mixing of cattle. Ideally animals should be conditioned before they move to the rearing farm by giving the feed to be fed outside before moving them in. They should have been weaned for at least a fortnight. Often cattle are best kept outside for two weeks after first entry to the farm. The animals should be in small groups to reduce stress and spread of infection. Sometimes long-acting penicillin or oxytetracycline may be useful but often these are best used about a week after entry. Vaccination may be of use provided it is given before movement. Pasteurella vaccines can be used. They are dead and require two doses, 2 to 3 weeks apart. Multicomponent virus vaccines may also be used, but again two doses are required at a 2 to 4-week interval. Any dehorning, castration, ear-tagging, etc. should be left until about a month after entry or two weeks after the last cases of shipping fever.

TABLE 3.5

Therapy for Shipping Fever

Drug	Method of Administration	Dose mg/kg	Dose mg/1b	Duration
Ampicillin trihydrate	s.c.,i.m.	5-10mg/kg	2.5-5mg/1b	Daily for 3 days
Chloramphenicol	i.m.	10mg/kg	5mg/1b	3-4 times daily for 3 days
Erythromycin	i.v.,i.m.	5mg/kg	2.5mg/1b	Daily for 3 days
Oxytetracycline	i.v.,s.c.,i.m.	10mg/kg	5mg/1b	Daily for 3 days
Penicillin/ dihydrostreptomycin	i.m.	20-30,000iu/kg 20mg/kg	10-15,000iu/1b 10mg/1b	Daily for 3 days
Spectinomycin	i.v.,i.m.	10-20mg/kg	5-10mg/1b	Daily for 3-4 days
Spiramycin	i.m.	20mg/kg	10mg/1b	Daily for 2-3 days
Sulphadimidine	i.v.,s.c.,oral	150mg/kg	75mg/1b	Daily for 3 days
Trimethoprim and sulphadiazine	i.m.	4mg/kg 20mg/kg	2mg/1b 10mg/1b	Daily for 3-5 days
Trimethoprim and sulphadoxine	i.v.,i.m.	3mg/kg 12.5mg/kg	1.5mg/1b 6mg/1b	Daily for 3-5 days
Tylosin	i.m., Mass medication	4-10mg/kg	2-5mg/1b	Daily for 3-5 days
Oxytetracycline	Oral	3-5mg/kg	1-3mg/1b	Daily for 5-7 days
Sulphadimidine	Oral	100mg/kg	50mg/1b	Daily for 5-7 days
Trimethoprim and sulphadiazine	Oral	5mg/kg 25mg/kg	2.5mg/1b 12.5mg/1b	Daily for 5 days

All animals should be provided with good quality feed and adequate ventilation. Corticosteroids, e.g. betamethasone, dexamethasone, are often found to help in reducing the level of exudation. Flunixin meglumide may be useful in reducing inflammation, and Pasteurella antisera may also be helpful.

Thrombosis of the Caudal Vena Cava

Aetiology

A septic focus, usually in the liver, results in a septic thrombus in the caudal vena cava from which there is the haematogenous spread of infection to the lungs.

Occurrence

An uncommon condition affecting single animals over one year old although many cases occur in the growing animal. A few cases of thrombosis of the cranial vena cava have been recorded with similar signs. Most cases result from a liver abscess. This causes a localised phlebitis, usually in the area of the vena cava, adjacent to the liver. Septic emboli pass to the lungs where they can produce chronic suppurative pneumonia and multiple lung abscesses or they can cause pulmonary arterial lesions. Endarteritis, arteritis and thromboembolism occur, resulting in aneurysms of the pulmonary artery which then rupture causing haemorrhage in the bronchi and alveoli. Usually there is a history of sudden onset of respiratory disease although in some cases there is a history of chronic loss of weight and coughing. A few cases have obstruction of the hepatic venous return with chronic venous congestion of the liver, its enlargement and there is no access to the collateral venous drainage. Bacteriological examination often reveals little because of previous therapy. However, some cases reveal staphylococci, *Corynebacterium pyogenes* and *Fusiformis necrophorus*.

Signs

Peracute

An animal suddenly dies with no premonitory signs but usually there is a pool of blood in front of it.

Acute

Most cattle with the condition show respiratory disease for a few days or some months with tachypnoea and shallow breathing. The cattle develop haemoptysis and frothy blood can be found in the nasal passages and mouth. There are often blood stains around the animal and in many cases there is melaena. There is a variable amount of thoracic pain with abduction of the elbows. On auscultation there is a widespread whistle, with wheezing sounds.

Chronic

Some animals develop congestive cardiac failure and ascites with an enlarged liver which may be palpated on the right sublumbar fossa. This often occurs some time before haemoptysis is present.

Necropsy

Often one or more abscesses are found in the liver, and usually the caudal vena cava thrombosis is in the area of the liver. Multiple septic emboli are normally present within the pulmonary artery. In the lung itself there is usually embolic suppurative pneumonia, intra-pulmonary haemorrhage, often concentric and globular in shape, and multiple red areas where blood has been aspirated. When there is obstruction of the hepatic veins then there is marked hepatomegaly and ascites.

Prognosis

Once animals start to show haemoptysis then death will ensue, usually within a week or two but occasionally it may take up to 40 days.

Diagnosis

1. History of loss of condition and respiratory signs in a single animal.
2. Signs, particularly haemoptysis with thoracic pain, are almost pathognomonic.
3. *Post mortem* findings with thrombosis of vena cava, emboli in pulmonary artery and intra-pulmonary haemorrhage.
4. Packed cell volume is often low (11.0 - 22.5 *per cent*).

Differential diagnosis

1. Accident, but highly unlikely to show signs unless immediate history of trauma.
2. Tuberculosis, but tuberculin test would reveal this.

Treatment

There is no effective therapy. Cattle can be casualty slaughtered after a course of four or five days antibiotic therapy using a broad spectrum compound.

Control

None is possible, but any septic focus should be treated adequately as soon as it occurs. Make sure that all changes in feeding are undertaken slowly so as to avoid the possibility of acidosis.

Bovine Tuberculosis

Aetiology

Infection with *Mycobacterium bovis* (Gram-positive, acid-fast rods).

Occurrence

At one time the condition was very common in Britain, but following tuberculin testing, pasteurisation of milk and adequate meat inspection the condition is today uncommon but is still seen periodically in dairy herds. In most cases infection breaks out in the growing heifers or younger cows. The condition tends to be more prevalent in south-west England, particularly Gloucestershire, Avon and Cornwall. However, outbreaks have occurred in other areas. In many regions infection has reappeared and is associated with the finding of tuberculosis in the badger (*Meles meles*). The organism is killed by sunlight but it is resistant to desiccation and can survive in a wide range of acids and alkalis. It is also able to remain viable for long periods in soil which is moist and warm. In cattle faeces *M. bovis* can survive for as little as a week or as long as eight weeks. Man can occasionally be infected and the disease can occur in goats and pigs, and very occasionally in horses and sheep.

When infection is by inhalation a lesion often occurs at the point of entry and the local lymph node. When ingestion is the route of entry, alimentary lesions are rare but lesions may be present in the tonsils, pharyngeal or mesenteric lymph nodes. Lesions may then disseminate from the primary areas to others.

When the badger is involved, most infection is thought to be by ingestion, but a higher infection level is necessary to establish alimentary than respiratory infection. In most cases infection is respiratory and is thought to be due to the inhalation of ruminal gases.

Source of infection

The organism can be present in sputum, milk, faeces, urine, vaginal and uterine discharges and any discharging lesions.

Route of entry

Usually inhalation (especially if housed) or ingestion (when outside or badgers source of infection).

Transmission of infection

Once in a herd, infection probably spreads from cow to cow by inhalation. However, spread from cows to calves may be via the milk. Occasionally intrauterine infection has resulted from a coital transfer.

Signs

Respiratory

Often signs are few and usually are confined to the respiratory tract. There is a soft, productive, chronic cough occurring once or twice at a time. It can be elicited by pressure on the pharynx. If the condition continues there is a marked increase in the depth and rate of respirations as well as dyspnoea. In advanced cases, areas of dullness in the chest are heard on auscultation or percussion. In other cases there are squeaks and whistles. A snoring respiration can occur.

Alimentary

Usually there are few signs but occasional diarrhoea occurs. Bloat can occur through enlargement of the mediastinal and bronchial lymph nodes.

Other lesions

Mammary involvement tends to be rare but results in udder induration and the supramammary lymph node is enlarged. The uterine form is also uncommon. Swelling of various lymph nodes can occasionally occur, and abortion is sometimes found.

Generalised

Often signs occur following calving. There is a progressive loss of condition with a variable appetite. There may be a variable rectal temperature but usually it is only about 39.7°C (103.5°F). The animals are more docile than normal but still bright and alert.

Necropsy

A focus of infection occurs within a week of bacteria entering the cow and, after the third week, calcification can occur. Depending on the route of entry, and where the condition becomes generalised, one or several lymph nodes may contain tuberculous granulomas. In the respiratory system it is the mediastinal or bronchial lymph nodes that are involved, possibly with abscesses in the lungs. The pus is thick, cheese-like and yellow or orange in colour. Sometimes the pleura and peritoneum contain nodules.

In practice an attempt is made to determine whether infection is active and if cases are "open" and therefore likely to infect other animals. Active infection is designated by lung infection with limited encapsulation and hyperaemia. Other organs often show small, transparent, shot-like lesions and these may also be present in the lymph nodes. Tuberculous cystitis and metritis tend to be open cases. Closed infection is seen as discrete lesions enclosed within well-developed capsules. The enclosed pus tends to be caseous and yellow or orange in colour.

Diagnosis

1. History, area where tuberculosis occurs in badgers or cattle.
2. Lesions - often chronic respiratory lesions with loss of condition and a soft, productive, single cough.
3. Comparative tuberculin test. Uses avian (0.5 mg/ml) and bovine tuberculin purified protein derivative (1.0 mg/ml) injected into the neck skin. There is a greater skin thickness increase in the bovine than avian tuberculin. Interpretation depends on whether no history of reactions, one or more reactions without confirmation at *post mortem* examination or herd with a recent history of reactions confirmed *post mortem*.

   Johne's disease, skin tuberculosis or avian tuberculosis can result in false positives but usually the avian reaction rises more than the bovine. False negatives occur following protracted infection, desensitisation following tuberculin testing, early cases of infection, old cows and those animals recently calved.

4. Single tuberculin test involving bovine tuberculin is the accepted EEC test. This depends on a skin thickness increase but gives a false positive reaction in cases of Johne's disease, avian and skin tuberculosis.
5. Other tests used elsewhere have included short thermal test (4 ml tuberculin injected subcutaneously and a temperature rise recorded), intravenous tuberculin (a temperature rise in four to six hours), Stormont test (intradermal injection into the neck followed by a second one at the same site one week later, resulting in a skin thickness increase in 24 hours).
6. Serological tests include complement fixation, fluorescent antibody, direct bacterial agglutination, precipitinoid haemagglutination test.

Differential diagnosis

1. Sporadic bovine leukosis - usually one animal, often young.
2. Enzootic bovine leukosis but agar gel immunodiffusion test will distinguish.
3. Lung abscess.
4. Chronic inhalation pneumonia but history of drenching.
5. Thrombosis of the caudal vena cava but an individual animal and haemoptysis.
6. Traumatic reticulitis but usually an initial severe attack of illness.
7. Actinobacillosis can result in lymph node enlargement.

Treatment

No form of therapy is undertaken in Britain.

Control

Herd

Routine tuberculin testing every 60 days until all reactors found. In infected herds testing of the herd usually occurs every six months until three clear tests produced. Then it becomes an annual test and after it remains clear, tests become biennial and eventually only take place every three years.

National

All cattle must be identified by a herd number and individual number unless slaughtered within 14 days of birth. Routine tuberculin testing occurs every three years in uninfected herds and only involves selected animals, i.e. bulls, cows, calves indoors and bought-in animals. Routine meat inspection also helps to identify infection. Badgers found dead are requested to be sent to Veterinary Investigation Centres for *post mortem* examination. In cattle in infected areas tests are undertaken to see if badgers are the source of infection.

CHAPTER 4

OTHER INFECTIONS AND INFESTATIONS

Anthrax

Aetiology

Infection with the bacterium *Bacillus anthracis* (Gram-positive, square-ended, spore-forming rod).

Occurrence

This disease is notifiable. Infection in cattle is now uncommon but in the period 1946-1958 there were many cases with the increase in the amount of feedingstuffs imported into Britain. The organism is encapsulated and spore-forming, it is non acid-fast and with polychrome methylene blue (MacFadyean's stain) the capsules are stained pink. Spores are only formed in the presence of oxygen and so as dead animals contain little oxygen, the bacteria are killed in a few days by the putrefactive process. When carcases are opened up, spores form which can survive for ten years or more. The spores are resistant to most environmental conditions but some are killed by boiling in water for 10 minutes or dry heat at 120°C for an hour. The organism can grow on vegetable matter and sporulate. The spores tend to be killed off in an acid soil but are viable for long periods in alkaline soils. Spores are killed after two days in five *per cent* lysol or 5 to 10 *per cent* formalin, 5 to 10 *per cent* sodium hydroxide and three *per cent* peracetic acid. Spores can be decontaminated by placing them in a plastic bag with ethylene oxide.

Most infection in Britain is via imported feedingstuffs but there are still a few areas where disease occurs sporadically following previous cases or downstream to tanneries or brush manufacturers which use imported animal products. Cattle and horses are most likely to be infected, but pigs, cats and dogs are relatively resistant. Man can become diseased but is more resistant to infection than cattle. In humans, most infection occurs as chronic skin disease (malignant carbuncle) but occasionally severe forms such as pulmonary (wool sorter's disease), intestinal and meningeal occur.

Following ingestion of infection it can traverse intact mucous membranes or pass through injuries or defects in the epithelium. Phagocytes transfer the bacterium to lymph nodes where it proliferates and then passes via the lymph vessels to the blood. A septicaemia occurs with toxin formation and death due to renal failure and shock.

Portal of entry

Ingestion, inhalation or via the skin.

Source of infection

Usually infected feedingstuffs, occasionally infected soil. Biting flies may help spread.

Signs

Peracute

Animal found dead which appeared to be well previously. Discharges may be present at the external orifices, i.e. mouth, nostrils, vulva and anus. Live animals are extremely ill with pyrexia 41.5°C (107°F), congested mucous membranes, dyspnoea. It is not long before the animal collapses and dies.

Acute

The duration of the disease is about 48 hours. The cattle again show pyrexia 41.5°C (107°F), dullness, anorexia, rapid hyperpnoeic breathing, and an increased heart rate. There is ruminal stasis and the mucous membranes are often haemorrhagic and congested. Some cases show diarrhoea or dysentery and there is sometimes oedema of the flanks, perineum, sternum, neck and tongue.

Abortion

Abortion may often occur in the acute syndrome.

Necropsy

Opening up the carcase will cause spore formation and so post mortem examination should not be undertaken. However, the carcase does not show rigor mortis and in many cases there may be a thick blood arising from the nostrils, mouth, anus and vulva. The spleen tends to be grossly enlarged with blood-stained fluid in most body cavities and ecchymotic haemorrhages throughout the tissues.

Diagnosis

1. History - sudden death.
2. Signs - thick, tarry blood from the external orifices, pyrexia, depression, congested mucous membranes.
3. Blood samples - stain samples taken from ear and tail (wear gloves) with polychrome methylene blue.
4. Take swabs for culture (Medusa-head shaped colonies).

Differential diagnosis

1. Lightning strike - usually close to fence, trees, etc. History of storm, burn marks.
2. Clostridial conditions- usually much gas present and ecchymotic haemorrhages.
3. Blackleg - usually gas in the muscles affected, ecchymotic haemorrhages.
4. Bloat - distended rumen.
5. Acidosis - rumen pH is usually below 5 and history helps.
6. Staphylococcal mastitis - udder signs useful.
7. Coliform mastitis - usually signs of toxaemia, milk and udder changes.
8. Summer mastitis - usually obvious signs in udder.
9. Pasteurellosis - lung involvement.
10. Lead poisoning - ecchymotic haemorrhages, high lead levels in kidney.
11. Nitrate/nitrite poisoning - methaemoglobin - chocolate blood.
12. Bracken poisoning - multiple, massive haemorrhages.
13. Yew poisoning - usually few signs but yew in rumen.
14. Drowning - often history, water in lungs.

15. Asphyxiation - history - often cause of blockage of larynx/ trachea found.

16. Anaphylaxis - history with pulmonary oedema and vascular engorgement.

17. Hypomagnesaemia - history, usually signs of struggling.

Treatment

High doses of antibiotics are effective in the early stages. Penicillin (10,000 units/kg BW - 5,000 units/lb BW) twice daily can be successful. It should be given intramuscularly and not intravenously because of the possibility of blood spillage. Anti-anthrax serum has been used intravenously in the past but it is no longer available.

Control

In the event of sudden death with no obvious cause, animals should be checked for anthrax. A farmer is not obliged to report sudden death in animals but he must report if he suspects anthrax. Once a case has occurred, take the temperatures of all cattle twice daily. When a rise occurs with no obvious cause, then inject penicillin and streptomycin. Temperature-taking should continue until two weeks after the last death and/or last temperature rise. Vaccination of stock is possible but should only be undertaken after the end of an outbreak and when other cases are likely to occur. The vaccine is a suspension of living encapsulated spores and is given subcutaneously. Immunity develops in one to two weeks but persists for 9 to 12 months. As it is a live vaccine, antibacterial therapy should not be used for 14 days after injection.

Aujeszky's Disease

Also known as pseudorabies.

Aetiology

An infection caused by a herpes virus.

Occurrence

The infection is only occasionally seen in cattle but, until the recent eradication campaign, infection was present in the pig population. The organism is resistant to changes in pH, although it is inactivated by heat. The virus can remain in meat for up to five weeks and can remain in the environment for two to seven weeks. Various disinfectants will kill the organism in a short period including formalin, hypochlorite, five per cent phenol and one per cent sodium hydroxide. Morbidity is very low but mortality of affected animals approaches 95 to 100 per cent.

Incubation period

Three to six days.

Portal of entry

Infection enters via abrasions of the skin or nasal mucosa.

Source of infection

Contaminated feed or water.

Signs

Peracute

Sudden death with no previous signs.

Acute

These cases show pyrexia of 40-41°C (104-106°F) although the temperature falls when close to death. There is excessive licking, cleaning, biting and kicking at the affected area, which is often on the head, flanks or limbs. Reactions result in hair loss, haemorrhage and excoriation. The animals lose condition as they do not eat or drink and there is drooling of saliva, sweating and teeth grinding. Paralysis occurs, followed by death.

Necropsy

Local lesions of hyperaemia and haemorrhage are seen. The central nervous system shows venous congestion. There are haemorrhages in the lungs and other serosal surfaces in some cattle. Histologically there is damage of the brain and spinal cord. There is perivascular cuffing and focal necrosis in the grey matter in the cerebral cortex, possibly with intra-articular inclusion bodies.

Diagnosis

1. Signs - severe itching and self-mutilation.
2. Inoculation of emulsified spinal cord into rabbits. After 36 to 48 hours, produces severe pruritis and death in 12 to 24 hours.

Differential diagnosis

1. Nervous acetonaemia but history helps and high ketone levels.

Treatment

None.

Prevention

Keep cattle away from pigs. Destroy all rodents. Cases are notifiable under the Aujeszky's Disease Order 1979.

Babesiasis

This is also known as redwater fever.

Aetiology

The condition is due to the piroplasm Babesia divergens, although Babesia major also occurs.

Occurrence

The disease involves a tick vector and so the condition is present in those areas where the tick is found. B. divergens is associated with the tick Ixodes ricinus which is mainly present in the hilly areas of Scotland, Northern England, Wales, Devon, Cornwall, Dorset and Hampshire. The condition is otherwise very rare in lowland parts of Britain. In Northern Ireland the number of clinical cases is 4,000 per annum with a prevalence of antibodies being 31.8 per cent, ranging in some counties from 21.8 to 59.5 per cent (Taylor, 1983). B. major is found in the tick Haemophysalis punctata which occurs in the coastal regions of Anglesey, North and South Wales, Kent and Essex.

The disease is seasonal as it is dependent on tick activity. I. ricinus is inactive below 7°C (45°F) and above 16°C (60°F) and it tends to hide to avoid desiccation. The tick requires moisture and the relative humidity needed is greater than 80 per cent for an unfed tick, and 85 per cent for an engorged tick. Activity tends to commence from March to the end of May (but up to July in Scotland). It ceases, and ticks are hard to find, during the hot summer months. Activity recommences from August to November.

Cattle reared in tick areas are rarely affected with redwater. Passive immunity is passed to the calf in the colostrum of the dam. Then a gradual exposure to infection results in premunity. Provided animals remain in the tick area, immunity is permanent. When cattle are removed from infected areas the protozoa are lost from the blood after about six months. There is then a sterile immunity for six months, following which the animal is susceptible to infection.

Disease in cattle is usually the result of moving cattle into an area which is infected from a non-tick area, or because they are in marginal tick areas with a variable tick population so that in some years the ticks may die out, thereby exposing the animals to future infection. Liver fluke is not considered to exacerbate babesiasis.

I. ricinus females lay up to 2,000 eggs. These hatch into larvae which spend the winter on the ground amid damp vegetation. They seek out a suitable host the following spring. They feed off suitable hosts such as sheep or cattle and then fall back to the ground. They remain for a year until they reach the nymph stage when the process is repeated. The following year the adults emerge. The parasite can persist through all stages of the life cycle including the egg stage. In a life cycle of over three years only about 17 days are spent on the host.

Cases of disease occur most frequently in animals between six and 12 months old. Those under six months tend to be less susceptible, even when from outside tick areas. Infection occurs less frequently in animals over five years old. Following infection the parasite multiplies in the peripheral blood vessels and they reach a peak at the time when clinical signs occur. There is haemolysis and death is probably the result of anoxia. Animals which survive subsequently possess a subclinical infection.

When Erlichia phagocytophila infection occurs before B. divergens, it reduces the severity of infection as well as increasing the incubation period. Where babesia infection is before E. phagocytophila then there is no effect.

Incubation period

This is variable, but is usually 14 to 21 days.

Morbidity

This can often be 100 per cent in susceptible animals.

Mortality

Can be very high, 95 to 100 per cent if untreated, but it is only about 50 per cent in those treated early. The average mortality in Northern Ireland is 12.5 per cent (Taylor, 1983).

Signs

Early

There is slight dullness with a pyrexia often of 40.5 - 41°C (105-106°F). The animal shows diarrhoea and because of spasm of the anal sphincter there is a narrow stream of diarrhoea (pipe-stem diarrhoea). There is also haemoglobinuria. Slight dehydration is often seen as a slightly sunken eye.

Mid

After 24 to 36 hours the mucous membranes tend to become pale and the pulse rate is increased. The animals tend to slow up and there is a reduction in appetite and thirst. The urine tends to become very dark in colour and reduced in quantity. The faeces may return to normal but less tends to be passed although there is still spasm of the anus.

Late

In another 24 to 36 hours the rectal temperature is often subnormal with the animal having blanched mucous membranes, a poor appetite and drinking little. There is marked constipation and a greatly increased heart rate.

Abortion

Pregnant cows may abort following infection.

Necropsy

The carcase may be very blanched and there is sometimes jaundice. The liver is often swollen and pulpy, with the kidneys dark and enlarged. The bladder contains red-brown urine. There are ecchymotic haemorrhages under the epicardium and endocardium.

Diagnosis

1. History - area of country, tick regions, time of year - spring and autumn.
2. Signs - haemoglobinuria, early pyrexia, pipe-stem diarrhoea.
3. Thick blood smears can be stained to detect the parasite. In dead animals smears can be made from peripheral or heart blood or the kidney.

4. Erythrocyte counts may be low - 2 million/mm^3.
5. Haemoglobin levels may be low - 3 g/100 ml.
6. Serology has been used, including complement fixation test, passive agglutination test, indirect fluorescent antibody test, indirect haemagglutination test. Other tests include a capillary count and slide agglutination.
7. Necropsy showing pale mucous membranes, splenomegaly, haemoglobinuria.

Differential diagnosis

1. Bacillary haemoglobinuria - often very short duration before death.
2. Leptospirosis has a shorter duration but usually jaundice.
3. Haemolytic anaemia due to kale or other cruciferous crops - history.
4. Enzootic haematuria but haematuria and bracken areas.
5. Cystitis but frequent micturition and haematuria.
6. Pyelonephritis but polyuria and blood in urine.
7. Cold water haemolytic anaemia - young cattle consuming large quantities of cold water.
8. Chronic copper poisoning - no fever but jaundice, haemoglobinuria and blood copper levels.

Treatment

Quinuronium sulphate is a useful drug and is used at a rate of 1 ml/ 50 kg (1 ml/100 lb) up to a maximum of 6 ml. The injection is given subcutaneously. When toxicity occurs it can be alarming, with salivation, sweating, diarrhoea, panting, collapse and death. When quinuronium sulphate poisoning occurs, the antidote is atropine sulphate. Amicarbelide isethionate can be used at a dose of 5 mg/kg (2 mg/lb). It is an acridine derivative. It is possible to double the dose in peracute cases. When haemoglobinuria persists for more than 24 hours a second dose should be given. Imidocarb dihydrochloride, an aromatic diamidine, is used in other countries at a dose of 1 mg/kg (0.5 mg/lb), and another therapeutic agent is phenamidine isethionate, used as 40 per cent solution. The dose of 1 ml per 45 kg (100 lb) is given subcutaneously.

Blood transfusions may be required in mid and late cases (MacKellar, 1962). Blood was collected using 3½ per cent sodium acid citrate and five per cent dextrose to prevent clotting. The blood flow is kept slow for two or three minutes, then it is run in at one litre per 5 to 8 minutes, using a 2.4 mm needle for animals under a year and 3 to 4 minutes using a 3 mm needle for older cattle. Repeat if necessary twice daily for 5 to 7 days.

Iron and vitamin B_{12} injections can be useful in acting as haematinics. Stimulants may be given such as etamiphylline camsylate. As constipation can be a problem, purgatives may be necessary, e.g. Epsom salts (magnesium sulphate).

Control

The only real method is the eradication of ticks. This can be done by improving pastures. Ploughing up pastures, burning bracken, removing natural fauna and rotational grazing all assist. Chemicals are not used to control ticks in Britain although abroad dips are often used. Bracken provides a suitable environment for tick survival and can be removed by spraying. Such pastures can then be improved and re-seeded.

Cattle in affected areas should only be bought from other known tick areas. Otherwise calves should be bought and exposed to infection early in life. In Australia, diluted blood containing 10^7 parasitised erythrocytes has been used. It would seem that injection only extends the prepatent period. Cobalt ^{60} irradiated blood containing 10^{10} (irradiated at a level of 28 K rads) parasitised erythrocytes appears to protect cattle. The use of two cypermethrin-impregnated ear tags in cattle has reduced tick numbers on them, but did not alter _B. divergens_ levels (Taylor, Kenny, Mallon, Elliott, McMurray and Blanchflower, 1984).

References

MacKELLAR, J C (1962) Veterinary Record, 74, 763-765.

TAYLOR, S M (1983) Veterinary Record, 112, 247-256.

TAYLOR, S M, KENNY, J, MALLON, T R, ELLIOTT, C T, McMURRAY, C and BLANCHFLOWER, J (1984) Veterinary Record, 114, 454-455.

Bacillary Haemoglobinuria

Also known as bacterial redwater.

Aetiology

A toxaemia due to infection with Clostridium haemolyticum (Cl. oedematiens type D), a Gram-positive, anaerobic bacterium.

Occurrence

The condition is very uncommon and it will usually involve animals in good condition. Spores are found in the soil and can survive at least a year. Infection is spread by carrier animals and flooding, and is obtained by ingestion. Invasion of the body occurs with the organisms passing to the liver. An activating factor, such as liver fluke or anti-tetanus injections cause disease to occur. In most outbreaks, disease only involves about 5 to 10 per cent of animals. There is toxaemia, and most animals die of this.

Incubation period

Usually 7 to 10 days.

Signs

Sometimes cattle are found dead. Signs tend to be of longer duration in dry cows than in those close to calving. More often cattle have a short illness with anorexia, reduced defaecation and rumination. The animal shows abdominal pain with an arched back and shuffling gait. Grunting occurs on walking. There is initially fever (39 - 41°C; 102 - 106°F), with rapid, shallow respirations. The brisket may show oedema. The faeces become dark brown in colour and in some cases there is diarrhoea. The urine is often red and there is jaundice which is hard to distinguish. Pregnant cows may abort. Death is preceded by dyspnoea and occurs within four days.

Necropsy

There is rapid rigor mortis with oedema and extensive, diffuse haemorrhages occur in the subcutaneous tissue. Jaundice is seen to a varying degree and haemoglobinuria. There are usually large amounts of fluid, often blood-stained, in the peritoneal, pleural or pericardial cavities. Diffuse, subserous haemorrhages are seen and in the epicardium there is haemoglobinuria. The abomasum and intestines show inflammation with blood in the lumen. The liver contains anaemic infarcts with a central zone of necrosis, surrounded by hyperaemia.

Diagnosis

1. Presence of haemoglobinuria.
2. Signs of pyrexia, abdominal pain, cessation of rumination, feeding and defaecation.
3. Post mortem findings of anaemic infarcts in liver.
4. Cl. haemolyticum isolated from liver infarct or heart blood.
5. Blood shows reduced erythrocyte count, 1-4 million/mm^3.
6. Haemoglobin level is 3-8 g/100 ml.

7. Leucocytosis with 10,000 - 16,000 $/mm^3$.
8. Neutrophilia.
9. Blood glucose level elevated (5.6 - 6.7 mmol/1; 100 - 120 mg/dl).
10. Serum agglutination levels rise after a week of illness from 1:20 to 1:400.

Differential diagnosis

1. Sudden death - Anthrax - polychrome methylene blue staining.
2. Blackleg but usually muscular signs.
3. Infectious necrotic hepatitis but usually signs of liver fluke damage.
4. Bloat but distended rumen.
5. Acute leptospirosis but usually jaundice.
6. Post-parturient haemoglobinuria but low blood phosphorus levels.
7. Haemolytic anaemia due to kale or other cruciferous plants.
8. Babesiasis - organism can be stained in blood smears.
9. Enzootic haematuria - haematuria in bracken areas.
10. Cystitis but frequent micturition and haematuria.
11. Pyelonephritis - polyuria, blood in urine.

Treatment

High doses of penicillin, oxytetracycline, ampicillin, amoxycillin and potentiated sulphonamides. In many cases blood transfusions can be given or electrolytes injected.

Control

Vaccination is possible with a combined vaccine for *Cl. septicum*, *Cl. chauvoei*, *Cl. novyi*, *Cl. tetani* as well as *Cl. haemolyticum*. The vaccination course involves two injections spread at least six weeks apart. Vaccination should be completed at least two weeks before the period of risk. Revaccination may be required at intervals of six months.

Blackleg

Also known as black quarter.

Aetiology

The cause of true blackleg is *Clostridium chauvoei*, an anaerobic, Gram-positive, spore-forming rod.

Occurrence

The condition occurs occasionally but some farms have a recurring problem. In some cases there are mixed infections of *Cl. chauvoei* and *Cl. septicum*. The organism is present in soil and is thought to enter the body via contaminated feed and it then passes through the alimentary mucosa. Organisms can be found in various tissues and disease occurs when there is proliferation of the organisms following activation of the spores. *Cl. chauvoei* produces a toxin which causes necrotizing myositis locally, and systemic toxaemia.

Most cases occur in cattle between six months and two years old. Animals are usually in good condition on a high plane of nutrition. The condition tends to be more common in the summer months of the year. In some cases problems occur following soil disturbance. Although morbidity tends to be low at 5 to 10 *per cent*, mortality is towards 100 *per cent*.

Signs

Most cases are dead when seen and death occurs in 12 to 36 hours after signs develop. In animals seen alive there is severe lameness, normally involving the upper part of the leg. Although most cases involve the limbs, other muscles can be involved, including the diaphragm, back , tongue, heart, brisket and udder. There is severe depression, anorexia, ruminal stasis, pyrexia 41°C (106°F) with a rapid pulse rate (100 to 120 per minute). The swollen area in the initial stages is painful and warm but later the skin becomes dry, cracked, cold and painless. In the later stages the area is swollen with oedema and emphysema.

Necropsy

Post mortem decomposition occurs rapidly so examination should be made as soon as possible. The animal may be found on its side with the affected limb extended. The affected area, when cut, shows dark, swollen tissue with serosanguinous fluid, emphysema, a bad smell and a metallic sheen to the cut surface. The animal tends to bloat quickly and bloody froth exudes from the nostrils and anus. In some cases, muscles other than those of the limbs may be involved and so a careful examination of other muscles should be made as the lesion may be small. Muscles of the lumbar region, tongue, diaphragm and brisket should be examined. The liver contains gas and the body cavities contain excess fluid, often with blood and fibrin.

Diagnosis

1. *Post mortem* findings.
2. Previous disease on farm.
3. Presence of organism in lesions at *post mortem* or obtained by swabbing of wounds or needle puncture.
4. SGOT (AST) levels raised.

5. SGPT (ALT) levels raised.
6. Serum lactic dehydrogenase levels raised.
7. Hypovolaemia - occurs late in the disease.

Differential diagnosis

1. Anthrax - detected by polychrome methylene blue stain of blood.
2. Lightning strike but scorch marks.
3. Bacillary haemoglobinuria but the liver contains infarcts and haemoglobinuria.
4. Hypomagnesaemia but often signs of struggling and haemorrhage.
5. Acute lead poisoning.

Treatment

Usually the condition is too far advanced to be treated. In early cases the use of intravenous crystalline penicillin at 10,000 units/kg BW (5,000 units/lb) is helpful, followed by procaine penicillin. Where the affected area is accessible then some of the antibiotic should be administered into it. The other cattle should be removed from the affected pasture. Animals which die should be burnt or buried in a deep pit.

Control

When more than the odd case occurs on the farm, vaccination should be considered. One vaccine, commonly used, also immunises against *Cl. septicum*, *Cl. novyi*, *Cl. haemolyticum* and *Cl. tetani*. The primary vaccination course involves two injections at least six weeks apart and should be completed at least two weeks before maximum immunity is required. For continuous protection, injections should be given at six-monthly intervals.

Botulism

Aetiology

Ingestion of toxin produced by Clostridium botulinum (Gram-positive spore-forming rod). Antigenically the organism is divided into distinct types, namely A, B, C, D and F.

Occurrence

Disease in British cattle is very rare and usually involves types C and D. In dry summers there are often many reports of the disease in wildfowl. Recently the disease has been reported in horses fed baled silage. The organism can occur as an inhabitant of the herbivore gut and faecal contamination of soil and water may result. Infection mostly arises from decomposing animal carcases but this is irrelevant in Britain. However, cases can occur following proliferation of Cl. botulinum in decaying vegetable matter such as spoiled hay or silage or the dead grass at the bottom of tussocks.

Cl. botulinum produces a neurotoxin which results in a functional flaccid paralysis. It is thought that there is interference with acetyl choline which is the chemical mediator for nerve impulse transmission at the synapses of the efferent parasympathetic and somatic motor nerves. The toxin apparently can be digested by proteolytic enzymes in the gut and perhaps this is why botulism is so rare in British cattle.

Incubation period

Depends on the amount of toxin produced and is usually 3 to 7 days.

Signs

Peracute

Sudden death due to respiratory paralysis, usually with no premonitory signs.

Subacute

Most cases are of this type. The condition is one of a progressive muscular paralysis starting in the hind limbs and progressing to the fore limbs, head and neck. The animal is conscious throughout and responds to painful stimuli. As the hind and front limb muscles are affected there is a progressive incoordination, stumbling, ataxia and knuckling of the limbs, followed by recumbency. The neck is involved after the limbs and the animal cannot lift its head and so a cow may be recumbent with its neck on the ground or turned into a flank. The muscles of the head are then affected, particularly those of the jaw and throat. The tongue tends to protrude and saliva is drooled. The animal is then unable to eat or drink. There is no pyrexia. The animal can often defaecate and urinate normally. The respiratory muscles become involved, resulting in abdominal breathing and then death due to respiratory paralysis about 1 to 4 days after signs develop.

Chronic

Some animals can develop a few signs of paralysis of the limbs with restlessness, incoordination, stumbling and ataxia, but recover spontaneously over several weeks. Often the animals tend to remain recumbent although they can rise. During the illness the cattle are often initially anorexic and do not drink but will then eat silage or concentrates but not hay. Some of the animals develop a roaring noise on inspiration.

Necropsy

There are no specific lesions although there may be haemorrhages subendocardially and subepicardially. The intestinal mucosa and serosa may be congested. The toxin produces no histological lesions. However the brain in some animals shows perivascular haemorrhages, particularly involving the cerebrum, cerebellum and corpus striatum. In a few cases the Purkinje cells of the cerebellum are destroyed.

Diagnosis

Definite diagnosis is often difficult.

1. History of ingestion of decaying grass or conserved grass.
2. Signs of progressive muscular paralysis involving the hind limbs, then front limbs, neck and head. Sensation and consciousness are normal with no pyrexia.
3. Presence of Cl. botulinum toxin in feed is an indication, as also is the presence of toxin in the alimentary tract. However, a negative finding may occur if the toxin has already been absorbed. The existence of toxin in the liver is considered diagnostic. Toxin presence can be tested for in experimental animals and useful evidence can be obtained by feeding suspect feed to susceptible animals.
4. Presence of Cl. botulinum bacteria in the gut in the presence of suitable signs is also an indication of infection. However, the organism may occur in normal animals.

Differential diagnosis

1. Parturient paresis but history and some signs should help distinguish, plus low plasma calcium levels.

Prognosis

This is usually very poor but in those cases where signs develop slowly it may be worthwhile. Remove the animal and all in-contacts from any suspect feed.

Treatment

It is probably best to provide some form of antibiotic therapy such as amoxycillin, ampicillin, penicillin, oxytetracycline. This should be used in a form to provide adequate antibiotic levels in the gut. Purgation may help to remove toxin from the gut. The animal may need to be given mild central nervous system stimulants such as xanthines, and it should be encouraged to eat, probably silage, cut grass, greenstuffs or concentrates are best. If prehension is not possible, feeding by stomach tube and parenterally may need to be undertaken. Ideally, Cl. botulinum antitoxin should be given. It is, however, hard to obtain unless access to some human hospital supply is available.

Control

As this condition is rare it will not usually be envisaged. However, all cattle should be removed from the suspect feed and it should not be used until toxin tests have been undertaken and the feed found safe. Vaccination with toxoid, usually combining types C and D, is used in parts of the world where the condition is enzootic.

Bovine Papular Stomatitis

Aetiology

This is caused by a paravaccinia virus in the pox group.

Occurrence

The condition is very common and the lesions of pseudocowpox on the teats of cows are possibly due to the same virus. The disease occurs most frequently in cattle between two weeks and two years old. Stomatitis signs have occurred in calves sucking cows with pseudocowpox. The virus is related to that causing milker's nodule in man and orf in sheep. Immunity following infection appears to be poor. As lesions can occur in isolated animals, this suggests the virus can remain quiescent. Morbidity in some herds may be up to 100 per cent, but mortality is nil.

Incubation period

Although this is not known, lesions have occured in calves at seven days old.

Signs

Severe

This form is not very common and usually occurs when the animal is debilitated with an intercurrent disease, e.g. parasitism. Lesions tend to be diffuse, slightly raised and roughened and of a yellow or grey colour. The lesions can occur anywhere in the mouth. In most cases there are also more discrete papular stomatitis lesions. As the more diffuse lesions regress there is often an underlying circular form. In some cases saliva is held in the mouth and there is wetness around the lips.

Mild

This is the most common form of the condition. The animal is healthy, eating well with no evidence of pyrexia, diarrhoea or respiratory signs. Ring-like lesions occur which are pathognomonic. They are rounded or oval. The periphery of the lesion is a thin red zone of congestion, within which is a white, slightly raised zone of hyperplasia. The centre is an area of tissue necrosis with a yellow or brown surface. Lesions heal from the centre outwards. Lesions tend to be confined to the rhinarium and mouth, in which they can occur anywhere but are often found near erupting teeth; those on the tongue tend to be found on the underside. A second type of lesion is a brown papule which is usually as large as the ring lesions. It heals from the centre outwards, producing a circle or horseshoe shape. The individual lesions only last about four days to two weeks, but in some cases there are successive crops of lesions and the condition can last for one or two months.

Necropsy

It is rare for an animal to die of bovine papular stomatitis. There are no macroscopic vesicles, but lesions may be found in the mouth and rhinarium. Less frequently lesions are present in the oesophagus, rumen, reticulum and abomasum. Histologically there is ballooning degeneration of the stratum spinosum cells which may contain eosinophilic intra-cytoplasmic inclusion bodies. There is an inflammatory response of the dermis.

Diagnosis

1. The animal is healthy.
2. There are typical lesions.
3. Histology of the lesions.

Differential diagnosis

1. Foot-and-mouth disease but there are vesicles and systemic reaction.
2. Mucosal disease but the animal is often ill and there is diarrhoea.
3. Malignant catarrhal fever, but there is stomatitis, pyrexia and diarrhoea.

Treatment

None is of use.

Control

This is not practicable.

Brain Abscess

Aetiology

An abscess which can result from haematogenous infection or localised spread.

Occurrence

The condition is uncommon. It can follow the progression of a localised infection such as middle ear disease, nasal infection or dehorning and in this case there is usually one localised lesion. Others can follow haematogenous spread with organisms such as *Actinomyces bovis*, *Mycobacterium bovis*, *Mycobacterium avium*, *Fusiformis necrophorus*.

Signs

These depend partly on the site of the lesion. Early on there is a transient fever which may be intermittent. There may be periods of excitement. Later convulsions tend to occur, head pressing, and depression. Some animals are unilaterally or totally blind. Many show delayed pupillary reflexes and nystagmus. Other signs may include circling, head deviation and hemiplegia.

Necropsy

One or more abscesses are present and if on the surface there is meningitis. Sometimes the abscesses are only apparent on microscopic examination.

Diagnosis

Often this is difficult.

1. Previous localised area of infection.
2. Leucocytosis may occur.
3. The cerebrospinal fluid has a high white cell count.

Treatment

Large doses of antibiotics may be successful. However, often response to therapy is poor.

Control

Ensure all local lesions are treated thoroughly.

Chorioptic Mange

Also known as tail mange.

Aetiology

This is caused by the mite *Chorioptes bovis*.

Occurrence

The infestation occurs quite commonly especially in growing and older cattle. The life cycle takes about three weeks to complete and unlike *Sarcoptes* spp. the adult mites remain on the skin surface, although the larvae burrow into the skin causing irritation. Most cases occur in housed cattle whereas animals outdoors are rarely affected. Infestation is usually transmitted by contact or indirectly by scratching posts, etc. Normally only one or two animals are affected.

Signs

The condition is usually mild in nature with lesions at the base of the tail, legs, udder and escutcheon. The lesions are usually small scabs.

Diagnosis

1. There is some pruritus.
2. The sites of the scabs.
3. Examination of the scabs will show the mites.

Differential diagnosis

1. Sarcoptic mange but the condition is more severe.
2. Psoroptic mange, but this is also more severe.
3. Ringworm but there is no pruritus.
4. Chlorinated naphthalene poisoning but there is no pruritus.

Treatment

The use of gamma benzene hexachloride baths or washes, or organophosphorus pour-on compounds will usually be effective. Bromocyclen can be used as a wash, bath or spray. Ivermectin compounds can be used.

Control

This is at present not possible.

Demodectic Mange

Aetiology

Infestation with _Demodex bovis_ (also known as _Demodex folliculārum_ var. _bovis_).

Occurrence

It is a relatively common infestation of cattle but most cases go undetected. However, infection interferes with the tanning of the hide resulting in its downgrading as it contains small pinholes. It can occur in animals of any age and signs are more likely to be observed in the autumn or winter. Cattle in poor condition tend to be more affected, but the condition is easiest to detect in animals with a thin coat of hair.

All stages of the life cycle take place on the host with the adult mites in hair follicles and sebaceous glands. Often there is a secondary staphylococcal infection resulting in the formation of small abscesses. Most infection is probably transmitted early in life.

Spread of infection

Contact.

Signs

Hard, small (3 mm diameter) lesions develop on the skin surface. In severe cases there is a loss of hair and a thickening of the skin. Lesions can occur anywhere on the body but are commonly found on the shoulders, brisket, lower neck and forearm. Some lesions are visible whereas others are only palpable. Pressure on the lesion produces a white, cheesy pus although in large pustules the pus is more fluid. Pruritus is not usually apparent.

Necropsy

Lesions are palpable and contain the parasite in swollen hair follicles or sebaceous glands.

Diagnosis

1. Signs - nodules.
2. Presence of parasite in pus.
3. Presence of parasite in skin biopsy.

Differential diagnosis

1. Non-specific staphylococcal skin infection - no parasite present.
2. Ringworm.
3. Pediculosis.

Treatment

Often this is disappointing, but the use of "pour-on" organophosphorus compounds can be helpful, at intervals of a week to ten days.

Local application can be made more frequently to the worst-affected areas.

Control

This is difficult and must involve isolation of known infested animals.

Foot-and-Mouth Disease

Aetiology

Caused by an enterovirus with seven main types: O, A, C, South African Type (SAT) 1, SAT 2, SAT 3 and ASIA 1.

Occurrence

The disease is notifiable. Although the disease is common in some parts of the world, it occurs only very sporadically in Britain. The last outbreak was on the Isle of Wight in 1981 with the last major one in 1967-68 when 211,800 cattle were slaughtered. The disease is highly contagious. Other susceptible species include sheep, pigs, wild ruminants (deer) and to a lesser extent hedgehogs, coypu, other rodents (rats). Human infection is rare and usually not very severe.

Each type of virus has various subgroups and immunity is only obtained to the specific type and lasts one to four years. The organism multiplies in living tissue but can survive on dead matter, e.g. 4 months on hay, 3½ months on rubber boots, 3 months on boot leather, 1 month on cow hair, ½ month on wool. It survives cooling well but is killed off by acidity in muscles following slaughter. The virus is killed by sunlight, changes in pH, most disinfectants, four per cent sodium carbonate, 1 to 2 per cent formalin. It survives 18 hours in milk and for a month in semen at -79°C (-110°F). All cattle are susceptible but immature animals and those in good health are particularly vulnerable.

The virus can be present in the blood or milk before any vesicles are apparent. It can survive up to 3 to 7 weeks in udder tissue but animals are not very infective four days after the vesicles rupture, although the organism may still be present on the hair and skin.

Incubation period

3 to 8 days (occasionally up to 21 days).

Source of British infection

Usually infected meat, otherwise migratory birds or wind-borne.

Farm to farm spread

Direct, via movement of infected animals; indirect, via movement of milk, animal products, wind, bedding, meat, clothing, car tyres, boots, harnesses, etc.

Mode of entry

Inhalation or ingestion.

Morbidity

Up to 100 per cent.

Mortality

2 to 15 per cent.

Signs

Early

In most cases several cattle are affected. Animals are usually dull and dejected with pyrexia 40 - 41°C (104-106°F) and anorexia. The lesions on the feet and in the mouth usually develop together although sometimes one set is first. There are signs of lip smacking and drooling of saliva in ropy strings, and difficulty in eating. Lameness may be apparent with shaking of the legs, kicking and paddling. The vesicles are usually 1 to 2 cm in diameter (½ - 1") and are seen on the tongue, buccal mucosa and dental pad, around the coronet and in the interdigital space. The vesicles normally rupture within 24 hours and are healed in seven days.

Later

Once the vesicles rupture, the temperature falls and the animal eats and moves more freely.

Chronic

There can be a rapid loss of condition. There may be separation of the horn-skin junction. New horn forms and replaces the old horn, allowing it to be shed. Other forms are occasionally seen, viz:-

Abortion

Pregnant heifers may abort.

Alimentary form

There is diarrhoea and dysentery.

Paralytic

An ascending posterior paralysis occurs.

Myocardial

There is dyspnoea, weak, irregular pulse and death.

Necropsy

The main lesions are apparent in the mouth and on the feet. These may be vesicles, ruptured vesicles or denuded epithelium with areas of healing. Lesions are found mainly on the tongue, buccal mucosa and dental pad, around the coronet and in the interdigital space. Some lesions may occur in the oesophagus, pharynx, intestines, reticulo-rumen, trachea and bronchi. The myocardial form presents a widespread myocarditis.

Diagnosis

1. History - area, presence of infection in country, several animals affected.
2. Lesions and vesicles in mouth or on feet, pyrexia.
3. Virus presence - fluorescent antibody, complement fixation on antigen in vesicular epithelium - virus morphology.
4. Tissue culture - used on negative samples with embryonated hens' eggs.

5. Animal test - infection of unweaned white mice or intradermal injection of guinea-pigs' pads.
6. Serology - but in recovery phase.

Differential diagnosis

1. Mucosal disease - lesions erosions not vesicles.
2. Rinderpest - lesions erosions plus alimentary involvement with diarrhoea, dysentery, etc.
3. Bovine malignant catarrh - usually single animals, often there are nervous signs, ocular lesions and lymph node enlargement.
4. Actinomycosis - usually swelling of jaw, and single animal.
5. Actinobacillosis - usually swelling of tongue, and single animal.
6. Calf diphtheria, lesions in mouth, little pyrexia, and a single animal.

Treatment

No therapy is undertaken in Britain. Experimentally,double standard RNA has helped by promoting interferon production. If the infection is suspected, the local MAFF Animal Health Office must be notified. If found to be positive, animals must be slaughtered and burnt or buried.

Control

Slaughter policy at present in operation. Following an outbreak an epidemiology team would study the course of the disease. At an early stage, if considered necessary, a ring vaccination policy might be introduced. In countries with endemic problems vaccination is the main form of control. A killed trivalent vaccine is available for O, A, C strains but immunity lasts only 6 to 8 months from a single injection. Live attenuated vaccines are also used.

Disease is kept out of Britain by only importing meat from areas where the disease is not present. From many countries only boneless meat can be imported. All cattle entering the country have a 28-day quarantine period.

Haemophilus Somnus Infection

Aetiology

Infection with Haemophilus somnus (Gram-negative, small rod-shaped organism).

Occurrence

The condition was recorded in Britain in the mid-1970's and clinical disease wasnot common. It has subsequently been found in many outbreaks of disease, affecting several animals at the same time. Most cases in Britain involve the respiratory tract, although other infections may give rise to septicaemia and localisation in various organs, including the brain. Outbreaks of respiratory disease occur, but on occasions only one animal may be affected. Serological surveys suggest that large numbers of cattle can be infected subclinically. Most cases involving pneumonia are seen in the autumn and winter and are more often associated with housed animals. It is more usual for calves or yearlings to be affected.

Portal of entry

Usually considered to be the respiratory tract. Transmission is probably by aerosol.

Signs

Peracute

Death of one or more animals with no previous signs.

Acute

Sleeper syndrome or thrombo-embolic meningo-encephalitis (TEME).
Initial The animals show nervous signs with normally a marked pyrexia 40 - 42°C (104 - 108°F). They are usually depressed and in sternal or lateral recumbency and may be unable to rise. The eyes may be partially or completely closed, hence the name 'sleeper'. The animals may show blindness, usually unilateral and there are often retinal haemorrhages and exudate accumulation in the posterior chamber. Weak animals may show ataxia, hind fetlock knuckling and often collapse after a few steps. Cattle treated early will often recover.

Late Other nervous signs may be present, including opisthotonus, hyperaesthesia, nystagmus. Although convulsions may occur there is usually muscular weakness or paralysis. Most cases which are recumbent will die.

Synovitis

This can affect any joint but most commonly the hock or stifle. The joint tends to be distended. Lameness is at first low-grade but later becomes severe with recumbency.

Pneumonia

Many cases show pneumonia but also pleurisy, tracheitis or laryngitis may be found. There is often tachypnoea and hyperpnoea, with dyspnoea. Some cases only result in mild respiratory signs, conjunctivitis and ocular discharge.

Abortion

Can occur in pregnant animals.

Bloat

A chronic, gaseous bloat can occur.

Necropsy

There may be focal or diffuse meningitis of the cerebrum with characteristically haemorrhagic infarcts in any part of the brain. There may be haemorrhages in other organs such as the kidneys, skeletal muscles, myocardium, reticulo-rumen, abomasum and intestines. In arthritis the joints have oedematous synovial membranes with petechial haemorrhages. There is inflammation of the pleura, peritoneum and pericardium which may be fibrinous or serofibrinous. The larynx and trachea may show ulceration, and the lungs may be consolidated. Histologically there is vasculitis and thrombosis, often with infarctions and accumulations of neutrophils.

Diagnosis

1. Signs - sudden onset of pyrexia, sleeping animals with nervous signs.
2. Neutropaenia and leucopaenia occur in severe acute cases. Others may show a neutrophilia and a shift to the left.
3. Presence of organism in blood, synovial fluid or cerebrospinal fluid.
4. Serology - complement fixation test or haemagglutination test.
5. Synovial fluid contains many neutrophils.
6. Cerebrospinal fluid gives a marked positive to the Pandy globulin test.
7. Animals make a rapid response to appropriate antibiotic therapy in the early stages.

Differential diagnosis

1. Meningitis of other origin - isolation of organism.
2. Listeriosis - often a unilateral facial paralysis, head deviation and normal or near-normal rectal temperature.
3. CCN - there is usually a normal temperature, blindness with nystagmus and opisthotonus.
4. Vitamin A deficiency - usually sudden syncope or convulsions of short duration.

Prognosis

Recumbent cattle often do not recover despite therapy. If there is no response in any animal after three days' therapy, the condition is probably irreversible.

Treatment

Often intravenous oxytetracycline (10 mg/kg; 5 mg/lb) is used. Other suitable antimicrobial agents include chloramphenicol, penicillin-streptomycin combinations, sulphonamides, trimethoprim and sulphadoxine and trimethoprim and sulphadiazine. Therapy should be undertaken initially twice daily. When an outbreak occurs, then in-contact animals should be examined at least twice daily for a fortnight. When ocular discharge and conjunctivitis are the main lesions, intrapalpebral injections of chloramphenicol may be helpful (Lamont and Hunt, 1982).

Control

Details of the environmental requirements of the organism have not been fully established and in consequence recommendations for control have not been devised. When cases are diagnosed, strict observation of in-contacts must be undertaken. In America vaccination is possible.

Reference

LAMONT, H H and HUNT, B W (1982) Veterinary Record, 111, 21.

Hypoderma spp. Infestation

This infection is known as warbles, and the parasite is known as the warble fly.

Aetiology

Infestation with one of two insects, Hypoderma bovis or Hypoderma lineata.

Occurrence

The parasite used to be common with up to 40 per cent of young animals infested in years following hot summers. H. bovis was more prevalent than H. lineata, the latter tending to be mainly seen in the South-West or Scotland. H. bovis is a large fly and has a larger larva. It is also present later on in the season than H. lineata. Occasionally cases of infection occur in horses, particularly in the saddle region. Cases in sheep tend to be of the deer type, H. diana. Man has occasionally been infested. Infestation is more common in young animals. It would seem that immunity following infestation is good in that older cattle usually show few warble fly grubs in the spring. The condition is notifiable.

The life cycle is complex with the flies being active for 2 to 4 weeks in the spring or summer. The adults do not possess mouth parts and so cannot feed. After mating, the fly lays several hundred eggs, each of which is attached to the shaft of a hair. H. lineata lays its eggs in lines on the hair whereas H. bovis does it singly. Larvae hatch from the eggs in 4 to 6 days and then penetrate the skin of the host. They migrate over a considerable period to one of two 'winter resting sites' - the spinal cord (H. bovis) or the oesophagus (H. lineata). They remain in these sites from December to March, after which they migrate to the subcutaneous fat on either side of the spinal column. They produce a breathing hole by puncturing the skin. They develop from first stage to third stage larvae over a period of one to two months. Then the larvae pass through the skin, drop to the ground and pupate. Pupation lasts three to five weeks, then the adult flies emerge.

Signs

The main signs are the presence of "warbles" on the backs of animals in spring and summer. These are swollen areas which cause the animal some pain. When the flies are on the wing, cattle may be seen running around the fields "gadding". There is a loss in milk production and condition of the animals. In the winter occasional cases of posterior paralysis or bloat can occur.

Necropsy

When under the skin of the back there is liquefaction of the fat which may become green and gelatinous, producing "butchers' jelly" and such meat is known as "licked beef". The larvae are found in a yellow fluid. In some cases haemorrhagic or green tracts can be seen in muscles following larval migration.

Diagnosis

1. History - time of year.
2. Signs - warbles.

Treatment

The use of organophosphorus compounds as "pour-on" preparations can overcome the problem. These include fenthion, phosmet and famphur. Ivermectin can be used as an injection. In the past, derris was used. Synthetic pyrethroids are now also used in "pour-on" forms.

Control

In Britain at present there is an eradication campaign which was initiated by the Warble Fly (England and Wales) Order 1978 and the Warble Fly (Scotland) Order 1978. The disease became notifiable in 1982 and requires that all cases of warble fly infestation must be notified to the Ministry. Subsequent to notification, between 15th March and 31st July all cattle over three months old on the infected premises may be required to be treated with an approved compound. Movement restrictions are placed on the farm until the treatment has been satisfactorily undertaken. Subsequently, in the autumn, all cattle on the farm may be required to be treated and orders can be placed to require treatment on adjoining farms or on farms where animals have been sent from the infected farm. There is also the provision for setting up infected areas and these require that all cattle in the area are treated with an approved compound in the autumn. In general terms, treatment in the autumn is better than in the spring because it kills off the larvae before any damage is done, efficacy is better and there is less possibility of side effects.

Infectious Bovine Keratoconjunctivitis (IBKC)

This can also be known as New Forest eye or pinkeye.

Aetiology

Many different organisms have been isolated and appear to cause keratitis or conjunctivitis (see Table 4.1). The most important appear to be *Moraxella bovis* (Gram-negative small rods), particularly the haemolytic form, with or without *Neisseria* spp. (Gram-negative cocci).

TABLE 4.1

Organisms Isolated from Cases of Bovine Keratitis and Conjunctivitis

Bacteria	*Moraxella bovis* *Neisseria catarrhalis* *Neisseria* spp. *Escherichia coli* *Staphylococci* spp. *Streptococci* spp. Diphtheroids *Pasteurella multocida*
Mycoplasma	T-mycoplasma *Mycoplasma laidlawii* *Mycoplasma bovirhinis* *Mycoplasma bovoculi*
Rickettsia-like organisms	
Chlamydia	
Viruses	Infectious bovine rhinotracheitis Herpes virus Cancer eye Adenoviruses Mucosal disease Malignant catarrhal fever
Thelazia	*Thelazia skrjabinii* *Thelazia gulosa*
Predisposing agents	Ultra-violet light Insects (flies, etc.) Dust

Occurrence

This is an extremely common condition of cattle, particularly young animals. It will also occur in older animals if the population is susceptible. At one time the condition was recorded as occurring in the summer months, but it is now seen all the year round. It can be present in animals indoors or outside. The Hereford and Hereford cross are thought to be more prone to infection than other breeds. One study suggested that the disease occurred more frequently in summer months when the temperature is above the seasonal normal. Morbidity can be very high with large outbreaks but mortality is almost nil.

Certain flies probably act as vectors of the disease. Affected animals may have reduced weight gain due to the pain and reduced feed intake. It is possible for an animal to be affected more than once.

Incubation period

Usually this is two or three days, but it may be up to three weeks.

Signs

In most cases only one eye is affected at a time, although the second may subsequently become involved. Normally the animals will have a unilateral copious serous lachrymal discharge with some photophobia and blepharospasm. If the eye is examined there will be some oedema of the conjunctiva and congestion of the corneal vessels and a reddened conjunctiva. The animal tends to stand about with the eye half-closed and is disinclined to move and consequently to eat. After one or two days a small, white opacity appears in the corneal centre. This may then disappear or progress to become larger and then corneal ulceration occurs. The ulcer tends to be white or yellow and often spreads. If the ulcer deepens and extends into the stromal layer the intra-ocular pressure causes a swelling of the cornea, a keratocoele and there is the possibility of panophthalmitis. The puncture is plugged with the iris forming a staphyloma.

Following ulceration there is marked congestion of the corneal scleral blood vessels and some of the vessels at the limbus become directed towards the ulcer which eventually becomes surrounded, producing a red-purple border of varying density. This reddening forms part of the healing process which can take anything from 2 to 5 weeks to complete. Following recovery there is, in most cases, little residual opacity except for a white pin-point scar usually towards the centre of the cornea. In a few cases, there is a slight rise in temperature to 39.5°C (103.5°F), during the early stages of the disease, but otherwise no systemic involvement occurs.

Necropsy

Unless there is rupture of the cornea and panophthalmitis leading to an ascending infection of the optic tract then death does not occur. This sequel is extremely rare.

Diagnosis

1. Keratoconjunctivitis is present, often with a central area of ulceration.
2. There is little pyrexia.
3. Usually many animals are affected.
4. Swabs from the conjunctival sac can be cultured for M. bovis or Neisseria spp.

Differential diagnosis

1. A hay seed, barley aulm or piece of straw may be in the conjunctival sac, but this is a single case, often the foreign material is visible, and frequently it occurs when the cattle have to pull out the feed from hayracks above their normal head-carrying height.

2. Respiratory infections could confuse but usually there is pyrexia and respiratory signs.

3. IBR: especially in the early stages there is a profuse conjunctival discharge but in many animals there will be a pyrexia and there is no keratitis or corneal ulceration.

4. Mucosal disease, but in this condition there is often pyrexia, severe depression, mouth ulceration and diarrhoea.

5. Photosensitivity keratitis where the main cause was phenothiazine, which is no longer available, but it can result from swelling of the eyelids and subsequent entropion.

6. Malignant catarrhal fever but in this condition only a single animal is affected and there is no ulceration of the cornea.

7. Entropion is seen from birth or soon thereafter and the offending cilia can be seen in contact with the conjunctiva.

Treatment

Antibiotic ophthalmic ointments can be used, such as chlortetracycline, oxytetracycline, or chloramphenicol. However, the last should only be used if the organisms present are shown to be sensitive to this antibiotic. No ointment should be used containing corticosteroids as this will delay the healing process. Ointments tend to be removed quickly (about 30 minutes) from the eye by normal lachrymal secretion and they also require the animal to be caught for their application. Antibiotic powders can be used such as oxytetracycline. These do not require the animal to be caught. They suffer the same disadvantages in that the antibiotic is soon washed out of the conjunctival sac and again it is best not to use powders containing corticosteroids. Recently intra-conjunctival injections have been used either into the third eyelid, the palpebral conjunctiva or through the palpebral skin. Injections of penicillin and streptomycin, oxytetracycline and chloramphenicol have been used. The last should again only be used following antibiotic sensitivity testing. Although many practitioners include corticosteroids in the injection, these are contraindicated. Recently the single application of oil-based benzathine cloxacillin topically in the bovine eye has provided clinical recovery and produced useful concentrations in the lachrymal fluid for up to 56 hours (Buswell, Bywater and Hewett, 1982). The provision of systemic antibacterial activity with sulphadimidine has been advocated (Bedford, 1976) and has much to recommend it in those cases with severe pain.

Another problem with therapy is that the best result is often achieved the earlier the treatment is given. However, if treatment is undertaken at an initial stage it is possible that immunity to the infection will be impaired and so the eye may be susceptible to a second attack. The use of a nictating membrane flap gives a good result in severe cases. It should be kept in position for two weeks or longer.

Control

Infected animals should be removed from the herd to help reduce the spread of infection. Until more is known about the epidemiology, little can be offered in methods of specific protection. M. bovis vaccines are available in America and have given some useful results. As flies are, at least in the summer, incriminated in the spread of the disease, the application of insecticides to the animals may be of use, particularly the new synthetic pyrethroids such as cypermethrin and permethrin or the organophosphorus compound crotoxyphos. Recently ear tags containing insecticide (cypermethrin, fenvalerate, permethrin, tetrachlorvinphos) have become available. In the past, fly repellant was often applied to the posterior surface of the ears of cattle in the hope that some would be applied to the faces of other cattle at the time of trough feeding.

References

BEDFORD, P G C (1976) Veterinary Record 98, 134-135.

BUSWELL, J F, BYWATER, R J and HEWETT, G R (1982) Proceedings of Twelfth World Congress on Diseases of Cattle. International Congrescentrum RAI, Amsterdam, The Netherlands. 7-10th September. Volume II. pp. 1122-1126.

Infectious Necrotic Hepatitis

Black disease is the usual name given to the condition.

Aetiology

Infection in damaged liver tissue with *Clostridium novyi* (*Cl. oedematiens* type B), a Gram-positive, anaerobic bacterium.

Occurrence

It is very uncommon in cattle. Usually there is some form of damage to the liver, resulting in necrosis, and this allows the organism to multiply and produce a toxaemia. In many cases the condition may have non-specific precipitating causes. Animals, particularly sheep, can be carriers of the disease and can produce contaminated faeces. The spores are ingested and pass to the liver via the lymphatic system, for subsequent activation which can be by liver fluke passage or other cause. The disease results in toxins causing liver and vascular damage.

Signs

Some cases are found dead overnight without showing previous signs of illness. However, in cattle, illness may last for 24 to 48 hours. There is usually depression, weakness, with a normal or subnormal temperature, the respirations tend to be rapid and shallow, often with hyperaesthesia. The animal may be in sternal recumbency and palpation of the liver region is painful. There is muffling of the heart sounds and the faeces are semi-solid. There may be periorbital oedema.

Necropsy

There is rapid putrefaction of the carcase and blood-stained fluid may come down the nostrils. The subcutaneous tissues show engorgement of the blood vessels as well as oedema. The liver tends to be swollen and dark red-black in colour. There are areas of hyperaemia which enclose necrosis and are often linear. There may be a gelatinous exudate between the abdominal muscle layers. Often there is evidence of liver fluke invasion. Blood-stained fluid is present in the abdominal, pleural and pericardial cavities and subendocardial and subepicardial haemorrhages are often seen. In a few animals there is congestion of the subcutaneous tissue and muscles of the shoulder.

Diagnosis

1. Usually *post mortem* examination with necrotic areas in an enlarged liver. In some cases young liver flukes are present.
2. Fluorescent antibody techniques can be useful.
3. The organism can be isolated from the area close to the liver lesions.

Differential diagnosis

1. Anthrax.
2. Blackleg.
3. Enterotoxaemia.
4. Malignant oedema.

Treatment

Therapy is usually unsuccessful but large doses of penicillin, ampicillin, amoxycillin, oxytetracycline or potentiated sulphonamides may be useful.

Control

Ensure that young cattle are kept away from habitats where *Limnaea truncatula* lives, or the areas are drained. Regular therapy for liver fluke can be helpful. The condition can also be caused by sudden changes in feeding or heavy cereal feeding and so all alterations in diet should be made gradually. The cattle can be vaccinated against *Cl. novyi* with a mixed potash alum precipitated vaccine. Two doses are injected subcutaneously at an interval of at least six weeks.

Interdigital Pododermatitis

This is often known as foul-of-the-foot, clit-ill or foot-rot.

Aetiology

The cause is *Fusiformis necrophorus* (*Fusobacterium necrophorum*, *Sphaerophorus necrophorus*) a filamentous, anaerobic, Gram-negative organism.

Occurrence

It is a common cause of lameness in growing cattle. Infection enters cuts and abrasions of the skin in the lower part of the foot, and such damage is more likely to occur when the skin is soft from continued wetting. It is seen in animals kept outside when the ground is wet, particularly where gateways are muddy or stony. Indoors, the condition is often seen in straw yards or where there is dung build-up with it caking to the feet, drying and damaging the skin above the horn of the hoof. Morbidity can be up to 25 *per cent* but mortality does not occur unless joints become involved and the animal has to be slaughtered.

Signs

It can occur in any front or back foot and usually involves one limb at a time. There is sudden, severe lameness and little weight is put on the affected foot. There may be pyrexia, 39.5 - 40°C (103 - 104°F) and some inappetance. There is usually swelling around the coronary band and the two claws are often parted. A split, usually with protruding sides, is found at the top of the interdigital cleft, but it can be on the side of the cleft. Palpation of the cleft is painful. There is normally only a small amount of pus, but the necrotic edges of the fissure may produce an offensive smell. Some cases heal spontaneously but in others complications may occur, including infection of the tendon sheaths and the interdigital joints. In these cases the leg may be carried and there is usually much swelling, extending a varying amount above the coronary band.

Necropsy

The lesions are essentially a necrosis of the skin and subcutaneous tissues.

Diagnosis

1. There is little systemic involvement.
2. The lesions are usually typical.
3. Bacteriology of the lesions can be performed.

Differential diagnosis

1. Laminitis, but normally two or more limbs are affected.
2. Penetration of the foot, but there is an area of necrosis at the site of puncture.
3. Bruising of the sole but there is some discolouration.

Treatment

The use of sulphadimidine intravenously or subcutaneously may help at a dose of 1 g/kg BW (0.5 g/lb). Sulphamethoxypyridazine (22 mg/kg BW, 11 mg/lb BW) and sulphapyrazole (0.03 - 0.1 g/kg BW, 0.02 - 0.05 g/lb) may be beneficial. Penicillin can be injected at 10,000 units per kg BW (5,000 units/lb BW), or oxytetracycline (5 - 10 mg/kg BW, 2.5 - 5 mg/lb BW). Locally the lesions should be washed, cleaned and in severe cases curetted, and antibiotic or copper sprays can then be applied. Oral zinc preparations are of use. It is often useful to keep the animal indoors on deep, clean straw until the lesions are healing.

Prevention

Make sure that there is plenty of clean bedding in yards. Muddy and stony patches should be filled in. Footbaths with five per cent formaldehyde, five per cent copper sulphate or zinc sulphate can help to reduce the problem.

Leptospiral Infections

Aetiology

Many different serotypes can infect cattle including *Leptospira interrogans* serotype *canicola* and *L. interrogans* serotype *icterohaemorrhagiae* (spiral organisms). Recently leptospires of the Pomona group have been isolated from cattle but are antigenically distinct from *L. pomona*.

Occurrence

The majority of positive findings on serology are in the Hebdomadis group and are probably related to *L. interrogans* serotype *hardjo* (see page 208). However, other serotypes are occasionally associated with disease. Often infection follows gross contamination by rodents, etc. Once infection is present in a herd most signs occur in the heifers. Usually morbidity is low but mortality in those affected can be high.

Incubation period

3 to 7 days.

Abortion rate

Up to 15 *per cent*.

Signs

When infection first enters a herd there may be occasional cases of septicaemia with marked pyrexia, 40 - 41°C (104 - 107°F), anorexia, jaundice, haemoglobinuria and pale mucous membranes. There may be marked anaemia with an increase in heart rate and the intensity of the heart sounds. Often dyspnoea is present. Some animals show dysentery, mastitis or lameness due to synovitis.

Abortion

This can result from the systemic reaction.

Necropsy

There are subserous and submucosal haemorrhages with jaundice, anaemia and haemoglobinuria. In a few cases there is pulmonary oedema and emphysema. Histologically there may be a progressive interstitial nephritis and centrilobular hepatic necrosis.

Diagnosis

1. Signs - haemoglobinuria, jaundice.
2. Bacteriology, isolation and culture of urine.
3. Serology.

Differential diagnosis

1. Babesiasis but the area helps and the time of year.
2. Kale poisoning but feed history helps.
3. Bacillary haemoglobinuria.

Treatment

High levels of streptomycin for three days are helpful, as also can be oxytetracycline. Blood transfusions may be required in some severely affected cases.

Control

Remove all rodents as these are a likely source of infection. If infection has just entered a herd it may be possible to blood test all the herd and remove the serologically positive animals. Otherwise, if many are infected, all cattle could be treated with antibiotics or the urine can be collected and examined for bacteria. The positively infected cows could then be culled.

Listeriosis

Aetiology

Infection with *Listeria monocytogenes* (Gram-positive and non-spore forming organism).

Occurrence

The condition is usually seen as sporadic cases. The bacterium is a saprophyte and can remain outside the body for long periods, a year in damp soil and two years in dry soil. The organism survives in good silage of pH 4 - 4.5 and in the badly-made product at pH 5.5 it survives and multiplies. Many species can be infected, including man, but probably sheep are most commonly involved. Any age of cattle can be infected but most cattle involved are young. Carrier animals probably occur and transmit infection to new premises. Cattle incidents peak in March, April and May but most abortions are seen in January and February.

Portal of entry

Probably oral or venereal in abortion but via inhalation or conjunctival in cases of meningoencephalitis.

Morbidity

Usually low, up to 10 *per cent*.

Mortality

Approaches 100 *per cent* if left untreated.

Incubation period

Probably 7 to 14 days.

Signs

Various syndromes occur.

Septicaemia

This is relatively rare and is seen mainly in calves although occasionally in the growing or adult animal. There is depression, anorexia and, in some cases, pyrexia and diarrhoea. Nervous signs are absent.

Meningoencephalitis

This is the commonest form in the growing or adult animal. Usually there is pyrexia, 40 - 42°C (104 - 107°F) but this subsides as other signs develop. Varying nervous signs are present with dullness and often sleepiness, head pressing, circling and head deviation. Some animals show unilateral facial paralysis with drooping of the mouth, eyelid and ear. Hypopyon and panophthalmitis occur in some animals following a few days' infection.

Late signs

Recumbency with a normal rectal temperature. Death is due to respiratory failure. Usually the course is not longer than two weeks.

Abortion

This is sporadic and uncommon. Usually abortion is at about seven months of pregnancy with retention of the afterbirth often occurring. The animal may show signs of illness, including pyrexia 40°C (104°F).

Prognosis

The quicker therapy is initiated the more likely it is to be successful.

Necropsy

Septicaemia

There may be multiple necrotic foci in organs such as the myocardium, endocardium, liver and spleen.

Meningoencephalitis

Congestion of meningeal vessels with clouding of the cerebrospinal fluid and panophthalmitis. Histologically microabscesses are present in the brain stem and they may be unilateral.

Abortion

The aborted foetus tends to be oedematous. Necrotic foci can occur in many organs.

Diagnosis

1. History - access to silage, one or a small group affected. History of disease on farm.
2. Age - usually growing animals.
3. Signs - nervous signs such as head pressing, severe dullness, pyrexia in early stages; facial paralysis and panophthalmitis.
4. Bacteriological culture from *post mortem* material, placental or foetuses. The organism is best isolated after maceration and refridgeration for a long period. Isolation from vaginal secretions possible after abortion.
5. *Post mortem* findings - necrotic foci in organs, microabscesses in brain on histology.
6. Cerebrospinal fluid may contain bacteria and neutrophils.
7. Serology - agglutination and complement fixation test but some infected animals give negative results.

Differential diagnosis

1. Nervous acetonaemia but soon after calving, blindness and intermittent convulsions. No facial paralysis or panophthalmitis. Ketone bodies in milk and blood.
2. Brain abscess - signs slowly develop and are progressive, often over a long time.
3. Rabies - usually signs progress relatively rapidly and death soon occurs. There is no facial paralysis or panophthalmitis.

Treatment

Intravenous injections of oxytetracycline (10 mg/kg BW; 5 mg/lb) or chlortetracycline (10 mg/kg BW; 5 mg/lb) (no veterinary form now available in the United Kingdom) can be used. Injections should continue for about five days. Other antimicrobial agents which may be useful include chloramphenicol and combined penicillin and streptomycin injections. It is essential that therapy is started early in order for it to be successful.

Control

No vaccine is available in Britain and it would be unlikely to be much used because of the sporadic nature of the disease. Once cases have occurred, the cattle should be checked carefully twice daily and animals showing any signs should be treated effectively and immediately. If silage is fed then the amount should be reduced. In subsequent years, try to ensure silage is made well and is of acceptable acidity (pH 4.0). There should be minimal soil contamination of the silage.

Louping Ill

Aetiology

The cause is an arbovirus.

Occurrence

Almost all cases occur in Scotland and the response in cattle is less than in sheep. Infection depends on transmission by the tick *Ixodes ricinus*.

Incubation period

About 7 days.

Signs

There is a staggering gait, with frequent collapsing and then sternal recumbency. The animal tends to eat and drink normally.

Necropsy

There are no gross signs. Histologically there is a non-suppurative meningoencephalomyelitis.

Diagnosis

1. Area of the country - tick area.
2. Signs - pyrexia, staggering gait.
3. Serology - haemagglutination inhibition antibody.
4. Virus isolation from the brain is often difficult.

Treatment

There is no specific treatment although in the early stages of infection specific antiserum can be used. Nursing and symptomatic therapy are of use.

Control

Keep cattle out of tick areas. Improve the pasture and use bracken killers. Vaccination can be undertaken with an inactivated louping ill virus oily emulsion vaccine which is also used in sheep. Injections should be not less than three weeks apart and not more than six months apart. The injection course should be completed at least two weeks before exposure to infection. Pregnant cows should have the course completed by the last month of pregnancy. Revaccination should occur annually.

Malignant Oedema

This is also known as gas gangrene.

Aetiology

An acute infection by organisms of the genus *Clostridium*, which are anaerobic, Gram-positive, spore-forming organisms, following entry through a wound. The bacteria concerned include *Cl. chauvoei*, *Cl. septicum*, *Cl. novyi* (*oedematiens* type B) or *Cl. welchii* (*perfringens*).

Occurrence

The condition occurs occasionally following entry of infection via wounds. In most cases infection results from a dirty environment. "False blackleg" can also occur with infection due to *Cl. septicum* and *Cl. novyi*. Most infection is soil-borne and spores tend to survive for long periods in the soil. The organisms normally enter the body following severe trauma or deep puncture wounds. Infection can sometimes be the result of bad injection technique, calving or contamination of surgical wounds following castration, etc. The bacteria produce toxins which cause illness in the animal once absorbed into the blood. There is also severe local damage caused by the toxins.

Incubation period

12 to 48 hours.

Signs

Most cases will die unless early therapy is provided. The signs at the site of entry of the organism are of erythema with a soft swelling. In some cases there is crepitation due to emphysema (but not in *Cl. novyi* infection) and the skin over the area becomes stretched and dark-coloured. There is often pyrexia, 40.5 - 42°C (105 - 107°F) with the animal showing signs of weakness and depression. If a limb is involved there might be lameness. Animals that are infected normally die in 12 to 48 hours after signs develop.

Necropsy

There is rapid putrefaction of the affected areas after death. Over the affected area is usually skin gangrene, and oedema of the subcutaneous and intramuscular connective tissue. Emphysema may be present. Unlike blackleg there is usually minimal muscle involvement. There are usually fairly generalised sub-serous haemorrhages with the body cavities containing sero-sanguinous fluid.

Diagnosis

1. Signs - there is local inflammation and emphysema with toxaemia but little muscle involvement.
2. Animals may have received some clostridial vaccination programme e.g. for blackleg.
3. Presence of organisms in the lesions.

Differential diagnosis

1. Blackleg - but the muscle is affected.

Treatment

Therapy must be given early in the course of the disease to be effective. Large doses of penicillin or broad spectrum antibiotics such as ampicillin, amoxycillin, oxytetracycline, trimethoprim and sulphadoxine are also useful. Any infected wound should be incised, drained and irrigated with hydrogen peroxide.

Control

When animals are injected, calved or castrated, a sound hygienic technique must be used. Several vaccines can be used, including a specific combined clostridial cattle vaccine for *Cl. chauvoei*, *Cl. septicum*, *Cl. novyi*, *Cl. haemolyticum* and *Cl. tetani*. Vaccination involves two doses at least six weeks apart and should be completed at least two weeks before the period of risk. Revaccination in areas of high infection should take place every six months.

Mycotic Dermatitis

Streptochricosis.

Aetiology

The cause is *Dermatophilus congolensis.*

Occurrence

The condition is seen infrequently and can affect animals of all ages although it is more likely to be seen in young cattle. It usually occurs when the weather is wet and warm. The organism can remain in soil for at least four months. It usually enters small abrasive wounds. Flies are believed to act as carriers in some cases.

Signs

The lesions usually occur on the rump but they may also be seen on the body and the sides of the legs as well as the back of the udder and down the thorax. There is usually a matting together of the hairs, often circular in shape, with a diameter of 2 to 5 cm (1 to 2 in). On the skin there is a yellow crust of exudate which becomes thick and hard. As the condition continues the exudate lifts off the skin surface. The hair may be lost.

Necropsy

Cattle do not die from infection.

Diagnosis

1. History of damp, warm weather.
2. Lesions are characteristic with thick crusting, particularly dorsal on the rump and back.
3. Scrapings or skin biopsy may show the organism.
4. Impression smear from the ventral surface of the scab which is then stained with methylene blue.

Differential diagnosis

1. Ringworm.

Treatment

Parenteral antibiotics are of use, such as penicillin and streptomycin at high levels or oxytetracycline. The animal can be treated topically with solutions of 1 in 200 dilution of quaternary ammonium compounds, one *per cent* solution of alum (potassium aluminium sulphate), 0.2 *per cent* copper sulphate or 0.2 - 0.5 *per cent* zinc sulphate.

Control

Improve ventilation if condition occurs in wet, humid buildings. Do not use grooming kits of infected animals on other cattle.

Otitis

Aetiology

This is unknown, but often there has been a history of enzootic pneumonia in the herd and it is possible that it is an ascending infection of the Eustachian tube. In the form involving the external ear, *Staphylococcus* spp. and *Streptococcus* spp. may be isolated, whereas that involving the middle ear normally contains *Pasteurella* spp. or *Haemophilus* spp.

Occurrence

It has been reported mainly in calf-rearing centres. Usually there has been a respiratory disease outbreak. Up to 30 *per cent* of calves may show signs but in housed cattle at the yearling stage the level of infection is low at about 1 in 2,000 (Jensen, Maki, Laverman, Raths, Swift, Flack, Hoff, Hancock, Tucker, Horton and Weibel, 1983).

Signs

There are two forms, namely discharging and non-discharging. Both types may be bilateral or unilateral.

Discharging

In this form the ear is dropped and there is a foul-smelling discharge. The animal is bright with a normal temperature and it eats well.

Non-discharging

Provided the infection is unilateral the head is rotated, there is some incoordination and on radiography there may be some rarefaction of the tympanic bulla. There is no discharge from the ear. The animal is often dull and there is some inappetance.

Diagnosis

1. The signs are useful.
2. Bacteriological culture and antibiotic sensitivity are helpful.

Differential diagnosis

1. Brain abscess, but there is head deviation rather than rotation.
2. Brain injury also produces head deviation and not rotation.
3. Meningitis, but with this there is pyrexia.

Treatment

The discharging form normally improves well with application of ointments such as intramammary tubes. Usually penicillin and streptomycin, chlortetracycline and cloxacillin are all efficacious. Therapy of the non-discharging form is often of limited success, but the tympanic membrane should be punctured and systemic antibiotic therapy used with compounds such as tetracyclines,ampicillin or amoxycillin.

Control

As little is known about the condition's aetiology, advice has to be limited, but all cases of enzootic pneumonia should receive adequate therapy.

Reference

JENSEN, R, MAKI, L R, LAUERMAN, L H, RATHS, W R, SWIFT, B L, FLACK, D E, HOFF, R L, HANCOCK, H A, TUCKER, J O, HORTON, D P and WEIBEL, J L (1983) Journal of American Veterinary Medical Association, 182, 967-972.

Psoroptic Mange

Aetiology

The cause is the mite *Psoroptes communis* var. *bovis*.

Occurrence

The condition is not as common as sarcoptic mange and is very unusual in Britain. It occurs more frequently in animals older than calves. It appears mainly indoors and is highly contagious, with many animals being affected. The life cycle takes about 10 to 14 days. The mites live on the skin surface but pierce it so that tissue fluid exudes and this forms a scab. The mite can live up to three weeks off the host. The disease tends to be more common in winter and autumn as the rate of egg laying increases in moist, cold conditions. Signs are few in the summer and this may be because infection is latent. Spread is often by direct contact or indirectly via scratching posts, etc.

Signs

In the early stages signs may not be observed. Then there is pruritus and lesions first tend to be found in those areas with plenty of hair, e.g. withers, neck, base of the tail. However, in severe cases, the whole body may be affected and in such animals there may be loss of condition. The lesions are normally papules or scabs, but in severe infection the skin becomes widely covered with scabs and it is thickened and wrinkled.

Diagnosis

1. Pruritus.
2. The site of the lesions.
3. Examination of skin scrapings from the periphery of lesions for mites.

Differential diagnosis

1. Sarcoptic mange.
2. Chorioptic mange.
3. Pediculosis.

Treatment

The use of a gamma benzene hexachloride bath or wash has been successful in treatment. Organophosphorus compounds, bromocyclen or ivermectin can be utilised. Extra acaricide may be applied to the worst affected areas. It may be necessary to repeat therapy, which is often unsatisfactory.

Control

Infected animals should be separated from those not showing signs. An acaricide should be applied as a spray or bath to non-infested cattle.

Pediculosis

Lice infestation.

Aetiology

Four types of lice are present in Britain, Damalinia bovis (the biting louse) and three forms of the sucking lice, Haematopinus eurysternus (most irritant), Linognathus vituli (smaller than H. eurysternus) and Solenopodes capillatus (smallest biting louse).

Occurrence

Together the four species are the most common cause of skin disease in cattle. It occurs more frequently in calves and young cattle than older ones. Housed cattle are more affected, particularly those in poor condition or on a low plane of nutrition. The eggs normally take about one to two weeks to hatch on the host, but about three weeks if off the host. The adult stage is reached in 2 to 3 weeks and the life cycle from egg to egg is usually about 4 to 5 weeks. Infection is mainly spread by contact between animals, but as the parasite can live a week or two off the host, indirect infection can occur via rubbing posts, infected grooming equipment, etc.

Signs

Each type tends to cause considerable irritation which results in rubbing, increased licking and grooming and a loss of hair. D. bovis is particularly found at the withers, neck and base of the tail. Both L. vituli and H. eurysternus mainly infest the shoulders, upper part of the neck, head and base of the tail.

Diagnosis

1. Recovery of the parasite - D. bovis is small and light-brown. Sucking lice tend to be larger with heads buried in the skin and they are blue-grey or brown in colour.
2. The eggs should be looked for if the adults cannot be found. They are light-brown in colour and attached to the hairs. Egg cases, which are white, may also be seen and these are usually further from the epidermis than the unhatched eggs.

Differential diagnosis

1. Mange.
2. Ringworm, but there is little pruritus.

Treatment

The use of chlorinated hydrocarbons is helpful and they are normally used as a powder. An organophosphorus powder is also available. In some cases where there is heavy infestation, a bath may be of more use. Organophosphorus compounds can be used by the pour-on method, e.g. prolate, fenthion, famphur. Bromocyclen can be used as a spray, bath, or powder. Ivermectins can also be given, at present only by injection. Synthetic pyrethroids are now also used as washes or pour-on preparations.

With most of these preparations the eggs remain unharmed and so a second application is usually required two or three weeks later and this will then result in almost complete eradication. Any grooming kit used on the animals should also be treated and as the parasite survives up to two weeks off the host, the bedding should be treated.

Control

Ensure that there is adequate dusting or bathing of all cattle after entry to the farm with a suitable insecticide.

Ringworm

Aetiology

In most cases this fungal infection in cattle is caused by Trichophyton verrucosum. Occasionally other species, such as T. mentagrophytes, are present.

Occurrence

It is the second most common skin condition of cattle, and occurs mainly in calves and young animals. Infection can be indoors or outside, but often it appears to be more common in the winter months, possibly because of the increased amount of contact between the animals. It would appear that following infection a high degree of immunity is obtained, as re-infection is very unusual. The disease can affect man where lesions can cause considerable irritation and inflammation. The fungus is aerobic and infects keratinised structures, in particular hair fibres, and the stratum corneum. The disease in individual animals is of varying duration in that new lesions develop at times when others are healing. The duration on cattle can vary between two and about 26 weeks, depending on the degree of infection. In most cases duration is probably about 2 to 4 months. Little work has been undertaken on the duration of individual lesions, but in one study it was about half the time the individual animal was affected. Infection is normally spread by contact between animals but it can result from spore persistence in buildings. Spores can be present on the coats of cattle without causing infection.

Incubation period

This is variable but in most natural outbreaks it is between three and six weeks. Experimentally the period can be as little as a week. Incubation tends to be longer in younger animals.

Signs

Lesions are most commonly found around the eyes, on the head, neck and around the perineum, although almost any area of the body can be affected. The sites often coincide with areas where indirect contact occurs between animals, i.e. on the neck when fed through bars. The lesions tend to be circular in shape and consist of grey, thick encrustations. Pruritus is absent. The encrustations are eventually lost and there may be an area of alopecia or hair growth which usually starts from the centre outwards. Secondary bacterial invasion can occur. In some animals it is possible for all the body to become infected, possibly due to a hypersensitivity reaction.

Diagnosis

1. The lesions are typical.
2. There is no pruritus.
3. A skin scraping and hair sample can be taken and cleared by warming in 10 per cent potassium hydroxide and there are chains of round spores on the hair surface or in the cornified layers.
4. Culture of samples can be helpful. A rapid method of identification can be obtained using mycobiotic media cultured at 37°C (98.5°F).

Differential diagnosis

1. Dermatophilus infection, but the distribution often occurs on the back and areas exposed to the wet.

2. Mange, but there is pruritus.

3. Pediculosis.

Treatment

In most instances, ringworm infections appear to do little harm to the animal and treatment is undertaken usually for aesthetic reasons or to prevent human contamination. Various methods of therapy have been used. Topical applications have been widely tried in the past, but they are time-consuming, some are of dubious value and there is also the chance of possible infection of the stockman. In consequence, all people handling ringworm-infected cattle should wear rubber or plastic gloves and protective clothing. Ointments normally used contain undecylenic acid, as it has been shown in man that the skin pH is important. Thus most infection is in children when the pH is relatively high. At puberty the pH falls from 6.5 to 4.0 due to sebum secretion which contains fatty acids. Ointments work best when the crusts have been removed and then the medicament applied. Baths and applications have been used, including benzuldazic acid, hexetidine, and etisazole hydrochloride. A new product, enilconazole, has recently become available for topical application. It is claimed to have fungistatic and fungicidal properties.

Aerosols can be used, including copper naphthenate, dichlorophen and undecylenic acid, and 246 tribromo-3-hydroxytoluene and salicylic acid. Injections of 10 per cent sodium iodide at 1 g per 12 kg BW can be given intravenously and may need to be repeated at weekly intervals.

Antibiotics. Griseofulvin, available as a powder, can be added to feed for seven days, thereby preventing the need for contact with the animals. Another antibiotic can be used, namely natamycin, which is applied topically to the affected areas and repeated in 4 to 5 days. There have been few well-controlled trials on the efficacy of the various products against ringworm.

Control

Spore formation makes any form of prevention difficult. Buildings and equipment should be thoroughly washed and all organic matter removed. The buildings can then be thoroughly washed or sprayed with 2 to 4 per cent formalin solution. The solution is irritant and adequate waterproof protective clothing and gloves, and if spraying, a face mask, should be used. One per cent caustic soda, phenolic disinfectants, and sodium hypochlorite can be utilised. The diet should be adequate and high levels of dietary vitamin A (up to 50,000 units/animal/day) are said to be helpful.

If only infected animals are treated, griseofulvin will not stop infection spreading from these to the other cattle. When only one or two are affected it is best to isolate these animals, treat them and only return them to the group when the lesions have healed and they have been washed in a fungicide bath. If uninfected calves are treated with griseofulvin, there is some protection while therapy continues but the animals will not develop an immunity to ringworm and so infection can occur after the effects of preventive treatment have worn off. In such cases the building will need to be thoroughly cleaned and all the animals, whether infected or not, should be washed with 0.5 per cent formalin solution. Natamycin can kill spores and can be used to spray woodwork, equipment, etc.

Papillomatosis

Warts, Angleberries.

Aetiology

A papovavirus with at least five strains is responsible and is host-specific.

Occurrence

They are particularly numerous in young cattle. In some cases only one or two animals are affected, although in some outbreaks spread of infection among young cattle may be very extensive. Transmission of infection is more likely when the calves are housed than when they are outside. Warts can occur following skin damage as occurs following skin lacerations, previous ringworm or dermatophilus infection, or around ear tags, etc. Spread can be direct contact or indirectly by dehorners, ear taggers, stockman's hands or possibly pediculosis. Immunity following infection is in most instances effective and lasts for at least two years.

Incubation period

This is variable but normally it is about two months.

Signs

Varying types of warts are seen including those like rice grains and nodules. Lesions can occur on any part of the body, but commonly they occur on the muzzle, head, and neck although in some animals they occur on the penis or on the udder and teats. There is no pruritus.

Necropsy

The wart contains both connective tissue and epithelium. Those consisting mainly of connective tissue are called fibromata, those with mainly epitheloid tissue are papillomata and those containing both types of tissue are fibropapillomata.

Diagnosis

This is relatively easy.

1. The lesions involve the skin.
2. A biopsy.

Differential diagnosis

1. Ringworm
2. Dermatophilus infection.

Treatment

The warts will resolve spontaneously over a period of months. In the case of a few warts which are pedunculated, an elastrator ring can be applied to the neck of each wart. Surgical removal, often with cautery, can be undertaken with local anaesthesia. Salicylic acid can be tried, as also have deep intramuscular injections of lithium antimony thiomalate, about 5ml every 48 hours for 4 to 6 injections. Variable success has been obtained with this and the same occurs with autogenous vaccines which are usually prepared in formalin.

Control

Affected animals should be isolated.

Sarcoptic Mange

Aetiology

This is caused by the mange mite *Sarcoptes scabiei* var. *bovis*.

Occurrence

This infestation occurs quite frequently, but usually in older animals. It tends to be more common in housed cattle, particularly where there is overcrowding and this allows more contact spread. It is more frequent in winter than summer. The mites burrow under the outer epidermis and the life cycle from egg to mature adult is only about 14 days. The mites can survive up to three weeks off the host. The short life cycle means that the animal's body can become covered with infection within six weeks. Spread is both by direct contact and indirect on bedding, scratching posts, etc. Humans can become infected with the parasite.

Signs

The areas affected tend to be the inside of the hind legs and groin, inside the front legs, the brisket, underside of the neck and tail head. The lesions are small, raised, red papules and there is generalised reddening of the skin in the area. Pruritus is marked and the resulting trauma causes loss of hair, a thickened, wrinkled skin, which becomes covered in brown scabs. In untreated animals the constant irritation can lead to loss of condition, weakness and anorexia. Very occasionally affected cattle can die.

Diagnosis

1. Pruritus.
2. The medial aspects of the legs are usually affected first.
3. The skin shows thickening and brown encrustations.
4. A skin scraping which may be taken with potassium hydroxide shows mites. However, as mites may be few in number, several scrapings may be necessary.

Differential diagnosis

1. Ringworm infection but there is no pruritus.
2. Chlorinated naphthalene poisoning but there is no pruritus.
3. Chorioptic mange.
4. Psoroptic mange.
5. Pediculosis, but different areas are affected, i.e. withers, neck, etc. and the parasite can be seen.

Treatment

Gamma benzene hexachloride baths will help to eliminate infection, but will need to be repeated at weekly intervals. The whole animal should be bathed. A lotion of benzyl benzoate can be applied to the affected areas every two or three days. Bromocyclen can be applied as a bath or spray. Occasionally rotenone or sulphur may be used. Ivermectin has been used successfully by injection.

Control

Infected animals should be removed from the others as soon as possible. The environment should be treated with a suitable acaricide, e.g. benzene hexachloride, bromocyclen or coumaphos.

Skin Tuberculosis

Aetiology

Various acid-fast organisms can be involved. They tend to be non-pathogenic.

Occurrence

It is generally a condition of individual animals. It mainly causes problems because of its interference with the interpretation of the tuberculin test.

Entry of infection

Usually via abrasions or injections.

Signs

One or more lumps are present attached to the skin. They are most commonly found on the limbs, particularly the lower part, and mainly on the forelegs. Often the nodules are in chains along the local lymphatic vessels. The nodules tend to be 1 to 3 cm (½ to 1 in) in diameter and can rupture to release a thick, creamy pus.

Necropsy

The nodules consist of thick, fibrous capsules containing solid or thick, creamy pus. Calcification may be present.

Diagnosis

1. Lesions.
2. Tuberculin test reaction. Usually there is a greater avian response.

Differential diagnosis

1. Bovine tuberculosis.

Treatment

Usually not undertaken but nodules can be removed surgically.

Sporadic Bovine Leukosis

Aetiology

This has not been completely resolved although virus particles are often present.

Occurrence

This is a generalised form of neoplasia in cattle but is still uncommon. Most cases are seen in animals under two years old although the cutaneous form may be seen in older animals. The condition is very sporadic. Mortality approaches 95 per cent of those affected.

Signs

Cutaneous

This is seen as cutaneous plaques of varying size, 1-5 cm in diameter (½-2 inches) on the neck, back, thighs and croup. The hair tends to be lost from the lesions which are covered by greyish-white scabs with pitted centres. These start to reduce. The peripheral lymph nodes are often involved and are enlarged. Others show spontaneous recovery.

Prognosis

Cattle may die several months after the appearance of disease.

Generalised

It is usually seen in calves less than six months old. There is a loss of weight, depression and weakness. Lymph nodes are considerably enlarged. Death often occurs in two to eight weeks. Some cattle occasionally show pyrexia, tachycardia or posterior paralysis. There tends to be no ulceration of the overlying skin.

Prognosis

Most animals die within six weeks of clinical signs becoming apparent.

Thymic

This is usually present in animals between six months and two years old. There is massive thymus enlargement and local oedema may be present. Clinically a firm swelling is seen in the presternal area or ventral part of the neck with some subcutaneous oedema in the region. In some cases the swelling may only be apparent by carefully examining the thoracic inlet. There is often unilateral or bilateral muffling of the heart sounds and on percussion there is an increased area of dullness around the heart. In some cases there is enlargement of some superficial cervical or other lymph nodes but generalised size increase is rare. Respiratory distress can result from the thymic enlargement.

Prognosis

Most animals will survive several weeks although those with severe respiratory distress die quickly.

Adult multicentric

This occurs in the adult animal and has two main forms.

1. Generalised lymph node enlargement.
2. Assymmetrical or localised lymph node enlargement.

1. The signs include a loss of weight with depression, generalised lymph node enlargement and, in some cases, tachycardia or posterior paralysis are seen.

2. Varying nodes are enlarged and there is usually loss of condition. Other presenting signs depend on the lymph nodes involved.

Necropsy

Firm white masses may be present in the thymus, kidney, liver, spleen or the lymph nodes. Affected lymph nodes may be much enlarged and contain healthy and neoplastic tissue which is firm, white and may contain yellow necrotic areas. Histological examination reveals the neoplastic masses to consist of lymphocytic cells.

Diagnosis

1. History; usually animals under two years old.
2. Signs; lymph node or other organ enlargement.
3. There may be anorexia.
4. The leucocyte count may become high.
5. The percentage of lymphocytes may increase.
6. Biopsy - a superficially enlarged node.

Differential diagnosis

1. Enzootic bovine leukosis has similar signs but the animals are older and give a positive agar gel immunodiffusion test (AGIDT).
2. Tuberculosis but likely to be mainly respiratory and several animals may be infected.
3. Actinobacillosis but usually only a few nodes are involved.

Treatment

Therapy has not been attempted.

Control

Under the Enzootic Bovine Leukosis Order, 1980, all animals with suspected tumours other than haemangiomas, haemangiosarcomas and papillomas must be notified to MAFF. The condition of sporadic bovine leukosis is too uncommon to warrant control.

Summer Mastitis

This is also known as August bag, summer felon.

Aetiology

This is a clinical condition seen in heifers and non-lactating cows during the summer months. In many cases Corynebacterium pyogenes is isolated but other organisms may be involved.

TABLE 4.2

Organism	% of Cases where Organism Isolated
Corynebacterium pyogenes	80
Peptococcus indolicus	65
Streptococcus dysgalactiae	54
Micro-aerophilic coccus	45
C. pyogenes as sole organism	5
Mixed cultures	89

(Stuart, Buntain and Landridge, 1951)

Occurrence

The condition is relatively common and can affect up to 43 per cent of herds in any one year although incidence annually varies considerably. The percentage incidence of cattle affected in a herd varies from 2 to 10 per cent. Most cases (about 70 per cent) are seen in August with lesser numbers in July and September. Cases often occur more commonly in hot, humid weather (Marshall, 1981). More cattle are affected at pasture than indoors. The condition tends to be sporadic but some farms seem to be particularly vulnerable. High-risk areas include the south-western counties, North Wales, Northumberland and Southern Scotland (Yeoman and Warren, 1984).

Bacteriological isolates are variable (see Table 4.2). Most cases tend to reveal mixed infections with C. pyogenes, Peptococcus indolicus, Strep. dysgalactiae and an unnamed micro-aerophilic coccus. The consequence of this is that C. pyogenes cannot be completely accepted (Sorensen, 1978) as the cause of summer mastitis and furthermore, experimental infection with the organism produces variable results. Peptococcus indolicus tends to produce a foul smell.

Flies have long been incriminated in the transfer of infection. Various studies have indicated that most of the flies seen around the udder tend to be of the head fly species (Hydrotaea irritans). Many organisms have been isolated from the flies, including C. pyogenes, Pepto. indolicus and Strep. dysgalactiae. Other flies are less commonly found in the region of the teats.

Signs

Early Signs

It has been proposed that if numbers of flies are attracted to the teat orifice of a single teat then summer mastitis is present (Warren, 1976).

Peracute

In almost all cases disease is peracute (40.5-41°C, 105-106°F), with anorexia, severe depression and weakness. One or more quarters will be swollen and often the first sign noticed is that the animal is walking lame. The secretion produced tends to initially be watery and then a thick pus, usually with a putrid smell to it. The leg may be swollen. The heart rate tends to be raised.

Once the animal is in recovery the affected quarters become indurated, and contain abscesses which may discharge. In a few cases the gland will be sloughed.

Abortion

Animals may abort during the initial pyrexic stage. Intrauterine growth is often retarded.

Necropsy

The udder shows severe inflammatory change with pus present. Chronic cases reveal induration.

Diagnosis

1. History - heifers.
2. Severe systemic involvement, foul-smelling mammary discharge.
3. Bacteriology and antibiotic sensitivity.

Treatment

Therapy is concerned with saving the animal, the quarter is invariably lost. Systemic therapy can include intravenous use of penicillin, tetracyclines or sulphonamides followed by their continued use intramuscularly or subcutaneously. The quarter should be stripped regularly and intramammary infusions, usually of a broad antibacterial spectrum, are used.

Control

Problems tend to arise because the dry cattle and heifers are not inspected as frequently as they might be. In addition, they are often grazed in fields furthest from the buildings and close to woods, which are the habitat of H. irritans. Ideally heifers coming up to calving should be put through the parlour at least once a day. This has the purpose of familiarising the heifers with the parlour. In addition, if the teats are dipped, it means the udder is inspected. Any teat injuries should be quickly and thoroughly treated. In the months of July to September on farms where summer mastitis is a problem, heifers should not be placed on suspect fields.

Dry cow therapy can be used at three-week intervals in the dry period. The nozzle is placed against the teat orifice and the antibiotic is forced through the streak canal. It is not necessary to enter the canal to do this and so damage to the canal need not occur. Fly control can be undertaken with one of a number of sprays and it has been suggested that this must start before the insects build up. The organophosphorus compound, crotoxyphos, can be used, as well as synthetic pyrethroids such as cypermethrin and permethrin. Spraying usually needs to be repeated at intervals of two weeks. Plastic ear tags, impregnated with pyrethroids, have been used with variable results, but it does seem that in most cases one per ear is required to have any effect on summer mastitis.

References

MARSHALL, A B (1981) Mastitis Control and Herd Management. National Institute for Research in Dairying, Reading and Hannah Research Institute, Ayr. Technical Bulletin No. 4. pp. 81-94.

SORENSEN, G H (1978) Nordisk Veterinaermedicin, 30, 199-204.

STUART, P, BUNTAIN, D and LANDRIDGE, R G (1951) Veterinary Record, 63, 451-453.

WARREN, W A (1976) Farmers' Weekly, 84 (17), 44-45 (letter).

YEOMAN, G H and WARREN, B C (1984) British Veterinary Journal, 140, 232-243.

Tetanus

Aetiology

The signs result from toxins produced by the organism *Clostridium tetani*, a Gram-positive rod, forming terminal spores.

Occurrence

The condition is not common but can cause outbreaks, particularly on some farms. The spores are very resistant with some resisting steam at 100°C (212°F) for 30 to 60 minutes, but they are destroyed by heating to 115°C (239°F) for 20 minutes. The spores can be destroyed by chemical disinfectants such as phenols in 10 to 13 hours or 0.5 *per cent* hydrochloric acid in two hours. The organism is found in the soil and can also be present in the faeces of some animals, particularly the horse, so that there tends to be a higher level of spores in soils contaminated by this species. Cattle are relatively resistant to infection, and entry of infection to the body is considered to be via a wound. The spores may remain dormant for long periods, only producing disease when conditions are suitable. Although some infections appear to follow injury or surgical interference such as castration, dehorning, etc., in many cases no external lesions are seen. It is usually considered that in such cases entry of infection is oral and the organism enters the body via minute abrasions which occur following the feeding of rough or fibrous feeds. Occasionally small outbreaks of disease occur in cattle and this is often associated with a change in feeding.

The organism tends to remain at the site of entry and multiply. Its growth is dependent on the right environment, i.e. anaerobic conditions or a lowered oxygen tension. Signs occur rapidly if the infection is introduced at a time of trauma but otherwise the spores may be dormant for long periods. An exotoxin is produced which passes via the peripheral nerves to the central nervous system.

Incubation period

This is variable, usually 1 to 3 weeks. However, it can be delayed for many months.

Signs

The first signs are usually of an increase in stiffness of the animal with muscle tremor and an increase in reflex response. The temperature is normal or slightly raised, 38.5 - 39.5°C (101.5 - 103°F). The gait tends to be somewhat unsteady and there is usually a raising of the tail. In some cases the animal will attempt to eat and drink but it will have difficulty in swallowing and prehension. Prolapse of the third eyelid may occur but is absent in many cases. The animal does tend to have an anxious expression with staring eyes and a set jaw, dilated nostrils and erect ears.

As the disease progresses the back is held straight or slightly arched, the tail is elevated. Bloat often occurs at this stage. Later on the tetany increases considerably with the hind limbs stuck out in front and the forelimbs forward with the head and neck extended. If the animal falls, which can happen if it is startled, the limbs still tend to be held rigid. Death usually occurs in 3 to 10 days after signs develop.

Necropsy

There are no specific gross findings other than that a wound may be present which can indicate the site of infection. Histology is unproductive.

Diagnosis

1. The signs are relatively distinct.
2. Culture of organism from site of infection.
3. Serum can be obtained from suspect animals and injected into mice.

Differential diagnosis

1. Acute laminitis but there is no tetany.
2. Hypomagnesaemia usually produces marked hyperaesthesia and severe convulsions without bloat.
3. Muscular dystrophy but there is no tetany.
4. Meningitis but in such animals there is usually depression.

Treatment

Penicillin should be used in large doses - 10,000 units/kg BW (5,000 units/lb BW). The animal should receive tetanus antitoxin intravenously (100,000 units) followed by 50,000 iu subcutaneously. It is best to give the antitoxin prior to any local treatment. Any suspect wound should then be opened up, cleaned, debrided and irrigated with hydrogen peroxide. Penicillin and antitoxin can be injected locally. Sedation may be required, particularly in the early stages, with either acepromazine or xylazine. If the animal is unable to prehend then intravenous glucose saline can be used at the rate of five litres per day. As the animal improves this can be replaced by feeding via a stomach tube, although this can cause considerable upset to the animal in the early stages. Hexamine is said to be of use in helping to overcome the blood/brain barrier to the antitoxin and penicillin.

Control

If due to an elective procedure such as docking or castration, then care must be undertaken to ensure strict disinfection. However, on some farms where problems occur it is prudent to use routine tetanus antitoxin following all surgical interferences unless the cattle are vaccinated. Vaccination can provide cover only for tetanus, or it may be combined with protection against *Cl. chauvoei*, *Cl. novyi*, *Cl. haemolyticum* or *Cl. septicum*. The vaccine is an alum-precipitated formalin-treated toxin. Usually the primary vaccination programme involves two doses at least four weeks apart with immunity reaching its maximum about two weeks after the second injection. A booster injection is usually given after a year and then subsequently about every three years.

Tickborne Fever

Aetiology

A rickettsial agent known as Erlichia phagocytophila but also known as Cytoecetes phagocytophila, Rickettsia bovina and Rickettsia ovina. It is considered that there are two strains because it is difficult to infect sheep with the bovine strain, and vice versa.

Occurrence

The disease is transmitted by the tick - Ixodes ricinus - and so is only found in tick areas. It therefore tends to be seasonal in occurrence, being seen in the spring or autumn. Calves are less susceptible to infection than adults. Attempts to vaccinate cattle against the condition have been unsuccessful and knowledge of immunity is limited. Disease can occur in the same animal in succeeding years. It seems a partial resistance to further infection results from the presence of rickettsia in the blood causing a low-grade premunity. As the rickettsiae remain in the blood for a considerable time (from months to about two years) other cattle can become infected. Infection with E. phagocytophila before B. divergens tended to delay or reduce infection with B. divergens, but if B. divergens infection occurred first it had no effect on subsequent E. phagocytophila infection.

Incubation period

6 to 7 days.

Signs

Peracute

Sudden death can very occasionally be seen.

Acute

There is usually a marked pyrexia 40.5°C (105°F) or more and it lasts from about 2 to 8 days. The animals tend to be lethargic, with inappetance and tachypnoea. The temperature usually gradually declines but will often rise again with accompanying signs. Further bouts of pyrexia may occur, usually of short duration.

Abortion

Abortion sometimes occurs in animals during the last two months of pregnancy.

Necropsy

There are no gross lesions and histologically the only characteristic lesion is the draining of lymphocytes from lymphoid tissue.

Diagnosis

1. History - area - tick region, time of year - spring or autumn.
2. Presence of rickettsia in neutrophils and monocytes during pyrexia.
3. Serology - complement fixation test.
4. During the fever phase there is a leucopaenia, 5,000 cells/mm^3 or less with an associated neutropaenia.

5. At the start of illness there is a thrombocytopaenia.

Differential diagnosis

Any pyrexia with no other obvious signs.

Treatment

Antibacterial compounds are considered to be of help including oxytetracycline (2 - 5 mg/kg BW; 1 - 3 mg/lb) or 33.3 per cent sulphadimidine (15 - 30 ml/50 kg or 100 lb) intravenously.

Prevention

Reduce tick population by improving the pasture. Ploughing up pastures, burning bracken, or rotational grazing may assist. Bracken can be removed by spraying. The use of pyrethroid-impregnated ear tags has been tried to reduce tick-borne disease. Although numbers of ticks in tagged animals were fewer, they still developed tickborne fever (Taylor, Kenny, Mallon, Elliott, McMurray and Blanchflower, 1984).

Reference

TAYLOR, S M, KENNY, J, MALLON, T R, ELLIOTT, C T, McMURRAY, C and BLANCHFLOWER, J (1984) Veterinary Record 114, 454-455.

CHAPTER 5

UROGENITAL CONDITIONS

Brucellosis

The condition is also known as contagious abortion and Bang's disease.

Aetiology

Infection caused by *Brucella abortus* (Gram-negative rod).

Occurrence

The organism can persist on pasture for 100 days in winter and 30 days in summer. The bacteria are susceptible to heat, sunlight and standard dose disinfectants. The infection is currently the subject of a successful eradication campaign. It is also a reportable disease. In the 1970's it was the most diagnosed cause of abortion but is now rare. Infection can also occur in horses, resulting in fistulous withers or poll evil, occasionally sheep, goats, dogs and deer are infected. In man it results in undulant fever. In animals it has been suggested that erythritol produced by the foetus is capable of stimulating growth of *B. abortus* and this occurs in greatest quantities in the placental and foetal fluids. The organism has predilection sites for growth including the pregnant uterus, udder, testicles, accessory male sex glands, and less commonly the lymph nodes, joint capsules and bursae.

Congenital transmission of infection can occur but most is horizontal, directly via infected calves, foetuses or placentae or their fluids. Indirect transmission can be by flies, dogs, infected boots, clothing, etc. Bulls are unlikely to transmit the infection venereally. Once a cow has been infected it is likely to become a permanent carrier. When a herd becomes infected, typically there is a period when many cattle abort resulting in an abortion storm. Subsequently abortions are confined to heifers coming into the herd or a few other animals which abort for a second or third time. Occasionally in younger animals gonitis, i.e. arthritis of one or both stifle (femoro-tibial) joints, occurs. In many of these animals the reaction follows the use of Strain 19 vaccine.

Route of infection

Usually ingestion but can penetrate intact skin, the conjunctiva or contaminated udder.

Spread of infection

Introduction of an infected or carrier cow to the herd.

Source of infection

Contaminated uterine discharges, placental membranes, aborted foetuses or freshly-born infected calves.

Abortion rate

Up to 90 *per cent*.

Signs

Heifers

In most cases the signs are of abortion following the fifth month of pregnancy. Generally, subsequent pregnancies run to term although a few cattle will abort for a second or even a third time. Following abortion, retained placentae and metritis are common. Some cattle develop hygromas of the knee or capped hocks.

Bulls

In the bull there tends to be orchitis and epididymitis with one or both scrotal sacs swollen and painful. The seminal vesicles are enlarged on palpation.

Necropsy

Infected adults do not die but the foetus may show a pneumonia. The placenta may be oedematous with leathery plaques on the chorion and cotyledon necrosis. In the bull there may be liquefaction necrosis of the testicles.

Diagnosis

1. Stage of pregnancy, usually over seven months.
2. Culture of abomasal contents of the aborted foetus.
3. Culture of vaginal discharge, part of placenta, or milk.
4. Vaginal mucus can be used for an agglutination test.
5. Milk may be tested.
6. Blood testing using Rose Bengal Plate Test (RBPT), serum agglutination test (SAT), complement fixation test (CFT). During the eradication scheme problems arose in interpretation because of previous vaccination with Strain 19 or McEwan's 45/20 vaccine.

Differential diagnosis

1. Listeriosis.
2. *Leptospira hardjo* infection.
3. Salmonellosis.
4. Mucosal disease.
5. IBR.
6. *Campylobacter* spp. infection.

Treatment

This is not undertaken in Britain and in any case is usually unsuccessful.

Control

Britain has undertaken an eradication scheme to remove brucellosis from cattle. All abortions, i.e. calvings under 271 days gestation, must be reported to the Ministry. An abortion investigation is carried out on such animals. In dairy herds the bulk milk is routinely monitored by the milk ring test. All dairy cattle over 12 months old are blood tested except steers and those regularly being bulk milk tested. In beef herds all cattle except steers over 12 months old are tested. Blood tests are subjected to the RBPT and if a reaction is seen, SAT and CFT tests are undertaken. Reactors are removed from the herd and retesting undertaken at 30-day intervals until clear.

In the past, vaccination was used. Strain 19 was a live vaccine which prevented abortion storms but injected animals could give reactions to the serological tests, especially RBPT and SAT, although the CFT was less affected. The 45/20 vaccine was the McEwan strain of B. abortus and was a dead vaccine which tended to be used in infected herds with an abortion problem. Serological reaction depended on whether Strain 19 had previously been used in the herd and anamnestic reactions occurred if the cattle were infected. Usually the 45/20 strain produced no response to CFT but SAT and RBPT could reach the inconclusive level.

Corynebacterium Pyogenes Abortion

Aetiology

Infection with *Corynebacterium pyogenes*.

Occurrence

The condition is a very common cause of abortion. It is sporadic in occurrence and occurs at any stage of gestation.

Signs

There is abortion which occurs at any stage. There are usually no other signs.

Necropsy

Usually no signs are present.

Diagnosis

Bacteriology.

Treatment and Control

None.

Epizootic Abortion

Aetiology

The infection is with a chlamydia, an obligate, intracellular pathogen.

Occurrence

The condition is very rare in Britain. The organism is antigenically and morphologically similar to that causing enzootic abortion in ewes. Infection is usually sporadic and occasionally 20 per cent are affected. Infection enters by the mouth, parasitises the intestines and macrophages become infected. This results in a chlamydiaemia. Infection can be isolated from ticks as well as the semen of bulls. The chlamydia pass across the placenta and enter the foetus.

Route of entry

Oral or venereal.

Abortion rate

Up to 20 per cent.

Signs

Heifers

Usually there are few signs except occasional mastitis. Abortion is usually after six months' gestation or calves are stillborn or born weak. Early embryonic death occurs if infection is sexually transmitted.

Bulls

Infection may be seen as orchitis, epididymitis and accessory gland infections.

Necropsy

Under six months' gestation the placenta may show necrotic cotyledons and the entire intercotyledonary placentae are brownish-yellow, oedematous and gelatinous. Over six months' gestation the placenta is often leathery and red-white in colour, and the margins of the cotyledons show small necrotic foci. The under six-month foetus shows subcutaneous oedema which is blood-tinged, and increased reddish pleural or peritoneal fluid. Over six-month foetuses often show petechial haemorrhages of the thymus, mucous membranes and subcutaneous tissue. There is often distension of the abdomen with ascites, focal necrosis and localised inflammation of the liver, spleen, kidney, central nervous system, adrenals, lungs and intestines. Histologically there is usually vasculitis.

Diagnosis

1. Isolation of organism.
2. Culture of organism (use diethylamino ethyl dextran and cycloheximide).
3. Complement fixation test.

Treatment

The use of oxytetracycline prior to signs may be helpful, but is probably equivocal.

Control

At present the condition is too unusual for serious studies of how to control the infection to be undertaken.

Fungal Abortion

Aetiology

Infection with fungi (usually *Aspergillus* spp., *Absidia* spp. or *Mucor* spp.).

Occurrence

Fungi are a common cause of abortion but cases tend to be sporadic. The fungi concerned are saprophytes which live on organic material. Most cases are the result of feeding poor quality hay. Abortion in the winter is often associated with the amount of rain during June. Most abortions occur in the winter months in housed cows. It is rare for the disease tobe present in cattle at pasture all the year round. It is usually considered that the condition occurs because the environment has become heavily contaminated with spores from mouldy hay or silage.

Route of entry

Inhalation or possibly via lesions in the alimentary tract.

Abortion rate

Usually low, about six *per cent*.

Signs

Most cattle do not show any signs of illness but abortion occurs between three and seven months gestation.

Necropsy

The placenta shows necrosis of the maternal cotyledon with a yellow soft area. There may be small, yellow, raised, leathery lesions on inter-cotyledonary areas. The foetus may show small, raised, soft lesions on the skin. Other foetuses show diffuse white areas over the skin.

Diagnosis

1. History or poor hay being fed.
2. Signs in the cow are negative.
3. Examination of the cotyledons and foetal stomach for the presence of fungi.
4. Culture.

Differential diagnosis

1. Other causes of abortion.
2. Brucellosis.
3. Leptospirosis.
4. Mucosal disease.
5. IBR.
6. *Campylobacter* spp. infection.

Treatment

It is not possible to treat.

Control

Improve hay-making methods. If hay is mouldy, ensure it is shaken out before being fed. Straw to be used for bedding should also be shaken out.

Granular Vulvovaginitis

Aetiology

It is probable that the condition is caused by ureaplasmas (T. mycoplasmas), having the proposed name *Ureaplasma diversum*.

Occurrence

The condition has caused problems in some herds in Scotland. At one time the disease was thought to be due to *Mycoplasma bovigenitalium* but ureaplasmas can be isolated from all cases of acute vulvitis although they can occur in normal animals (23 *per cent*). Most lesions last 30 days or more.

Incubation period

3 - 5 days.

Spread of infection

Venereal, direct by bull or indirect by contaminated catheters.

Signs

There is no pyrexia but lesions develop in the vulva and there is a posterior vaginitis with a mucopurulent discharge for 4 to 10 days after healing. The vulva looks hyperaemic with small hard nodules present in the vulva and posterior vagina. The animals may become repeat breeders with, in some cases, extended inter-service intervals.

Diagnosis

Signs.

Differential diagnosis

1. Infectious bovine vulvovaginitis.
2. *Mycoplasma bovis* vulvovaginitis.

Treatment

In an infected herd use artificial insemination. Infuse 1 g of oxytetracycline into the uterus the day after service. Infected bulls should be treated with antibiotics for five days and receive an extended period of sexual rest lasting three months.

Control

Insemination pipettes should be covered with a polythene sanitary sleeve. Bulls should have semen taken from them and minocycline hydrochloride added at the rate of 500 μg/ml. Semen can then be inseminated.

Leptospira Hardjo Infection

Also known as 'flabby bag'.

Aetiology

Infection with *Leptospira interrogans* serotype *hardjo* (spiral organism).

Occurrence

A common cause of abortion in Britain, although it is one which has only recently been readily diagnosed. In Northern Ireland 41.6 *per cent* of randomly-selected aborted foetuses were infected (Ellis, O'Brien, Neill, Ferguson and Hannan, 1982) and the level rose to 68.9 *per cent* of foetuses from farms with abortion problems. A very common problem in New Zealand, most cases are in the dairy herd rather than beef cattle. Humans can be infected but they must be exposed to concentrated infection, i.e. contact via urine while milking. Although infection is present in the milk, it quickly dies off once taken from the udder. Meat does not carry infection. Spread occurs more rapidly in wet seasons in low-lying areas. Colostrum-derived infection normally lasts about three months. Serological rises in *L. hardjo* titres following infection tend to be short-lived (i.e. a few months to a year or so).

Spread of infection

Cow to cow via urine, foetuses and uterine discharge. Bull to cow by infected semen.

Source of infection

Carrier cows or infected calves which may be chronically infected, but it may possibly be spread by contaminated water.

Abortion rate

Up to 25 *per cent*.

Signs

There are two main syndromes.

Udder form - severe

In a heifer the udder signs will not be apparent until the animal has calved. This form occurs soon after the infection enters a herd. There is a sudden drop in milk yield affecting all four quarters, with pyrexia usually between 40 - 41.5°C (104 - 107°F). The udder secretion becomes thickened and clotted, occasionally it is bloody or it can be yellow or colostrum-like. The udder itself is not swollen or inflamed but tends to be flaccid. In a 6 to 8-week period 30 to 50 *per cent* of the herd may be infected. The condition usually resolves over 7 to 10 days.

Udder form - mild

Many cows are infected and show only a slight drop in milk yield.

Abortion

This usually occurs 6 to 12 weeks after the dam is infected. Abortion can occur on its own or be preceded by the milk drop syndrome. Most cases of abortion occur in the second half of pregnancy. If infection occurs late in pregnancy then an infected calf may be born.

Necropsy

Abortion

There are usually no useful macroscopic features in the aborted foetus.

Diagnosis

Udder form

1. History, sudden onset of problem.
2. Signs, sudden loss of milk, flaccid udder.
3. Californian Milk Test positive and high white cell count.
4. Identification and culture of the organism from urine (it can occasionally be isolated from milk and blood in the acute stages).
5. Paired serum samples, complement fixation test, microscopic agglutination test, plate agglutination test.

Abortion

1. Identification of the bacterium in the foetus - fluorescent antibody studies.
2. Culture of the bacteria.
3. Foetal serology.
4. Serology of the dam.

Differential diagnosis

Udder form

1. Other leptospiral infections.
2. Salmonellosis.
3. Foot-and-mouth disease.
4. Mastitis.

Abortion

1. Salmonellosis.
2. Mucosal disease.
3. Brucellosis.
4. IBR.

Treatment

Large doses of streptomycin may help remove the organism and prevent kidney and liver damage.

Control

Vaccination is possible with a killed strain. It involves two initial doses at least four weeks apart. If cattle are young when vaccination commences then two doses are required after five months of age. An annual booster is recommended.

Reference

ELLIS, W A, O'BRIEN, J J, NEILL, S D, FERGUSON, M W and HANNA, J (1982) Veterinary Record, 110, 147-150.

Q Fever

Aetiology

Infection with the rickettsia *Coxiella burneti*.

Occurrence

The condition is uncommon. Most infections in cattle are without signs. However, humans can be infected.

Signs

Some cattle develop anorexia. Occasionally abortion occurs.

Diagnosis

Isolation of the organism from the aborted foetus.

Treatment

Usually not applicable, but oxytetracycline injections for five days may be useful.

Control

As the condition is unusual, control is impractical.

Sarcocystosis

Aetiology

Infection in cattle of other countries is with the intermediate stage of the coccidia *Sarcocystis cruzi* (*S. bovicanis*), *S. hirsuta* (*S. bovifelis*) and *S. hominis* (*S. bovihominis*).

Occurrence

Infection by *Sarcocystis* spp. until recently has been considered to be unimportant. The definite hosts are dog and fox for *S. cruzi*, cat for *S. hirsuta* and man and monkeys for *S. hominis*. Humans who eat uncooked infected meat can develop stomach pains and diarrhoea. Cattle are infected by ingesting an oocyst or sporocyst. These liberate sporozoites which penetrate the intestinal wall to enter arterial endothelial linings. After a period of dormancy, schizonts or meronts are produced which, when mature, contain merozoites. These merozoites enter the blood and produce second generation schizonts in the endothelium of capillaries. They are mature about 4 to 5 weeks after infection.

The mature schizonts enter the bloodstream and multiply by dividing into two progeny from which other generations are produced. Merozoites from second generation schizonts or zoites developing in the blood penetrate muscles and nerve cells. The parasite develops in a parasitopherous vacuole and encystment occurs 5 to 7 weeks after infection. The cyst contains mother cells (metrocytes) which divide into two globular metrocytes, which in turn divide to produce banana-shaped zoites. The mature cysts contain bradyzoites and these are found about 11 weeks after infection. Only bradyzoites are infective to the final host (Dubey and Fayer, 1984). When abortion occurs it is not certain whether it is due to pyrexia in the dam or a result of hormonal imbalance. It would appear that *Sarcocystis* infections are well tolerated by the intermediate host. A low-grade infection does not protect against a more massive infestation.

Signs

General

Experimentally there is fever, anorexia, anaemia, diarrhoea, excessive salivation, muscle weakness, muscle twitching, loss of hair and mild nervousness. The lymph nodes may be enlarged.

Abortion

This mainly occurs in animals which become ill.

Necropsy

There is a reduction in perirenal and pericardial fat. Organs tend to be pale or haemorrhagic. Haemorrhages can occur on the surface, particularly of the heart and serosal surface of the reticulum although they occur on other viscera, thymus and skeletal muscles as well as the sclera. The liver is pale and the lymph nodes may be oedematous, enlarged and with petechiae. The schizonts are often not present by the time the animal is ill. Foetal encephalitis is thought to occur (McCausland, Badman, Hides and Slee, 1984).

Diagnosis

Definite diagnosis is difficult but the following are helpful.

1. Clinical signs (anorexia, anaemia, pyrexia, swollen lymph nodes, salivation).
2. Biochemical testing - there are raised levels of lactic dehydrogenase (LDH), sorbitol dehydrogenase (SBDH), creatine phosphokinase (CPK) and blood urea nitrogen (BUN).
3. Serology (including indirect haemagglutination and enzyme-linked immunosorbent assay tests).
4. Necropsy (the presence of haemorrhages in muscles and elsewhere without inflammation).
5. Presence of schizonts (they are in or near blood vessels and in direct contact with the host cell cytoplasm).

Treatment

None is at present practical, although anticoccidials (amprolium, monensin, salinomycin) may reduce infection levels.

Control

Control is to reduce the shedding of *Sarcocystis* spp. in the faeces of the definite host, e.g. dogs, cats, foxes. Do not let carnivores eat dead carcases, cook all the meat and offal thoroughly. Prophylactic use of anticoccidials in cattle may be helpful and these include amprolium, halofuginase, monensin and salinomycin.

References

DUBEY, J P and FAYER, R (1983) British Veterinary Journal, 139, 371-377.

McCAUSLAND, I P, BADMAN, R T, HIDES, S and SLEE, K J (1984) The Cornell Veterinarian, 74, 146-154.

Trichomoniasis

Aetiology

Infection with the flagellated protozoan *Trichomonas foetus*.

Occurrence

This condition probably does not now occur in Britain. It used to be spread by coitus.

Source of infection

Introduction of an infected bull or cow.

Abortion rate

10 - 30 *per cent*.

Signs

Heifers

They are variable but cattle can conceive and carry a calf to term without any clinical signs. However, at the next conception there may be repeated returns to service without other obvious signs of infection. Other cattle at initial infection return regularly or irregularly to service. Some animals fail to conceive and develop a mucopurulent discharge with oedema of the endometrium. Cattle can conceive and abort at two to four months of gestation while others develop anoestrus and pyometra.

Bulls

Many bulls show no signs. Some will show a swelling of the penis with a discharge and presence of small red nodules on the penile mucosa.

Diagnosis

1. History of introducing cows.
2. Signs of infertility and early abortion.
3. Presence of protozoa in the vaginal mucus. The organism is usually surrounded by a large number of leucocytes. Cervical mucus agglutination test.
4. Serology (serum agglutination test, complement fixation test).
5. It is very difficult to detect infection in herds and usually serological tests are negative. It is prudent to ensure bulls are infected if the cows show infection.

Treatment

In the female there is usually spontaneous recovery. Bulls should be treated with sodium iodide at a level of 5 g/50 kg BW (1 oz/600 lb BW) in 500 cc of distilled water. It is given by intravenous injection at two-day intervals on five occasions. The herd should be divided into those known or possibly infected and those not infected (just-calved cows, maiden heifers). The non-infected heifers can be covered by a clean bull. Infected cows should be inseminated artificially. Recently treatment with dimetridazole orally or intravenously or ipronidazole hydrochloride intravenously have been advocated.

Control

Artificial insemination will prevent the problem occurring.

Vibriosis

Aetiology

Infection with Campylobacter (previously Vibreo) fetus, variety veneralis (Gram-negative curved bacillus).

Occurrence

Infection was at a high level in the 1950's but became very low by the 1960's. Recently, however, disease has started to increase. Spread of infection has been by travelling and shared bulls. Bulls up to three years old are less susceptible to infection, harder to diagnose and easier to treat. Following infection, cattle become immune.

Route of infection

Venereal.

Spread of infection

It can be direct or indirect between bulls via the hindquarters of teaser animals.

Abortion rate

Usually low, five *per cent* up to 20 *per cent*.

Signs

Heifer

There is infertility, irregular, moderately prolonged dioestrus, early embryonic death. Abortion occurs in about five to 20 *per cent* of animals at about five to six months of gestation.

Male

There is no effect on sperm quality or inflammation of the genital tract. Young bulls may recover spontaneously.

Necropsy

The placenta is semi-opaque with little thickening. There are petechial haemorrhages, localised areas of avascularity and oedema. The foetus may show flakes of pus on the visceral peritoneum.

Diagnosis

1. Culture of sheath washing and fluorescent antibody test.
2. Vaginal mucus agglutination test.
3. Culture of foetus and uterine discharges.
4. Blood agglutination test.
5. Test mating of a bull with maiden heifers induced to oestrus by prostaglandins to check infection.

Differential diagnosis

1. Brucellosis.
2. Leptospira hardjo infection.
3. Infectious bovine rhinotracheitis.
4. Mycotic abortion.

Treatment

The extruded penis of infected bulls can be treated with streptomycin and chlortetracycline. The prepucial cavity can be douched by use of cream in an artificial vagina. Otherwise the penis and prepuce can be irrigated for three days with streptomycin and penicillin. Following treatment, bulls should be test-mated with unexposed heifers.

Control

The use of artificial insemination for two pregnancies will overcome the problem. Various means can be used. Firstly, bulls can be disposed of and artificial insemination used. Otherwise the infected bull should be used in the infected part of the herd and a clean bull in a clean part of the herd. A third option is to treat all infected bulls with antibiotics and then use artificial insemination from the bulls.

Amyloidosis

Aetiology

This is uncertain but is the result of a hyperglobulinaemia probably resulting in an abnormal antigen-antibody response.

Occurrence

It is a rare condition which is not fully understood. Most cases occur sporadically and spontaneously following prolonged suppurative infections. The origin of amyloid, which is a glycoprotein, is not certain, but is thought to be due to an abnormality of the antigen-antibody reaction. Although renal amyloidosis is the most commonly-recognised condition, amyloid can also be deposited in the liver and spleen. When the main organ affected is the liver, there tends to be proteinuria. This leads to hypoproteinaemia and then oedema of organs, resulting in marked anasarca. The diarrhoea produced is partly due to amyloid deposition and oedema of the intestinal wall. Many of the animals affected are in the growing phase.

Signs

Usually the animal is thin and emaciated. In most cases there is marked anasarca with an enlarged liver palpated in the right sublumbar fossa and an enlarged kidney with loss of its lobular structure palpated per rectum. There is usually polydipsia and a profuse, watery diarrhoea. The animals later become uraemic, recumbent and comatosed. Death occurs two to five weeks after the onset of signs.

Necropsy

There are usually one or more chronic suppurative processes present in the organs. The carcase is emaciated with usually marked oedema. The affected organs are enlarged and pale in colour. The kidney and liver have diffuse amyloid infiltration while in the spleen it is more localised. The amyloid can be shown by aqueous iodine staining.

Diagnosis

1. Signs.

Treatment

No therapy has proved of value and so the cattle should be slaughtered.

Contagious Bovine Pyelonephritis

Aetiology

The cause is Corynebacterium renale (Gram-positive) which probably has four serotypes, of which Type 1 is the most pathogenic.

Occurrence

It is the most common cause of identifiable nephritis in cattle but it is still an unusual condition. Cases tend to be seen sporadically. C. renale is susceptible to physical and chemical agents. The organism can be cultured from the urine of infected cows or carriers and in some cases other organisms may be present such as Staphylococcus aureus, Corynebacterium pyogenes and Escherichia coli.

Route of entry

Via the vulva with ascending infection to bladder and kidney.

Spread of infection

Usually carrier or infected animals or contaminated catheters, or service by infected or contaminated bulls.

Signs

Subacute

Often infected animals are hard to identify in a large herd. There is firstly the passage of blood-stained urine with the blood being present on the hairs of the tail. The animal is otherwise normal but will develop occasional attacks of acute colic due to obstruction of the ureter or renal calyx with pus and tissue debris. Rectal palpation is often negative early on.

Chronic

There is a gradual, progressive loss of condition with a variable appetite and a fluctuating temperature of about 39.5°C (103°F). Urination tends to be more frequent than normal and contains, particularly in the last part, blood, pus and tissue debris. In some cases the urine will have periods of normality. The bladder and one or both ureters tend to be thickened on rectal palpation. The bladder may appear smaller than normal with the kidney painful and enlarged. If the condition is allowed to continue there is weakness, depression, recumbency with an increased heart and respiratory rate with anuria. Death occurs following coma and is due to uraemia.

Necropsy

There is often an emaciated carcase with the kidneys enlarged and with less prominent lobulation. The surface of the kidney may show pale necrotic areas with the ureters and renal pelvis containing pus, blood and debris. The walls of the bladder and urethra are thickened with oedema and haemorrhages.

Diagnosis

1. Signs - changes in the urine, palpably enlarged kidney.
2. Bacteriology - culture urine.
3. Antibiotic sensitivity.

Differential diagnosis

1. Traumatic reticulitis but urine changes are present and abdominal pain sporadic.
2. Enzootic haematuria but usually older suckler cows in a bracken area.
3. Kale poisoning but haemoglobinuria.

Treatment

Most serotypes are susceptible to penicillin and large doses of procaine penicillin should be used (15,000 iu/kg; 7,500 iu/lb for 10 days). Acidifying the urine with 100 g of monobasic sodium phosphate for several days can be helpful. While the infected animal is being treated it should be isolated and any bedding or litter destroyed.

Prevention

Although treatment is usually successful, it is best not to keep the animal as it may be a source of infection for the herd and so it should be slaughtered when convenient. If the cow is kept, it should not be served naturally but by artificial insemination.

Urolithiasis

Aetiology

Urinary calculi are either organic or inorganic. The organic ones are less common and form casts or urinary deposits. The inorganic ones tend to be crystalline and are more common.

Occurrence

The condition normally is seen in cattle which are housed and with milk substitute as their only source of feed, or in weaned animals fed high levels of concentrates. There are a few areas in Britain, i.e. Southern Scotland, where urolithiasis occurs in animals at pasture. Most calculi can contain calcium or magnesium ammonium phosphate, although struvite and oxalate deposits occur at times. The condition is mainly seen in the male because signs are not normally observed unless some form of urethral blockage occurs. More cases are found in those castrated than those entire. Calculi can lodge anywhere in the urethra but occur most commonly at the sigmoid flexure of the penis with the region of the ischial arch being the second most common site.

Signs

Most signs are associated with partial or complete blockage of the urethra. This is seen as frequent attempts to urinate which may be accompanied by the passage of small amounts of urine, often blood-tinged or the attempts are unproductive. Calculi may be present on the prepucial orifice hairs. There is usually evidence of mild to severe colic with kicking at the belly, paddling movements and tail swishing. In most untreated cases with complete urethral obstruction, there will be perforation of the urethra or bladder rupture. When either takes place there is usually a period of relief from abdominal pain. When bladder rupture has occurred then the urine enters the abdomen which becomes distended and there is a fluid thrill present on percussion. In those with urethral perforation, urine tends to dribble under the skin, causing ventral abdominal distension, which will start to progress anteriorly. In most cases there is some toxaemia and possible uraemia and this is seen as inappetance, with increasing dullness of the animal, which will ultimately become comatosed and die.

Necropsy

There is usually some degree of cystitis, often with urinary deposits present in the bladder. When the bladder ruptures there is much fluid in the abdomen and in those cases of urethral perforation there will be erosion in the area of the calculus and urine, possibly with cellulitis, present subcutaneously. The position of the calculus can be ascertained by the passage of a catheter.

Diagnosis

1. The history helps, particularly the area of the country and the type of diet fed.
2. The signs.
3. It normally occurs in the male.
4. The passage of a urethral catheter meets an obstruction.

5. If there is bladder rupture or urethral erosion then the presence of any fluid swelling can be investigated with a hypodermic needle.

6. The urine crystals can be analysed.

Differential diagnosis

1. Ascites.

2. Intussusception.

3. Constipation.

Treatment

If an animal is nearing slaughter then casualty slaughter may be the best policy. It may be possible to perform a urethrotomy and remove the calculi. Provided the stones are distal to the ischial arch then the provision of a urethrotomy in the perineal region may overcome the problem and if it proves impossible to remove the calculi the opening can be made permanent. Medical treatment can include hyoscine butylbromide injected intravenously or intramuscularly at a dose of 20 - 40 mg per animal, or 5 - 10 ml of protein-free pancreatic extract. Withdrawal of concentrates may assist the condition and the provision of salt water following relief of the blockage is useful.

Control

Precipitation of phosphate can be avoided by having a correct ratio of calcium to phosphorus which should be at least 1.2:1, but levels up to 2.5:1 have been suggested. The concentration of magnesium in the diet should be 1.4 mg/kg dry matter and this means that the most magnesium oxide which should be added to the diet is 200 g/tonne (½ lb/tonne) of feed. Three per cent salt in the concentrates has been recommended and it is thought to have an ionic effect rather than just causing diuresis. Such diets should only be used where there is always free access to water.

White Heifer Disease

The condition used to be common in the white Shorthorn with up to 10 *per cent* of them being affected. It is now rare, but can be found in other breeds. There are varying degrees of involvement. In all cases there is partial or complete persistence of the hymen. This may be the only abnormality, but in other animals there are abnormalities cranial to the hymen. These defects may include the absence of the cranial vaginal cervix, uterine body or horns. The ovaries are functional and in most cases there is a distension of the normal organs due to the accumulation of the products of secretion.

Prolonged Gestation

This has been recorded in most dairy breeds and in some cases it has an inherited origin. There are two main forms of the condition.

(a) Prolonged gestation with foetal giantism. In these animals the foetus continues to grow *in utero* before parturition 21 to 100 days late. The cow usually calves with no udder development, or ligament relaxation, and usually first stage labour is minimal, necessitating a Caesarean section. The calves tend to be heavy, have well-erupted teeth and a good coat growth. The adrenals of the calves are hypoplastic and following delivery most are weak and die in hypoglycaemic crisis. The condition is the result of an autosomal recessive gene.

(b) Prolonged gestation with adrenohypophyseal hypoplasia. This is due to a recessive gene and it is mainly recorded in the Channel Island breeds. The gestation length is increased by weeks or months and parturition occurs about 7 to 14 days after the calf's death. There is again no udder development and few signs of parturition. The calf in this case is small and ceases to grow after the seventh month of gestation and so it can often be delivered by manual traction. It often shows a disproportionate dwarfism, cranio-facial defects which may cause hydrocephalus, alopecia, abdominal distension. There is no or only partial development of the adenohypophysis.

It should be remembered that the gestation of some of the larger beef breeds such as the Charolais, Simmental and Limousin is longer than for the Friesian or most native beef breeds.

Hermaphrodite

Both true and pseudohermaphrodites occur. In the true form there are gonads of both sexes, although they may be combined into an ovo-testis. In the pseudohermaphrodite the gonads are of one sex but some of the reproductive organs have characteristics of the opposite sex.

Chromosomal Translocations

There are always 60 chromosomes present in a normal bovine. Translocation is the fusion of two morphologically distinct chromosomes. The most common is 1/29 translocation where there is fusion between number 1 and 29 pairs; it is also referred to as the Robertsonian translocation. It has been recorded in the Swedish Red and White breed, Charolais, Red Poll and British White. The condition appears to be of importance in that there is reduced fertility in such animals due to early embryonic death.

Testicular Feminisation

It is characterised by a male (XY) genotype but an external female phonotype with abdominally placed testicles. The defect is a failure of the target organs to respond to the secretion of testosterone. In complete testicular feminisation there are abdominal testicles without Wolffian or Mullerian duct systems. Few cases have been reported other than an Ayrshire heifer (Long and David, 1981).

Signs

Usually there are no signs of oestrus but those of virilism. Rectal palpation reveals large gonads in the position of the ovary. The vulva tends to be small and the cervix non-existent on examination with a speculum.

Reference

LONG, S E and DAVID, J S E (1981) Veterinary Record, 109, 116-118.

XY Gonadal Dysgenesis

The external phenotype is female but there are no gonads.

CHAPTER 6

DEFICIENCY DISEASES

Calcium Deficiency

Aetiology

Primary deficiency is due to a lack of calcium in the diet and is very rare. Secondary problems are usually the result of high intakes of phosphorus and marginal levels of calcium.

Occurrence

The conditions are very uncommon today. Cases of deficiency do not occur at pasture but they can be recorded in intensively-fed cattle on high cereal diets. Pregnant cattle show a negative calcium balance towards the end of gestation. Calcium has several uses in the body in that besides being used in the blood-clotting mechanism, it maintains normal neuromuscular junction excitability and it is used in the production of bone and milk. Signs are more common in the growing animal than the adult.

Degenerative arthropathy

This is mainly found in young, growing beef bulls following rearing on a nurse cow, housing for long periods and feeding of a diet of cereals and other by-products high in phosphorus and low in calcium. There may be a slight inheritance to the condition. Signs can develop after six months of age although more commonly they are seen between one and two years old, and occasionally up to four years.

Signs

General

There is often a reduction in growth rate with dental abnormalities such as poor tooth development, excessive attrition and delayed eruption.

Degenerative arthropathy

One or both hind legs show lameness of gradual onset. In severely affected animals the limb may become useless. The hips are most affected and there is crepitus but other joints may also be involved such as the stifles. Muscular atrophy occurs but the joints are not swollen.

Necropsy

General

Osteoporosis and parathyroid hyperplasia are seen.

Degenerative arthropathy

There is articular cartilage erosion of the femoral head, often going as deep as the cancellous bone. The joint capsule is thickened and may contain calcified plaques and the synovial fluid is turbid and brown in colour. The periarticular surfaces may show bony exostoses. In stifle involvement the cartilaginous menisci are reduced in size.

Diagnosis

1. History, diet.
2. Signs - tooth abnormalities or progressive lameness.
3. Dietary analysis.
4. Bone ash is low (normal 60 *per cent*).

Differential diagnosis

1. Fluorosis.

Treatment

Ensure adequate calcium, phosphorus and vitamin D intake, and that there is a correct calcium:phosphorus ratio. This may mean a reduction in phosphorus level if it is excessive and increased calcium levels. The daily intake of calcium for growing animals should be from 9 - 30 g ($^1/_3$ - 1 oz) from 100 - 500 kg BW (220 - 1100 lb BW) and for phosphorus it is 7 - 23 g ($^1/_3$ - $^2/_3$ oz). A cheap source of calcium for diets is ground limestone.

Control

It should be ensured that adequate minerals and vitamin D are present in the diet. Bone meal and dicalcium phosphate are ideal sources of both calcium and phosphorus, but they are expensive. Ground limestone is a useful, cheap method of ensuring adequate calcium in the diet, but its overuse can result in other mineral deficiencies.

Cerebrocortical Necrosis

(CCN, polioencephalomalacia)

Aetiology

It is a deficiency of thiamine caused by endogenous thiaminase. Thiaminase has been found to be produced by *Clostridium sporongenes* and certain *Bacillus* spp. which can be found in cases of CCN. However this does not mean they are the only causal factors.

Occurrence

It is a sporadic condition which can occasionally occur as outbreaks. Most animals affected are fast-growing, well-nourished animals between six and 18 months old. It can occur following deprivation of food or water or sometimes about a week after a move from poor pasture to good grazing.

Similar syndromes can be produced experimentally by feeding large amounts of bracken or horsetail which contain high levels of thiaminase. Amprolium is also a specific thiamine antagonist and has also been used experimentally. Molasses toxicity results in a similar problem due to a fall in the proprionate levels. Thiamine is naturally synthesised in the rumen. It forms an essential component of several enzymes used in glucolysis in the brain. Deficiency in thiamine results in increased blood pyruvate levels and a decrease in the lactate:pyruvate ratio as well as a depression of the erythrocyte transketolase level. This causes an interference with normal carbohydrate metabolism and the cerebral cortex in particular requires the oxidative metabolism of glucose.

It is possible that thiamine deficiency might have a direct metabolic effect on the neurones, particularly in the calf which is very dependent on the pentose pathway of metabolism in which the transketolase enzyme limits the rate of activity. Thiamine pyrophosphate is a coenzyme for several carbohydrate metabolic reactions and it is associated with transketolase in the pentose pathway of glucose oxidation. There tends to be marked cerebral oedema and cerebral necrosis and the signs are mainly the result of an increase in intracranial pressure.

Morbidity

Usually low but occasionally up to 25 *per cent*.

Mortality

If not treated early it can be 25 to 50 *per cent*, with higher levels in young cattle (6 to 9 months) than older ones.

Signs

Acute

There is a sudden onset of nervous signs including blindness, muscle tremors particularly of the head and neck, head pressing, jaw champing and frothy salivation. Animals tend to be hard to handle and in the early stages signs may be intermittent. Although the animal appears blind, and the menace reflex is absent, the palpebral and pupillary reflexes are present. The convulsive signs soon become continuous with the animal becoming recumbent. The signs are then of opisthotonus, nystagmus, optic disc oedema, often strabismus and clonic tonic convulsions which become worse when the animal is stimulated. The temperature is normal, the ruminal movements are normal but the heart rate is variable. Calves often die in 1 to 2 days although older animals show signs for a longer period. Recovery following therapy may well take 2 to 4 days or longer.

Subacute

The signs last for a few hours to several days and include blindness, head pressing and standing. The condition will resolve in some cases.

Slight

In an outbreak of CCN some of the animals show anorexia, partial impairment of eyesight and a mild depression. Almost all of the animals recover within 24 hours of therapy.

Prognosis

Although recovery may occur, some animals may still remain blind. The longer the time between onset of signs and therapy, the less favourable the prognosis. When cattle remain dull and anorexic after three days' treatment they are unlikely to recover and should be slaughtered.

Necropsy

Most of the animals do not show any gross changes in the body other than the brain. There is usually increased intracranial pressure with a yellowing and compression of the dorsal cortical gyri. The cerebellum tends to be compressed into the foramen magnum and recovered animals show decortication of the motor area and occipital lobes. Histologically there is bilateral necrosis of the dorsal occipital and parietal cerebral cortex and also occasionally the thalamus, basal ganglia, lateral geniculate bodies and mesencephalic nuclei. Cerebellar lesions also occur.

Diagnosis

1. History - age of animals - change in feeding, good condition.
2. Signs - blindness, palpebral and pupillary reflexes normal; ruminal movements normal, normal temperature but otherwise many nervous signs.
3. Blood pyruvate and lactate levels are increased.
4. Urine pyruvate levels increased.
5. Erythrocyte transketolase activity reduced.
6. Pyruvate kinase levels are much increased.
7. Thiamine levels in erythrocytes, blood and plasma may be in the normal range.
8. Blood creatine phosphokinase (CPK) levels may occur.
9. Thiaminase levels increased in rumen liquor and in faeces.
10. Haematology virtually normal although total and differential counts may show a mild stress reaction.
11. Increased cerebrospinal fluid pressure, 200 - 350 mm saline (normal 120 - 160 mm saline).

12. Histology - bilateral necrosis in cerebral cortex (bisect brain longitudinally, put one half in buffered formalin, the other is deep-frozen).

13. Green fluorescence of brain then exposed to long-wave ultraviolet light.

TABLE 6.1

Differences in Thiamine Levels within Certain Tissues of the Body in Animals with or without Cerebrocortical Necrosis

	CCN (±SEM)	Not CCN (±SEM)
Liver dry (μg/g)	2.5 ± 0.43	11.1 ± 2.11
Heart dry (μg/g)	2.5 ± 0.56	13.2 ± 2.12
Brain dry (μg/g)	1.8 ± 0.37	7.7 ± 1.52
Erythrocyte transketolase (% TPP effect)	172	15

(After Edwin, Markson, Shreeve, Jackman and Carroll, 1979)

Differential diagnosis

1. Ragwort poisoning but severe diarrhoea, pale mucous membranes and sometimes jaundice.
2. Aflatoxicosis but usually diarrhoea and marked tenesmus.
3. Listeriosis but may be unilateral facial paralysis, pyrexia.
4. Lead poisoning but usually abdominal pain, diarrhoea, no pupillary reflex, no ruminal movements.
5. Coenuriasis usually slow onset, circling.
6. Molasses poisoning - signs and pathology similar but history of feeding large quantities and also glucose levels full whereas thiamine levels remain normal.
7. Amprolium poisoning - signs and pathology similar but history of feeding it.
8. Bracken or horsetail poisoning causes similar signs and pathology but they would be highly unlikely to cause such a manifestation other than experimentally. History of access to plants.
9. Haemophilus somnus infection but usually pyrexia, neutrophilia.

Treatment

Thiamine hydrochloride should be administered intravenously at a dose of 10 mg/kg (5 mg/lb) BW, the dosage should be repeated every three hours or so for five treatments. A response will occur in 24 hours if animals are caught in the early stages, otherwise recovery is slowly progressive over several days. Multivitamin injections are often used but although they are suitable for follow-up therapy, in the initial stages insufficient thiamine will be administered unless very large doses are given.

Nursing is important and the cattle should be presented with wholesome food including at least 50 per cent good quality roughage. Rumen liquor from cattle on predominantly roughage diets may be helpful. The use of dried brewers' grains can help the condition as they contain high levels of thiamine and others of the B vitamin group. Levels of 0.5 - 1.0 kg/ 300 kg BW (1 - 2 lb/6 cwt) have been suggested.

Control

The precipitating factors for CCN are still not known, which makes it difficult to recommend preventive measures. As the condition is the result of endogenous thiaminase activity, provision of extra thiamine is of limited value. Most natural feeds contain thiamine at a level of 2 ppm and this, plus the vitamin synthesised in the rumen, is normally sufficient. Provision of adequate amounts of roughage should prevent the condition and a level of 1.5 kg roughage per 100 kg BW is suggested.

Reference

EDWIN, E E, MARKSON, L M, SHREEVE, J, JACKMAN, R and CARROLL, P J (1979) Veterinary Record, 104, 4-8.

Cobalt Deficiency

Aetiology

This is due to a lack of cobalt in the diet.

Occurrence

Cattle are affected less than sheep and younger cattle are more susceptible than older animals. Almost all cattle affected are grazing and deficiency normally occurs at the end of the grazing season or soon after housing, i.e. after about six months on a deficient pasture. The condition occurs when soils are deficient in the element, although the types of such soils are very variable, from shale to granite. Deficient pastures are likely to occur where levels of cobalt are below 0.25 ppm. Factors reducing the available cobalt levels include liming and high manganese levels. The season influences cobalt and it tends to be leached out by high rainfall. Growing cattle require more than 0.04 mg/kg DM. Cobalt tends to be stored in the liver but its only major function appears to be in the production of cyanocobalamin (Vitamin B_{12}) which is used in the metabolism of proprionic acid. Animals may develop a high rate of ketosis.

Signs

Early

Deficiency results in a loss of appetite resulting in a loss of weight, wastage and unthriftiness. The coat tends to become staring and dry, with the skin tight. Sometimes cattle develop pica. The mucous membranes become pale. Ketosis may develop.

Late

The animals may show progressive fatigue, diarrhoea, excessive lachrymation and infertility. Ultimately there is weakness, emaciation and recumbency. Death normally results at least three months after signs develop.

Necropsy

The carcase shows no fat and is emaciated with muscular atrophy. Anaemia and oedema may be present. The spleen is often pigmented by the presence of large deposits of haemosiderin.

Diagnosis

1. History - occurs at grass after 3 to 12 months, area of country.
2. Signs of loss of condition, anaemia, etc.
3. *Post mortem* examination.
4. Low liver cobalt level - 0.05 ppm DM (normal 0.5 ppm DM or above).
5. Low liver Vitamin B_{12} level (deficiency at 0.01 μg/g; normal 0.3 μg/g).
6. Response to Vitamin B_{12} injections.
7. Anaemia - normochromic, normocytic (often hard to detect as haemoconcentration).
8. Low serum Vitamin B_{12} levels (deficiency 200-250 μg/ml, normal 800-1000 μg/ml).

9. Presence in urine of methylmalonic acid (MMA) - normally metabolised by Vitamin B_{12} and formininoglutamic acid (FIGLU) also used but the latter may be of doubtful value.

10. Biochemistry - often there is hypoglycaemia and low serum alkaline phosphatase.

Differential diagnosis

1. Copper deficiency - history, signs, blood copper levels help.

2. Selenium deficiency, area and muscular lesions in some animals, blood glutathione peroxidase levels may be useful.

3. Parasitic gastroenteritis - history, faecal egg counts and plasma pepsinogen levels.

4. Fascioliasis but faecal egg identification will assist.

Treatment

Immediate rectification of the problem can be obtained with the intramuscular injection of Vitamin B_{12} at a level of 2 - 4 mg/kg BW (1 - 2 mg/lb BW). Cobalt can be added to the diet in the form of cobalt sulphate or cobalt chloride to provide 0.2 - 1.0 mg cobalt daily.

Control

Diets containing 0.07 mg/kg DM cobalt should be satisfactory to prevent deficiency problems. Cobalt bullets containing 30 per cent cobalt oxide and 70 per cent iron grit can be used at the level of one per animal any age after eight weeks old. The bullet lodges in the reticulum and slowly releases cobalt. However, sometimes the bullets become covered in scale of calcium salts and so grinders or two pellets may be necessary to ensure adequate abrasive action. About five per cent of bullets fail to lodge in the reticulum. Vitamin B_{12} injections can be given monthly but require the regular handling of the animals. However, the top dressing of pasture with cobalt salts can be effective, using 400 - 600 g/ha (5 - 8 oz/acre) of cobalt sulphate annually, or 1.2 - 1.5 kg/ha (1 - 1.3 lb/acre) every three or four years. Cobalt can also be added to the drinking water and is now available in soluble glass ruminal boluses.

Copper Deficiency

Aetiology

Deficiency of copper in ruminants, either primary due to a lack in the diet, or more likely secondary deficiency following a failure to absorb or utilise the element.

Occurrence

Absorption of copper varies with age but once the rumen is functional only about 2 to 10 per cent is absorbed. Copper is absorbed in the small intestine and enters the bloodstream where it binds with plasma albumin. It enters the liver where it is stored, mainly in the parenchyma but also the reticulo-epithelial cells. Copper is excreted via the bile in the faeces and some of this is reabsorbed in the small intestine. Very small amounts are found in the urine and milk. Absorption is affected by genetic factors as well as elements. Most cases of deficiency occur in cattle grazing primarily or secondarily deficient areas and not receiving any form of proprietary concentrates. Oil cakes such as linseed or soya have high copper values.

Copper is concerned with the formation of cytochrome oxidase, which regulates oxidation processes and electron transfer in tissues. It is also part of the enzyme lysyl oxidase which is used for elastin or collagen synthesis and deficiency results in skeletal defects and blood vessel fragility. Copper is also present in caeruloplasmin which releases iron into plasma from stores for erythropoeisis and deficiency results in anaemia.

The primary deficiency is uncommon and is seen on the Chilterns, Berkshire Downs, East Anglian heaths and on soils derived from Old Red Sandstone. The secondary deficiency is relatively common and although dietary intake of copper is satisfactory, deficiency is due to the many interactions between it and other elements, e.g. molybdenum poisoning (see page 281). Molybdenum inhibits absorption of copper from the intestine and sulphur (as protein) increases this effect. High levels of iron, zinc, lead, cadmium and calcium carbonate also reduce copper absorption. Blood sampling of cattle has shown hypocupraemia to be common in most cattle-producing areas of England (Leech, Howarth, Thornton and Lewis, 1982).

Signs

Primary deficiency

The cattle have a reduced growth rate, sometimes there is a scour but not usually as pronounced as in secondary deficiency. There may be a stilted gait with some ataxia developing after exercise, but recovery occurs after rest. Ribs and limb bones may develop spontaneous fractures, the shaft thickness may be reduced and there is osteoporosis. Thickened epiphyses, particularly in the fetlock region, may be noted, and stiffness of the joints. The hair colour may be affected with red and black hair becoming bleached to a rusty-red or grey colour. In many cases the hair colour loss starts on the hindquarters and progresses forwards. Only in very severe cases does the "spectacle" effect of depigmentation of the periorbital hair occur. Very occasionally cases of sudden death due to cardiac lesions can occur. Temporary infertility is sometimes seen.

Secondary deficiency

In cattle there is again a stiff gait and unthriftiness. Molybdenosis is characterised by severe scours. Some calves become severely lame with epiphyses which are painful to palpate and usually the distal ends of the metapodial bones are enlarged. In some animals, depigmentation of the hair occurs.

Subclinical hypocuprosis

In some animals which are apparently normal the injection of copper results in improved weight gain.

Necropsy

There is usually emaciation with anaemia seen as thin, watery blood and pale tissues. Where copper levels are low there are deposits of haemosiderin in the liver, kidney and spleen. The limb bones may show evidence of rarefaction and fracture. A thickening of the epiphyseal plates, particularly of the metapodial bones, may be present. In the small intestine there may be villous atrophy. Histologically the bones show osteoporosis.

Diagnosis

1. The area of the country where it is seen.
2. It is usually seen at pasture.
3. The signs may give an indication.
4. Several animals are usually affected.
5. Anaemia which is macrocytic and hypochromic with a blood haemoglobin of 5 - 8 g/100 ml (normal level is 8.0 - 15.0 g/100 ml) and erythrocytes at a level of 2 - 4 million/µl (normal values are 5.0 - 10.0 million/µl).
6. Blood copper levels (see Table 6.2).
7. Liver copper levels (100 g of fresh liver are required for the estimation).

Both blood and liver copper levels tend to be lower in primary than secondary deficiency.

8. Low blood caeruloplasmin levels.
9. Soil analysis for copper and molybdenum levels.

Differential diagnosis

1. Coccidiosis but there is overcrowding and blood in the faeces.
2. Cobalt deficiency but low blood vitamin B_{12} levels.
3. Salmonellosis but can have blood present and bacteriology.
4. Parasitic gastroenteritis.
5. Fascioliasis but liver fluke eggs present.

Treatment

If therapy is undertaken, it is important to confirm the presence of copper deficiency, as overdosing is toxic. Weekly oral administration of 1.5 - 4 g copper sulphate is very useful, but requires constant handling of

TABLE 6.2

Blood Plasma and Liver Copper Levels

	ADEQUATE	MARGINAL	DEFICIENT
Plasma copper	>0.9 μg/ml (>15 μmol/l)	0.9-0.4 μg/ml (15-6 μmol/l)	<0.4 μg/ml (<6 μmol/l)
Liver copper	100-200 mg/kg DM		<50 mg/kg DM

the cattle. Parenteral administration of copper can overcome the problem. Copper sulphate has been used at a level of 0.75 - 1.0 g. A methionine copper complex can be administered as a deep intramuscular injection at a dose of 40 - 100 mg per animal, as also can diethylamine copper oxyquinoline sulphonate at a rate of 0.24 mg/kg (0.12 mg/lb) BW by subcutaneous injection and copper edetate as a subcutaneous injection of 50 - 100 mg, depending on the product and age of the animal.

Experiments in sheep have shown high doses of copper methionine subcutaneously to be safer than calcium copper edetate and diethylamine copper oxyquinoline (Mahmoud and Ford, 1981), but it was considered that this might have been the result of the rapidity of absorption depending on the route of injection. A comparison of the efficacy of copper preparations in cattle showed copper edetate to be best with copper diethylamine oxyquinoline sulphonate 19 per cent worse, aqueous copper methionate 36 - 48 per cent worse, and cupric sulphate producing the second best result. The injections also cause a local reaction with copper diethylamine oxyquinoline sulphonate giving least damage, copper edetate producing an intermediate reaction and copper methionate causing most swelling (Suttle, 1981b).

Prevention

Ensure that the level of copper in the diet of cattle is at least 10 mg/kg DM (10 ppm). When deficiency has been determined, it may be necessary to inject or drench the cattle routinely. However, no such programme should be undertaken unless a sample of the animals has been checked to ensure blood copper levels are low. The timing of the first injection (in severely affected herds) is at about six weeks old, but subsequent injections need to be based on further blood sampling. Copper sulphate can be used as a weekly drench of 1.5 - 4.0 g depending on size. Recently cupric oxide needles have been used to alleviate hypocupraemia in heifers (Suttle, 1981a) and a capsule containing 24 g has been advocated, administered with a bolus gun.

The use of pasture dressing annually with 5.6 kg/ha (5 lb/acre) copper sulphate is effective. As there is a possibility of poisoning, animals should not graze the pasture until after heavy rain or three weeks after application. The copper supplementation of water has been advocated (Farmer, Adams and Humphries, 1982). Recently an intraruminal bolus has been introduced which releases copper slowly from a soluble glass.

References

FARMER, P E, ADAMS, T E and HUMPHRIES, W R (1982) Veterinary Record, 111, 193-195.

LEECH, A, HOWARTH, R J, THORNTON, I and LEWIS, G (1982) Veterinary Record, 111, 203-204.

MAHMOUD, D H and FORD, E J H (1981) Veterinary Record, 108, 114-117.

SUTTLE, N F (1981a) Veterinary Record, 108, 417-420.

SUTTLE, N F (1981b) Veterinary Record, 109, 304-307.

Hypomagnesaemia

Staggers, Grass Staggers, Grass Tetanus.

Aetiology

This is due to reduced circulating levels of magnesium. In many cases there is also a hypocalcaemia.

Occurrence

Fewer cases occur in the growing animal than in calves on milk diets or cows, particularly between four and seven years old and often within two months of calving. The most susceptible growing animals are in-calf heifers. Most cases occur in animals turned out to a lush pasture in the springtime, or following some stress in outwintered cattle during the autumn or winter, or in cattle grazing green cereal crops. In the last case, high levels of serum potassium are often present and there may be competition for absorption between potassium and magnesium. In other cases the absorption of magnesium daily approaches that lost and available body reserves are small. In consequence any alteration in nutrition or even temporary starvation can initiate the condition, particularly in animals which are stressed in other ways, or at critical times of the year. Reduction in absorption or availability of magnesium can be caused by a number of factors including high usage of ammonia, nitrogen or potash fertilisers. Weather can also have effects with wind possibly increasing requirements, frost reducing feed intake and severe rain possibly stressing the animals.

Signs

Acute

Most of these cases occur in the spring or following stress to cattle with chronic hypomagnesaemia in the autumn. The animal initially may seem normal but will suddenly show a staring expression, with muscular tremors. Any stimulus is then likely to result in severe problems with excessive twitching, bellowing and running. Often, with movement, the animal develops a staggering gait and will then fall on its side. The animal will usually show frenzied paddling movements with its legs, opisthotonus, retraction of the eyelids, pricked ears, an exaggerated blink reflex, profuse salivation, champing of the jaws, urination and defaecation. Rectal temperature is often high, 40 - 41 $^{\circ}$C (104 - 106 $^{\circ}$F) with a rapid heart and respiratory rate. Usually the heart can be heard several paces from the animal. A convulsive episode will be followed by a quieter period which can be transformed into further convulsions by any stimulus. The animal often dies and this can be within an hour of the onset of signs.

Subacute

Signs develop over 2 to 4 days and are less dramatic. There is a reduced appetite, sporadic muscle tremors may occur, particularly on the head and neck, urination and defaecation are more frequent and there is often a wild facial expression. The ruminal movements are reduced and if the animal walks it often has a staggering gait with muscle tremors. Cattle may progress from subacute to acute signs, whereas others gradually return to normal.

Chronic

Many animals, particularly in autumn, have low serum magnesium levels but they do not show signs. Others show just a mild inappetance, with unthriftiness and dullness. Some of these animals may later develop acute or subacute signs. Conversely, some subacute cases later develop the chronic form of the disease.

Necropsy

There is often extensive congestion and haemorrhages in organs. Blood may be found in the subcutaneous tissues and in the pleura, peritoneum, intestinal mucosa, pericardium and endocardium. Emphysema may occur.

Diagnosis

1. History - the animal may be grazing lush pasture, or green cereal crops, exposed to bad weather or outwintered.
2. Signs are useful including hyperaesthesia, muscular tremors, rapid heart rate with loud beat.
3. Serum magnesium levels (normal 0.7 - 1.19 mmol/l, 1.7 - 2.9 mg/100 ml). Most cases have levels below 0.2 mmol/l (0.6 mg/100 ml). Blood samples taken close to or following death may give falsely high readings due to release of magnesium from damaged cells.
4. Creatine phosphokinase (CPK or CK) levels tend to be high - normal plasma levels are less than 40 iu/l.
5. Serum glutamine oxalotransaminase (SGOT) - Aspartate aminotransferase (AST) level tends to be raised, the normal value is 40 iu/l or below.
6. Heart muscle contains low magnesium on *post mortem* examination.
7. Magnesium levels in the cerebrospinal fluid are low.
8. Serum calcium levels are often reduced to 1.25 - 2 mmol/l (5 - 8 mg/100 ml) - normal level 2.5 mmol/l; 10 mg/100ml.
9. Hyperkalaemia may be seen in cattle with green cereal poisoning. (Normal level 3.9 - 5.8 mmol/l; 3.9 - 5.8 mequ/l).
10. Urine contains low magnesium levels.
11. The calcium:magnesium level of the rib bone or caudal vertebrae is useful but expensive. The normal ratio is 70:1 but a value of over 90:1 is indicative of a chronic problem.

Differential diagnosis

1. Tetanus but usually of a longer course with a raised tail head, bloat and possible prolapse of the third eyelid.
2. Lead poisoning but there is blindness, bellowing, colic.
3. Cerebrocortical necrosis but again blindness.

Treatment

Standard therapy is magnesium sulphate, usually as a 25 *per cent* solution, injected subcutaneously at a level of 200 - 400 ml. Serum magnesium levels rise rapidly to a normal level but subside in 3 to 6 hours. Intravenous injection is used by some practitioners but is very risky and can lead to cardiac arrest or medullary depression. It is not recommended that the intravenous route be used, but if it is, injection must be slow and the animal monitored. If the heart rate becomes very slow or fast, or there is respiratory distress, then the injection should be stopped and a calcium borogluconate injection given. If intravenous injection is to be given then it is probably best to use calcium rather than magnesium. Magnesium lactate and magnesium gluconate have been used to produce prolongation of the raised serum magnesium levels. Magnesium chloride has been given rectally.

Control

Management

When cases occur in the spring on lush pasture then the cattle should be kept on bare pasture and given hay which should be consumed before the animals are allowed on the pasture. Otherwise grazing should be for short periods or strip grazing may be undertaken. In the autumn, provision of extra roughage and other feed outside will help overcome the problem. Cattle should be supplied with adequate shelter for inclement weather.

Magnesium supplements

Feeding magnesium daily during the period of risk can help to overcome the problem. Provision of calcined magnesite 30 - 60 g (1 - 2 oz) depending on size, by drench, will prevent the problem. However, it requires much labour and the magnesite is not very palatable to cattle. This can be overcome by providing the calcined magnesite with molasses or the magnesium can be included in magnesium-rich concentrates or in palatable feed blocks. Magnesium acetate is more acceptable to cattle and again can be used in concentrates, licks or by provision in the drinking water. Magnesium bullets have also been used. Two bullets of appropriate size are used, each cylinder containing 86 *per cent* magnesium, 12 *per cent* aluminium and two *per cent* copper alloy. The cylinders are administered with a special balling gun and remain in the reticulum liberating small amounts of magnesium for about a month.

Pasture control

Potash fertilisers should not be used in the spring. The use of magnesium fertilisers can be helpful, such as calcined magnesite (1270 kg/ha - 1100 lb/acre) and last one year on heavy clay soils, but three years on light, sandy soils. Magnesium limestone can also be used but is administered at higher levels (6.3 tonne/ha; 2.4 ton/acre). A two *per cent* solution of magnesium sulphate can be sprayed on pasture being grazed every two weeks. Foliar dusting of grass can also be used with finely-ground calcined magnesite at a level of 30 kg/ha (28 lb/acre).

Iodine Deficiency

Aetiology

This can occur due to a primary lack of iodine. Secondary deficiency is recorded following high intakes of Brassica, high calcium ingestion, heavy bacterial contamination of feed or water, a low level intake of linseed meal or other plants containing cyanogenetic glycosides (Blood *et al*, 1983).

Occurrence

It is relatively uncommon in Britain. Primary deficiency is occasionally seen in some parts of Britain, e.g. Derbyshire. The condition is mainly seen in the newborn calf of a deficient dam. Iodine forms part of the hormone thyroxine, and a deficiency will result in the pituitary increasing the production of thyrotrophic hormone. Calves born alive are prone to die if chilled, etc. Heifers are more likely to produce goitrous offspring than cows.

Many cases occur in areas where high rainfall leaches the iodine. A high level of dietary calcium reduces the intestinal absorption of iodine. Thiocyanates, goitrogenic substances, are found in *Brassica* spp. including kale, rape and cabbage. Linseed oil contains an arachidoside, a goitrogenic glycoside, and soyabean by-products may also result in problems. Heavy bacterial or sewage contamination of water may reduce its iodine level.

Signs

Heifers

Oestrus may not be expressed. Some calves may be aborted or stillborn. Other calves are born weak and if assisted to suck they will usually survive. In both calves born dead or alive, the thyroid gland is enlarged and in some cases the gland can be felt to pulsate. Gestation length of stillborn calves is often increased. Occasionally there are areas of alopecia and if the thyroid becomes very large, respiratory obstruction can occur.

Bulls

Lack of libido.

Necropsy

The full-term calf thyroid glands are enlarged and heavier than usual (normal fresh weight 6.5 g). (Blood *et al*, 1983). Histologically there is thyroid hyperplasia.

Diagnosis

1. The area of the country.
2. The diet may contain goitrogenic plants.
3. Several cows in the herd may have aborted, or given birth to stillborn or weak calves.
4. There is generally thyroid enlargement.
5. Blood protein iodine levels are low (normal 2.4 - 4μg/100 ml plasma).

6. Iodine levels of soil and pasture will assist.
7. The thyroid weight at necropsy.
8. Iodine content of the thyroid gland (normal 0.1 per cent dry weight or 0.03 per cent fresh weight).

Differential diagnosis

The main problem is other causes of abortion.

1. Brucellosis.
2. Mycotic abortion.
3. *Salmonella dublin* infection.
4. Leptospiral abortion.
5. Mucosal disease.
6. IBR infection.
7. *Campylobacter fetus* infection.
8. Trichomonas infection.

Treatment

It should be ensured that the calf sucks and is kept in a warm, draught-free environment. Thyroid extract can be used at a dose of 1.0 - 2.0 mg/kg BW (0.5 - 1.0 mg/lb BW). Intravenous sodium iodide can be used at a dose of 5 - 7 g for the young calf, but it is not without risk; potassium iodide can be used orally at about 3 g per calf. Iodism (iodine poisoning) can sometimes develop (see page 272).

Control

Ensure adequate iodine in the diet of dams. A recommended level is 0.8 mg/kg DM for pregnant and lactating cows. The level for calves should be 0.12 mg/kg DM.

References

BLOOD, D C, RADOSTITS, O M and HENDERSON, J A (1983) "Veterinary Medicine" 6th edition. Bailliere Tindall, London. p.1031-1034.

Manganese Deficiency

Aetiology

Primary deficiency is due to a lack of manganese in the diet, it occurs in some enzootic areas and it is unusual. Secondary deficiency is due to a depression in the availability of ingested manganese.

Occurrence

Both primary and secondary deficiencies are very uncommon. Levels of manganese in the diet should be about 40 ppm and most pasture contains 50 - 100 ppm. Primary problems are likely to occur where soils contain less than 3 ppm of manganese. Secondary deficiency possibly occurs in diets with a high calcium/phosphorus excess. Soils with a high alkalinity tend to reduce availability of manganese and this starts at pH 6.0 in sandy soils and pH 7.0 in heavy soils. Heavy liming may also reduce manganese uptake by plants. The main uses of the element appear to be in cartilage synthesis and some infertility problems respond to manganese.

Signs

Growing animals

Mostly there is poor growth with poor coat formation and a loss of coat colour.

Infertility - Heifers

Manganese-responsive infertility has been recorded. On rectal palpation of these heifers, one or both ovaries may be found to be small in size. There may be a failure to exhibit oestrus or suboestrus, or a failure to conceive. Some calves born to deficient animals show congenital limb deformities such as enlarged joints, knuckling of the fetlocks and occasionally twisting of the limbs.

Infertility - Bulls

Poor quality semen may be produced.

Necropsy

Affected animals do not usually die. Calves born to deficient heifers may show congenital limb deformities and poor growth. Affected heifers show small ovaries.

Diagnosis

1. Signs - infertility is the most sensitive indicator.
2. Liver manganese levels (deficiency at 8 ppm DM; normal level 12 ppm DM).
3. Blood manganese level (normal 18 - 19 μg/100 ml).
4. Hair manganese levels (normal in non-pregnant heifers 12 ppm but this does fall during pregnancy to 4.5 ppm at the time of calving).
5. Response to manganese supplementation.

Treatment

The daily use of 4 g manganese sulphate has been found to be helpful.

Control

Feed 4 g manganese sulphate from nine weeks before to six weeks after first service. Very high levels of manganese can result in a reduction in the utilisation of zinc and cobalt.

Phosphorus Deficiency

Aetiology

Primary phosphorus deficiency can occur, as also does secondary, which is aggravated by a low vitamin D and possibly a high calcium intake.

Occurrence

Primary deficiency is highly unlikely to occur in Britain, and secondary problems are also very rare. The daily requirement of phosphorus is 7 - 23 g ($^1/_3$ - $^2/_3$ oz). Phosphorus is used to ensure adequate mineralisation of the teeth and bones. Inorganic phosphate is also utilised in the formation of protein, tissue enzymes and in the intermediate metabolism of carbohydrate and in reactions resulting in muscle contraction.

Signs

Rickets

A progressive stiffening of the gait with enlargement of the joints, particularly of the forelimbs and costro-chondral junctions. Lameness is variable and often the back is arched. In severe cases there is a tendency for recumbency. Dental abnormalities may occur with the teeth showing delayed eruption and excessive attrition, and pigmentation.

Infertility

There is a delay in sexual maturity with anoestrus, suboestrus and irregular oestrus.

Necropsy

The joints tend to be enlarged with increased epiphyseal cartilage, the bones tend to be shorter and thicker due to the deposition of osteoid tissue. Histologically there is defective mineralisation of the developing bone.

Diagnosis

1. Signs.
2. Analysis of diet.
3. Low bone ash (normal 60 per cent; ratio ash:organic matter 3:2).
4. Biochemistry - elevation of plasma alkaline phosphate levels occurs.
5. Serum phosphorus levels may be low (normal 1.4 - 2.1 mmol/l; 4 - 8 mg/100 ml) although serum calcium levels are normal until just before death.
6. Radiography shows reduced density of the bones and the long bones have indistinct ends.
7. Necropsy.

Differential diagnosis

1. Copper deficiency but low plasma copper levels.
2. Muscular dystrophy.

Treatment

Phosphorus deficiency can usually be treated by ensuring an adequate level in the diet and acceptable calcium:phosphorus ratio, with enough vitamin D present. Phosphorus levels of 7 - 23 g (1/3 - 2/3 oz) per 100 - 500 kg BW (220 - 110 lb BW) are recommended with 300 iu of vitamin D/kg (150 iu vitamin d/lb) dry matter intake. An injection of vitamin D_3 at 3000 - 5000 iu/kg BW (1500 - 2500 iu/lb BW) will provide an adequate level for one to three months.

Prevention

Ensure adequate minerals and vitamin D are present in the diet. Bone meal and dicalcium phosphate are good sources of both calcium and phosphorus in a correct ratio but they are expensive.

Sodium Chloride Deficiency

Aetiology

A dietary deficiency of sodium.

Occurrence

Although deficiency can occasionally occur in lactating cows, there is a possibility of a rare problem in rapidly growing cattle on low sodium diets containing high levels of cereals or in cattle grazing very sandy soils fertilised with potash. Pasture and ration should contain about 0.15 per cent sodium on a dry matter basis.

Signs

There is a craving and excessive licking of their own and other animals' coats, objects, etc. Appetite is often reduced and urine drinking may occur.

Necropsy

Death would only occur after a period of a year or so and it is therefore highly unlikely.

Diagnosis

1. Signs - licking excessively.
2. Serum sodium level (normal level 139 mmol/l; 139 mequ/l).
3. Saliva sodium level (normal 140 - 150 mmol/l - deficient = 100 mmol/l).
4. Response to salt supplementation.

Differential diagnosis

1. Lack of fibre in diet.

Treatment

Supplement the diet with sodium up to a level of 0.5 per cent. Salt licks or mixes may be introduced although individual cattle vary in their uptake by this method. Appetite should be encouraged with the use of stomach powders, e.g. nux vomica, ginger, gentian, ammonium bicarbonate.

Control

Ensure the diet contains at least 0.15 per cent sodium on a dry matter basis. Use salt licks or mixes if necessary. Salt can be sprayed at a level of 16 kg per hectare in 5,500 litres of water (14 lb in 500 gallons of water per acre).

Vitamin A Deficiency

Aetiology

The condition can be the result of a deficiency of the fat-soluble vitamin A, or carotene, which is its dietary precursor. Secondary deficiency can occur where, although there is sufficient vitamin in the diet, it does not reach normal tissue levels because of some failure in digestion or metabolism.

Occurrence

The condition is unusual these days. It can either be congenital or post-natal, but in most cases the latter requires feeding for several months on a deficient ration. Generally a diet of green feed will provide sufficient carotene and hence vitamin A. Diets likely to be deficient in vitamin A include sugar beet pulp, cereal straw and cereals. Skim milk and whey contain only small amounts of vitamin A, although proprietary milk substitites have added vitamin. The vitamin A requirement of a cow during pregnancy is at least twice that of the non-pregnant animal. Vitamin A is stored in the liver and to increase liver reserves of the foetus this is better accomplished by the feeding of vitamin A than carotene. Colostrum is the main source of the vitamin for the young animal and its vitamin A and carotene content can be increased by the introduction to the dam's diet of extra vitamin and carotene. High environmental temperature, "stressed animals" and fast-growing animals all require extra vitamin A. Many factors influence the vitamin A and carotene content of feeds. Thus vitamins C and E help to prevent vitamin A loss, and also the uptake of the vitamin is inversely proportional to the phosphate present in the diet. The vitamin is not very stable and so pelleting of the rations, storage at high temperatures and rancidity all decrease the content of the diet. Wood preservatives such as chlorinated naphthalenes inhibit carotene conversion to vitamin A and prolonged oral use of liquid paraffin or other mineral oils can produce a deficiency. Vitamin A is used to produce visual purple for the retina, normal epithelium and bone.

Signs

Post-natal

Classic xerophthalmia with thickening and clouding of the cornea is almost non-existent in practice. The main signs are usually a failure to grow, incoordination of gait, night-blindness or complete blindness. When blindness is apparent, it is usually permanent. Occasionally a nervous form involving sudden syncope (fainting) and convulsions with apparent complete recovery is seen. Diarrhoea may be seen in some cases. Probably the most common signs of marginal deficiency are brown, bran-like scales in the coat, particularly in fast-growing animals.

Reproductive efficiency

Heifers

The animal will usually conceive but there tends to be placental degeneration with the birth of weak or dead calves or abortion.

Males

Libido is normal but there is a reduction in the number of normal spermatozoa produced due to degeneration of the germinal epithelium of the seminiferous tubules.

Necropsy

Careful dissection may reveal stenosis of the optic foramen and necrosis of the optic nerve. Compression of other nerves may also be apparent. Histological examination will reveal squamous metaplasia of the interlobular and main ducts of the parotid salivary gland. This is considered pathognomonic for vitamin A deficiency, but it tends to resolve in two or three weeks of receiving adequate vitamin A. Secondary pneumonia and enteritis are common.

Diagnosis

1. There is a lack of green feed in the diet.
2. Night-blindness and a scaly skin are useful signs when apparent.
3. Cerebrospinal fluid pressure is increased from a normal of less than 100 mm of water to 200 mm or more.
4. Plasma vitamin A and carotene levels are low (see Table 6.3).
5. The vitamin A and carotene levels of the liver are low (see Table 6.3).
6. Squamous metaplasia of the parotid salivary gland duct, at post mortem examination, is pathognomonic.

TABLE 6.3

Vitamin A and Carotene Levels

	Normal	Minimum	Deficient
Plasma vitamin A per 100 ml	25 μg	10 μg	7 μg
Plasma carotene per 100 ml	150 μg	60 μg	9 μg
Liver vitamin A	800 μg/g	60 μg/g	2 μg/g
Liver carotene	400 μg/g	4.0 μg/g	0.5 μg/g

Differential diagnosis

Poor growth

1. Faulty feeding.
2. Parasitic gastroenteritis.
3. Fascioliasis.

Nervous

1. Hypomagnesaemia but the animal is not blind.
2. Lead poisoning, but there is grunting and abdominal pain.
3. Tetanus, but then there is no blindness and prolapse of the nictating membrane and bloat occur.
4. Cerebrocortical necrosis.

Treatment

An immediate injection of about 10 times the normal daily maintenance dose should be given. This is about 400 iu of vitamin A per kg BW (200 iu per lb BW).

Control

The daily vitamin A requirement of a calf and growing animal is 40 iu/kg BW (20 iu/lb BW). Intensive cereal beef and pregnant heifers require 80 iu/kg BW (40 iu/lb BW). Green feed or early cut hay, good silage or dried grass should be given. Injections of vitamin A can be given at the rate of about 5,000 iu/kg BW (2,500 iu/lb BW); depending on the preparation the dose may need repeating at one to three-monthly intervals.

Vitamin D Deficiency

Aetiology

Usually a lack of vitamin D (fat-soluble vitamin obtained by solar irradiation).

Occurrence

The clinical deficiency is uncommon because of improved nutrition. Vitamin D_3 (cholecalciferol) is produced by ultra-violet light irradiation on the skin. Vitamin D_2 is produced in sun-cured hay. Vitamin D levels in hay vary depending on how it is cured. Modern, rapid haymaking means levels of Vitamin D are at a minimum compared with exposure to sunlight for long periods. Ensilaged grass also tends to be low in the vitamin. Vitamin D levels in the diet should be 300 iu/kg (150 iu/lb) dry matter intake. Optimal daily intake is 7 - 12 iu/kg BW (3.5 - 6 iu/lb BW). Although sun-cured hay is high in vitamin D, green forages tend to be deficiency. One useful material to use is yeast. Cod and halibut liver oils are high in vitamin D but they reduce on pelleting and storage. Water-soluble vitamin D supplements are now available.

Hydroxylation of the vitamin occurs in the liver to 25-hydroxycholecalciferol and a second hydroxylation occurs in the kidney to 1,25 dihydroxycholecalciferol. The dihydroxylate form aids absorption of calcium from the gut and is used in bone mineralisation. The metabolite is also used in the regulation of absorption and loss of the phosphate in the kidney.

Signs

There may be a reduction in appetite and feed conversion efficiency with poor productivity.

Rickets

Late stages may involve rickets. Lameness may be present with enlargement of limb joints and the costrochondral junctions. Arching of the back may occur and as lameness progresses the animal may become recumbent.

Heifers

Reproductive efficiency may be reduced.

Necropsy

The animal may be in poor condition. The joints are enlarged with increased epiphyseal cartilage. The long bones tend to be thicker than normal with deposition of osteoid tissue subperiosteally.

Diagnosis

1. Signs.
2. Dietary analysis.
3. Biochemistry - raised plasma alkaline phosphatase levels.
4. Usually there is marked hypophosphataemia; later on there is also hypocalcaemia.

Treatment

Injections of vitamin D at 3,000 - 5,000 iu/kg BW (1,500 - 2,500 iu/lb BW) will give adequate levels for several months. Adequate levels of calcium and phosphorus should be given.

Control

Ensure adequate vitamin D is present in the diet or inject solutions of 11,000 units/kg (5,500 units/lb) BW which will maintain vitamin levels for 3 to 6 months. Storage of vitamin D in the body is limited and so daily provision of the vitamin is always the best method of supply. An intake of 7 - 12 iu/kg (3.5 - 6 iu/lb) BW is about optimum but doses of 20 - 45 iu/kg (10 - 22.5 iu/lb) are often used.

Vitamin E and Selenium Deficiency

This results in muscular dystrophy, also known as white muscle disease, fish flesh disease, degenerative myopathy or paralytic myoglobinuria.

Aetiology

Either vitamin E (fat-soluble) and/or selenium may be deficient.

Occurrence

It can be seen in cattle at any age after birth. Selenium deficiency is mainly dependent on the part of the country where crops are produced. The condition appears to be becoming increasingly important, probably due to the increased cost of bought-in feeds causing farmers to use more home-produced crops for their animals. The accepted level of selenium in feeds is 0.1 mg/kg DM. Selenium is mainly used by the body in the production of the enzyme glutathione peroxidase.

Vitamin E deficiency is much more dependent on the type of crop grown and its storage, etc. Vitamin E levels tend to be high in green pasture, silage, dried grass or kale. Adequate levels of the vitamin are also present in cereal grains, well-cured fresh hay, maize silage and brewers' grains, but deficiencies can occur on poor quality hay, straw or root crops unless there is a suitable supplement provided. Vitamin E tends to deplete with storage. Cattle diets high in unsaturated fatty acids, as can occur where cod liver oil, fish meal, soya bean meal or linseed oil are fed, may become deficient due to their oxidation, resulting in rancidity and the destruction of the vitamin E. Storage of grains when wet or with proprionic acid can also reduce the vitamin E level. Normal levels for growing cattle are considered to be 150 mg of αtocopherol, and for the calf, milk substitutes should contain antioxidants and 300 iu/kg DM.

The condition affects muscles, particularly cardiac, skeletal and diaphragmatic. Deficiency can occur in suckler calves sucking mothers with low selenium or vitamin E levels or artificially reared calves on deficient diets. The condition results from unsaturated fatty acids entering the muscle cells where they accumulate. They are oxidated to lipid peroxides which result in degeneration and calcification. It is believed vitamin E helps prevent lipid peroxide formation within the muscle cells whereas selenium, in the form of glutathione peroxidase, assists in its elimination. Those compounds with many unsaturated points are known as polyunsaturated fatty acids and these are particularly common in vegetable oils which therefore predispose to peroxide formation.

Cases in yearlings often follow turnout in spring after housing and feeding on poor quality roughage, and in some cases following the feeding of proprionic acid-treated cereals. In some areas of Britain where both grain and forage approach critical levels, addition of proprionic acid may result in the condition. Excessive muscular exertion, as often happens after turnout, may also be involved and helps produce myoglobinuria in some individual animals.

Signs

These vary considerably in degree.

Sudden death syndrome

This is where an animal literally drops dead in a matter of minutes and is almost exclusively seen in calves. Death is due to cardiac muscle involvement. A few cases of paralytic myoglobinuria are found dead with no premonitory signs.

Acute muscular dystrophy

This again is mainly present in the calf. The condition is sudden in origin. The animal becomes dull and lies in lateral recumbency. There is respiratory distress, a heart rate often elevated to 150 - 200 beats per minute and irregular. The rectal temperature is normal, the calf is fully conscious and has normal eye reflexes. Most calves die within 6 to 18 hours and the mortality approaches 100 per cent.

Subacute muscular dystrophy

This is the form most commonly encountered clinically in cattle. Most cases follow within one week of turnout in the spring. The signs depend on the muscles affected. Usually the animal stands stiffly with an arched back and it is reluctant to move. When it does it may have a stiff gait. The animal will usually eat well, but shows some sweating, and it may have a rectal temperature up to $40.5^{o}C$ ($105^{o}F$) with possible hyperpnoea and dyspnoea. Some cases show the red-brown urine of myoglobinuria. Often on palpation of the dorso-lumbar and gluteal muscles, these are found to be firm to the touch. Severely affected animals may become recumbent and death in some occurs within a few days.

Subclinical muscular dystrophy

This is seen in some animals in the same groups as those where subacute muscular dystrophy is encountered. Such cattle may show raised levels of plasma creatine phosphokinase (CPK) indicating muscle damage, but without other signs.

Ill-thrift

Some cases of poor growth and diarrhoea in older calves respond to selenium therapy.

Necropsy

Sudden death

Often in this form there are no macroscopic lesions present. In other cases there is congestion of the liver and lungs. The heart shows slight pallor of the myocardium. Histologically lesions not otherwise apparent can be detected with a haematoxylin basic fuchsin - picric acid method and these are considered to be a peracute myocardial degeneration.

Acute muscular dystrophy

There may be localised streaks in the diaphragm and skeletal muscles. In the skeletal muscles they tend to be bilaterally symmetrical white or grey areas. In the heart there may be cardiac hypertrophy and myocardial degeneration with pulmonary congestion and oedema. Histologically there is no inflammation but changes vary and include hyaline degeneration and coagulative necrosis.

Subacute muscular dystrophy

There is normally no cardiac involvement, but the skeletal muscles show bilateral white or grey areas.

Diagnosis

1. The diet provided, and the area of Britain.
2. The signs are of muscular involvement.
3. Often there is a raised heart rate even when apparently unaffected.
4. Blood or cell glutathione peroxidase levels (inadequate selenium status is indicated by erythrocyte glutathione peroxidase (GSHPx) activity of less than 15 units/ml cells). Recently a modified glutathione peroxidase spot test based on ultra violet light fluorescence has been introduced.
5. Raised plasma creatine phosphokinase (CPK or CK) levels in early stages (normal = 40 iu/l). The enzyme is specific for skeletal and cardiac muscle damage.
6. Raised plasma aspartate transaminase (AST, SGOT) levels remain high longer (normal less than 40 iu/l) than CPK. Levels are raised in muscle and liver damage.
7. Tocopherol level in the blood (normal 770 μg/100 ml) but this is not easy to analyse. Liver tocopherol can also be used.
8. Response to therapy.
9. Soil or herbage analysis.
10. Tissue levels of selenium (normal kidney cortex 1.0 ppm and 0.05 ppm wet matter for liver).

Differential diagnosis

Peracute

1. Blackleg.
2. Anthrax.

Subacute

1. Arthritis.
2. Laminitis.

Chronic

1. Copper deficiency.
2. Cobalt deficiency.
3. Parasitic gastroenteritis.

Treatment

Injections

Vitamin E. Numerous injections contain vitamin E in combination with vitamins A and D, the dose is about 6 iu of DL α-tocopherol per kg BW.

Selenium. An injection of 0.1 to 0.15 mg/kg BW (0.05 - 0.8 mg/lb BW) sodium selenate lasts six months (Allen, Little and Sansom, 1978) and one of 9 mg subcutaneously to calves has been recommended (Cowie, 1978).
A proprietary form of sodium selenite may be injected subcutaneously at the rate of 5 mg per 100 kg BW. In 1982 a long-acting injection of barium selenate was introduced at a dose of 50 mg selenium per 50 kg BW. The

rise in body selenium as measured by blood glutathione peroxidase levels often appears to fall far short of the "up to 12 months" suggested by the manufacturer. Additionally a high level of selenium remains at the site of subcutaneous injection which could possibly produce carcase spoilage and public health problems (Allen and Mallinson, 1984).

Combined Vitamin E and Selenium. Two injections are at present available. When used as recommended by the manufacturers then selenium levels are lower than those suggested to be necessary for response. Thus in some severe cases the therapeutic dose may need to be increased.

Bullets. Reticular bullets are available containing selenium.

Diet

Provide a diet high in vitamin E and selenium. Inject cows with calves at foot and those due to calve with the combined vitamin E and selenium injection.

Control - Animals

Growing calves should be given a supplement at the rate of 0.1 ppm selenium of the total ration and 150 mg per head of α-tocopherol daily. Cows should receive a supplement of vitamin E during the last two months of pregnancy and the first month of lactation.

Injections of selenium and vitamin E can be used, also selenium bullets are of value. Subcutaneous implants of selenium in optical glass to allow slow release of selenium have been used experimentally and an intraruminal form is now available commercially.

Control - Pasture

A top dressing of fertiliser containing sodium selenite 75 - 150 g/ha (1 - 2 oz/acre) or foliage dusting or spraying can be undertaken at 17.5 g/ha ($^1/_4$ oz/acre). Analysis of pasture should be undertaken to determine that toxic levels of selenium are not produced; this can occur at levels of 0.5 mg/kg. Selenium can be added to the drinking water.

References

ALLEN, W M, LITTLE, W and SANSOM, B F (1978) Veterinary Record, 102, 222-223.

ALLEN, W M and MALLINSON, C B (1984) Veterinary Record, 114, 451-454.

COWIE, R (1978) Veterinary Record, 102, 267-268.

Zinc Deficiency

Aetiology

This can be either primary due to a lack of zinc, or secondary due to impaired uptake.

Occurrence

It can be seen in cattle fed indoors or outside. Usually cattle do not show signs on diets containing 40 ppm of zinc, but it is probable that calcium and highly fibrous diets reduce zinc availability and perhaps low copper levels reduce uptake.

Signs

These usually occur about two weeks after the deficient diet is introduced. The main signs are of poor growth with possible stunting. There is alopecia and parakeratosis often affecting the limbs, muzzle, vulva, anus and tail head. There are fewer lesions on the main part of the body. In some cases any wounds or abrasions will take longer to heal.

Necropsy

Most animals do not die, but skin biopsies show increased thickness of all skin components and the stratum corneum contains nucleated epidermal cells.

Diagnosis

1. There is alopecia and skin thickening.
2. Biopsy shows parakeratosis.
3. Serum zinc levels (normal = 80 - 120 μg/100 ml).
4. Hair sample analysis.
5. A response to zinc therapy starts in about a week.

Differential diagnosis

1. Sarcoptic mange, but there is pruritus.
2. Pediculosis, but there is again pruritus.

Treatment

Oral medication with zinc sulphate weekly at a level of 2 g per week or 1 g weekly by injection is useful.

Control

A diet containing 50 ppm of zinc is usually adequate. Reduce levels of fibrous roughage or calcium in the diet. Weekly oral medication with 2 g zinc sulphate can be useful. Long term control can be obtained with zinc-containing fertiliser.

CHAPTER 7

POISONINGS

Cases in which poisoning is thought to have been involved tend to be uncommon. They provide about 1.3 per cent of all the diagnoses made at Veterinary Investigation Centres between 1975 and 1977 and of the poisonings, 79 per cent were due to chemicals. The majority of the diagnoses made were of lead poisoning (74 per cent), bracken poisoning (nine per cent) and ragwort poisoning (five per cent).

Aflatoxicosis

This is also known as groundnut poisoning.

Aetiology

This is caused by a series of hepatotoxins known as aflatoxins, which are produced by certain strains of *Aspergillus* spp.

Occurrence

The condition is uncommon in Britain. It is normally considered as occurring with groundnut meal, cotton seed cake or their derivatives, although the toxins have been found in other plant products. Calves of 3 to 6 months old are particularly susceptible. The onset of signs depends on the dose but they do not normally occur until about six weeks after the introduction of the contaminated feed.

Signs

There is usually dullness, loss of appetite, abdominal discomfort, teeth grinding, diarrhoea which may contain blood, jaundice, severe tenesmus and anal prolapse (Allcroft and Lewis, 1963). Nervous signs are common including apparent blindness, staring eyes and walking in circles. Death often takes place after convulsions and usually occurs within 48 hours.

Necropsy

There is jaundice, a swollen liver with fibrosis, ascites and visceral oedema.

Diagnosis

1. The diet fed may well be found to contain groundnut.
2. The signs are of use, especially tenesmus and nervous signs.
3. Serum alkaline phosphatase levels may be raised (normal value is 5 - 40 iu/l).
4. Liver vitamin A levels tend to be low.
5. Toxin detection in feed.

Differential diagnosis

1. Coccidiosis.
2. Mucosal disease.
3. Copper poisoning.

Treatment

Remove the ration. There is no specific therapy but supportive treatment for the liver including glucose or glucose saline i.v. or s.c. and multivitamin injections may be helpful.

Control

Only concentrates should be used which have acceptable levels or preferably no aflatoxin. Recent regulations have more or less resulted in a ban on the importation of groundnut, cottonseed and their derivatives for inclusion in feeding stuffs (Fertilisers and Feeding Stuffs (Amendment) Regulations, 1981). New regulations allow an import limit of 0.5 mg/kg in all feeding stuff compounding, and require the certification of aflatoxin levels for groundnut, palm kernel, cotton seed and their derivatives. Groundnut was also to be banned from use in dairy feeds (Veterinary Record, 1981).

References

ALLCROFT, T R and LEWIS, G (1963) Veterinary Record, 75, 487-493.

VETERINARY RECORD (1981) 109, 148.

Arsenic Poisoning

Aetiology

Arsenic salts which are soluble, e.g. sodium arsenite, are more toxic than the less soluble forms such as sodium arsenate and arsenic trioxide.

Occurrence

This can occur in cattle of any age depending on exposure. The chemical is little used in modern agriculture and so poisoning is very uncommon. Occasionally cases occur due to high soil levels, e.g. Cornwall. It is still, however, very rarely used as a weedkiller and in the form of monosodium acid methane-arsenate it has been used as a potato haulm killer. Previously it used to be used as an ectoparasiticide for dips and as an anthelmintic. An organic form of arsenic, sodium arsanilate, is used for the prevention of diarrhoea in pigs and poultry. Various individual animals show idiosyncracies and are able to take large amounts of arsenic without ill-effect. Cattle will often lick arsenic with apparent relish. Mortality on poisoning approaches 100 per cent.

Route of entry

This is usually oral but it can be via the skin, particularly if there are abrasions.

Signs

Most animals die quickly and the signs have been described (Blood et al, 1983).

Peracute

There is dullness, depression and early death.

Acute

There is marked abdominal pain, ruminal stasis, teeth grinding and passage of foetid diarrhoeic faeces. Respiratory and pulse rates are greatly increased. Death occurs in two or three days.

Subacute

The animals are ill for up to seven days, with diarrhoea, dysentery, complete anorexia, dehydration, thirst and no gut sounds. They are reluctant to move and have arched backs. Nervous signs may occur and these include muscular tremors, incoordination and terminally, coma.

Chronic

This is an uncommon form but when it occurs the calves show poor growth, poor coats and dullness. Erythema of the conjunctiva and other mucous membranes may be apparent together with, in some cases, ulceration.

Necropsy

The carcase does not undergo rapid putrefaction and on opening there is a garlic odour. Often a stomatitis and lesions of congestion and submucosal haemorrhages are present in the abomasum, duodenum and caecum. The mesenteric lymph nodes are enlarged and the liver and kidneys tend to be enlarged, friable and show fatty degeneration. The bladder blood vessels are swollen.

Diagnosis

1. Knowledge of exposure to arsenic.
2. The signs of severe enteritis, abdominal pain and some nervous signs may help.
3. An estimate of arsenic in the urine of live animals.
4. Liver and kidney from dead animals have high arsenic values of 5 to 15 parts per million (ppm) wet matter.

Differential diagnosis

There are many potential differentials including most of the conditions which involve the alimentary tract or the nervous system, for example:-

1. Lead poisoning.
2. Coccidiosis.
3. Mucosal disease.
4. Salmonellosis.
5. Antimony poisoning.

Treatment

The earlier treatment is started, the more likely is a successful outcome. Sulphur-containing drugs such as sodium thiosulphate are of use, the dose for cattle varies from 5 - 30 g in 50 - 200 ml water i.v., plus oral dosing with 15 - 60 g about four times a day. Liquid paraffin orally may help to remove arsenic from the gut. Fluid therapy should be undertaken and water supplies should be adequate. Younger animals should be encouraged to drink milk or milk substitutes and be kept warm.

Control

Always ensure arsenic compounds are handled carefully and stored correctly. It is probable that on some farms there are still supplies of arsenic dip and anthelmintic around, and these should be destroyed.

Reference

BLOOD, D C, RADOSTITS, O M and HENDERSON, J A (1983) "Veterinary Medicine" 6th edition, Bailliere Tindall, London. pp. 1098-1102.

Bracken Poisoning

Aetiology

Ingestion of bracken (*Pteridium aquilinum*). The toxin causing the problems in ruminants has not been identified but it does not seem to be the same as the thiaminase present in the plant. Acute toxicity can be produced with ptaquiloside, a norsequiterpene glucoside.

Occurrence

Although uncommon, it is the second most frequently-diagnosed form of poisoning, according to the Veterinary Investigation Centres. The plant tends to be most toxic when young, growing plants or their rhizomes are consumed. Usually a relatively large amount has to be ingested before any signs occur, and this usually happens when there is little other available forage. The condition results from a depression in bone marrow activity leading to a reduction in blood platelets and granular leucocytes, capillary fragility and terminally there is a reduction in erythrocytes. A depression in white cells often allows a bacteraemia to occur. Signs are not usually evident until the bracken has been consumed for two to eight weeks, so that cases can occur several weeks after the animals have been removed from the bracken. Usually only one or two animals are affected, but most of these die.

Signs

Often there is a loss of condition, with a dry skin. There is then the sudden appearance of dysentery or melaena with haemorrhages from the mouth, nose, vagina and eyes. Pyrexia usually occurs with a high temperature of 40.5 - 43°C (105 - 109°F) and respiratory and heart rates tend to be accelerated. Haemorrhages may be present under the mucosa and skin. Death usually occurs one to five days after signs develop.

Necropsy

Haemorrhages are usually found throughout the carcase and viscera and vary from petechial haemorrhages to large losses of blood. There may be necrosis and sloughing of the mucosa in various organs, particularly those of the alimentary tract. The liver, kidneys and lungs often show infarctions and necrotic areas.

Diagnosis

1. History of exposure to bracken.
2. Clinical signs.
3. Platelets usually reduced from about 500,000/mm^3 to 40,000/mm^3.
4. White cells are depressed from about 4,000 to 10,000/mm^3, to 1,000/mm^3.
5. Erythrocyte counts tend to fall terminally.
6. Urine may contain many erythrocytes and epithelial cells.

Differential diagnosis

1. Anthrax but organism not present.
2. Pasteurellosis but again organism not found.

3. Leptospirosis but there is no sign of this organism being present.
4. Babesiasis, but usually with this there are no haemorrhages.
5. Sweet vernal grass poisoning, but history should confirm.
6. Blackleg, but again haemorrhages are not a prominent feature.
7. Furazolidone poisoning.

Treatment

The injection of 1 g DL-batyl alcohol can be given daily intravenously or subcutaneously for four to five days in an attempt to stimulate the bone marrow. In all cases, because of the white cell depression, there should be adequate antibiotic cover. Blood transfusions can also be given.

Control

Bracken areas should be fenced off to prevent access and killed with a bracken killer. If access to bracken cannot be helped then adequate feed should be provided.

Brassica Species Poisoning

Kale poisoning, rape poisoning.

Aetiology

Most cases of cattle poisoning involve kale which results in a haemolytic anaemia due to conversion of S-methyl cysteine sulphoxide to dimethyl disulphide.

Occurrence

Although many cattle receive kale during the autumn and early winter, clinical cases of the condition are uncommon. Subclinical problems are, however, slightly more common with about six per cent of dairy cows having low haemoglobin values. Haemolytic anaemia results from the presence of S-methyl cysteine sulphoxide (SMCO) in the kale plant. Naturally-occurring bacteria in the rumen convert SMCO to dimethyl disulphide(DS). The higher the amount of kale fed the more severe and more rapidly does anaemia develop. SMCO levels tend to increase as the plant matures. Although the toxic principle is destroyed by heat or ensilaging, it remains in the frozen plant. Some cases are associated with cold weather and it is thought that cattle with a phosphorus deficiency are more likely to be affected.

The toxic dose of SMCO is 15 g/100 kg BW and this produces a fatal anaemia. Ingestion needs to continue for at least a week. In experiments the haemoglobin level took two to three weeks to fall to 5 g/100 ml (normal 8 - 15 g/100 ml) when only kale was fed, whereas it only fell to 6 - 7 g/100 ml in four to five weeks when kale formed a third of the dry matter intake. The DS precipitates haemoglobin producing Heinz-Ehrlich bodies. Signs tend to be more severe in the period just prior to or after calving, possibly associated with phosphorus deficiency. Bloat very occasionally occurs and may be due to cyanogenetic glycosides.

Signs

Peracute

A few animals will show such a severe anaemia that they collapse and die.

Acute

These animals tend to develop a haemoglobinuria usually three weeks after grazing the kale. They then become dull and weak with pale mucous membranes which may lead on to jaundice. Usually the rectal temperature is normal but it may rise to 40.5^{o}C (105°F) with tachycardia and a slight increase in the rate and depth of respirations. In some cases there is diarrhoea. Untreated cases will usually die whereas those treated often take a month to six weeks to fully recover.

Chronic

The animal is slightly dull and may have a slight red tinge to the urine which could be missed. There is a reduction in the blood haemoglobin level.

Subclinical

No signs are apparent but haematologically there is a mild anaemia.

Bloat

On some occasions bloat will occur with kale feeding.

Necropsy

The carcase may be pale or jaundiced. The blood tends to be thin and watery with haemoglobinuria. The kidneys and liver may be dark-coloured. On histology the liver shows necrosis.

Diagnosis

1. History of kale feeding.
2. Signs of anaemia, jaundice, haemoglobinuria.
3. Haematological examination shows a reduced erythrocyte count with Heinz-Ehrlich bodies present in the cells.
4. The haematocrit is low and the anaemia is macrocytic.
5. The white cell count tends to be reduced.
6. Haemoglobin levels are usually below 6 g/100 ml.
7. Biochemically there is often a hypophosphataemia (normal = 1.2 - 2.3 mmol/l - 4 - 7 mg/100 ml).

Differential diagnosis

1. Babesiasis, but depends on area of Britain and usually at a different time of year.
2. Bacillary haemoglobinuria but it is rare and there is a fever.
3. Post parturient haemoglobinuria but only in freshly-calved cows.
4. Leptospirosis but usually pyrexia and jaundice.
5. Chronic copper poisoning but history of copper feeding and blood and liver copper levels are high.

Treatment

Reduce or stop kale feeding and put the animals onto a highly nutritious diet. In the acute case, blood transfusion of at least 4.5 litres of blood will be required. Iron injections can be useful.

Prevention

Allow the animals access to good quality hay or silage before they are turned onto the kale. Cattle should be closely supervised once turned onto kale. A maximum of 20 kg (45 lb) of kale daily should be given to each cow.

Copper Poisoning

Aetiology

The main problem is exposure to large amounts of soluble copper salts.

Occurrence

The condition is uncommon but can occur in cattle of all ages. It may be seen in animals at pasture following the use of copper sulphate either during the control of the intermediate snail host (*Limnaea truncatula*) of liver fluke or to overcome copper deficiency. At present a more likely cause of the problem is the over-zealous use of copper preparations either by injection or as supplements to counteract marginal copper deficiency problems (Mylrea and Byrne, 1974). Occasionally high levels of copper occur in the diet and can cause problems. Acceptable levels of copper in feed are about 10 mg/kg DM. Mortality approaches 100 *per cent*. High oral ingestion of copper results in alimentary irritation and shock. In chronic cases there is a gradual accumulation of copper in the liver until a toxic level is reached when intravascular haemolysis occurs due to protein coagulation. The same signs also occur in acute cases which survive long enough. In most outbreaks several animals are affected at one time.

Signs

Acute

If the copper has been ingested there is severe alimentary mucosal irritation which results in diarrhoea with mucus, often with a blue-green tinge to it. There is also increased thirst and the animal shows bouts of abdominal pain with an arched back. In most cases there occurs a subnormal temperature, an increased heart rate and then collapse and death. Some cattle show dysentery and if the animal survives long enough, haemoglobinuria and jaundice appear. When the source of copper is introduced by injection the animals tend to be initially bright but show anorexia with increased dehydration, followed by haemoglobinuria, haemorrhages and ascites. Death in acute cases is often within a day of onset of signs.

Chronic

If relatively high values of copper have been taken in with the feed then there is no diarrhoea, but the sudden occurrence of jaundice, anorexia, depression and haemoglobinuria. The animal normally dies in 1 to 2 days.

Necropsy

In most cases there is jaundice, haemoglobinuria, an enlarged, yellow liver with a large gall bladder, a friable spleen and swollen friable kidneys. In acute cases, death may occur before these signs appear and then there is usually evidence of severe irritation of the alimentary mucosa with abomasitis, enteritis and often abomasal ulceration. When an injection is the source of the copper then there tends to be ascites, hydrothorax, hydropericardium, centrilobular necrosis of the liver and renal tubular necrosis (Mylrea and Byrne, 1974).

Diagnosis

This is often much easier than with many of the other poisonings.

1. Knowledge of copper usage on the farm or administration to the animal.

2. The signs of jaundice, haemoglobinuria and diarrhoea with a blue-green tinge.

3. The plasma copper levels will be high (the normal is 100 µg/100 ml; 15.7 mmol/l).

4. Liver copper levels will be high (the normal is about 350 ppm dry matter).

5. Kidney copper levels are high.

6. The packed cell volume decreases from the normal of about 35 per cent.

7. Aspartate transferase (AST, SGOT) levels are increased from the normal of 20 - 50 iu/l.

8. The urine should be checked for haemoglobinuria.

9. Laboratory analysis of the feed can be undertaken.

Differential diagnosis

This tends to be most difficult in animals with acute enteritis or following an injection when no jaundice or haemolytic crisis has occurred.

1. Fluorosis.
2. Arsenic poisoning.
3. Lead poisoning.
4. Mercury poisoning.

Treatment

British Anti-Lewisite (BAL) given at a level of 40 mg/kg BW as an injection is of some benefit and it should be repeated for three or four days. There is usually considerable reaction around the site of injection.

Control

Remove the ration if this is considered the source of the trouble, or take the cattle off the suspect pasture. Never give copper injections unless blood samples or liver biopsies taken from a sample of the group show a deficiency to be present.

Reference

MYLREA, P J and BYRNE, D T (1974) Australian Veterinary Journal, 50, 169-170.

Ergot Poisoning

Aetiology

It occurs following the ingestion of sclerotia of *Claviceps purpurea*, a fungus. *Claviceps* is a parasite of cereals such as barley, wheat and particularly rye, and also many grasses. The sclerotia are black, enlarged bodies of about 2 cm length. They occur soon after the plants produce their inflorescences. When ripe, the sclerotia fall to the ground. The ergots contain many alkaloids of which the water-soluble ergotamine and ergometrine, and the water-insoluble ergotoxine are the most important.

Occurrence

The condition only occurs if large quantities of contaminated grain are consumed. Ergotamine causes central nervous signs to occur. The chronic form is more common than the acute type. In the chronic form, signs occur about 2 to 4 weeks after starting to ingest the contaminated feed and they include vasoconstriction.

Signs

Acute - Severe

There may be periods of nervous depression and drowsiness. There may be intermittent blindness and deafness. The heart shows irregularities and there is occasionally diarrhoea. As the condition worsens, there are periods of convulsions and coma followed by apparent recovery. Many animals die, often during convulsions.

Mild

Some animals may show periods of reduced or increased skin sensitivity and intermittent periods of blindness and deafness.

Chronic

There is lameness of one or more limbs with the hind limbs being usually first affected. The areas involved, which are normally the fetlock regions of the limbs and the tail tip, become swollen and reddened. There is a loss of sensation and coldness to the area with an indented ring below the knee or hock as though a tourniquet had been placed on the leg. The hooves are shed in severe cases and also sometimes the tips of the ears and tail. In some cases there is alimentary tract discomfort with a tucked-up appearance and lethargy.

Necropsy

Acute

There may be capillary changes in the brain and other affected organs.

Chronic

Gangrene of the lower limbs, tail or ears.

Diagnosis

In the acute form specific diagnosis is hard, but in the chronic stage it is relatively easy.

1. The feed should be examined for the presence of sclerotia. This is best done by looking at the feed prior to milling.

Differential diagnosis

1. Other poisonings.
2. Chronic salmonella infection.

Treatment

There is no effective therapy. However, the feed should be discontinued.

Control

Pastures heavily infested with ergot should not be used. The grass can be cut at a time when the grasses first show their inflorescences, but special care must be taken of the grass near hedgerows, fences, etc.

Ethylenediamine Hydroiodide Poisoning

Aetiology

Overusage of the compound ethylenediamine hydroiodide.

Occurrence

The compound is used in America and Sweden (Andersson and Tornquist, 1983) to treat or prevent various conditions including interdigital pododermatitis, actinomycosis, infertility, mastitis and respiratory disease. It contains 80 per cent iodine. The material is little used in Britain.

The normal requirement of iodine for growing cattle is 0.25 mg/kg dry matter of the feed, which is equivalent to 0.01 mg/kg BW of iodine. A level of 1 mg/kg BW of ethylenediamine hydroiodide has produced signs similar to those of respiratory disease. This is thought to be due to impairment of the cell-mediated and humoral immune mechanisms (Haggard, Stowe, Conner and Johnson, 1980).

Signs

Signs are usually respiratory in nature with pyrexia (40-41°C; 104-106°F), nasal discharge, lachrymation and coughing. There may be reduced weight gain.

Diagnosis

History of usage of ethylenediamine hydroiodide.

Treatment

Withdraw the compound.

References

ANDERSSON, L and TORNQUIST, M (1983) Veterinary Record, 113, 215-216.

HAGGARD, D L, STOWE, H D, CONNER, G H and JOHNSON, D W (1980) American Journal of Veterinary Research, 41, 539.

Fluorosis

Aetiology

Various fluoride compounds differ in their toxicity. Thus sodium fluoride is very toxic whereas calcium fluoride and sodium fluosilicate are less so.

Occurrence

The condition is uncommon and is confined to certain areas, particularly near brickworks, iron foundries, etc. Grass in such areas, as well as hay and water, may become contaminated. Fluoride does not pass the placental barrier or appear in high levels in the milk so that intoxication in the calf is the direct result of ingestion. Plants do not absorb fluorine and so most of the problem arises from surface contamination. Some problems have arisen when feeding bone flour containing high levels of fluoride. Serious effects occur when ingestion levels are in the region of 30 ppm. Tooth problems occur at 10 ppm and a few lesions occur at a level of 5 ppm. Safe intakes of fluorine are less than 1 mg/kg BW. Most cases of intoxication have been in suckler herds or the result of concentrate mixtures with high fluoride levels. The signs of alimentary irritation are the result of the production of hydrofluoric acid. On absorption calcium fluoride is formed and so hyperaesthesia may occur.

Signs

Acute

The signs are usually of alimentary stasis with constipation or diarrhoea. Dyspnoea is common and nervous signs, including muscular tremor and weakness may be present. There is, later on, tetany leading to collapse and death.

Chronic

In the growing animal lesions of the teeth are the main signs. Because the element does not pass the placental barrier, lesions only occur in the permanent teeth. There is mottling or pigmentation (yellow, brown or black) of the teeth in the rostral or cheek teeth. The lesions may not be very evident until the teeth have erupted for a few months. Excessive attrition of the teeth may occur. Lameness and unthriftiness can also be seen. There may be stiffness and a painful gait. Any joint can be affected but usually it involves the hip or joints of the hind limbs.

Necropsy

Acute

A severe abomasitis and enteritis is present in acute cases. Degeneration of the liver, kidney and heart muscle may be present.

Chronic

There is hypoplasia of the enamel and dentine. The intra-articular structures can often show marked spur formation. Histologically there is defective and irregular calcification of newly-formed osseous tissue.

Diagnosis

This is extremely difficult unless there is a reason to believe fluoride is present.

1. Exposure to fluoride as near brickworks, etc.
2. There are high blood levels to fluorine, the normal is 0.2 mg/ 100 ml blood.
3. The urine level of fluorine is increased, the normal is 3-6 ppm.
4. The laboratory analysis of feed and herbage is useful (the level should be below 1 mg/kg BW of total feed intake).
5. Analysis of bones and teeth *post mortem*.

Differential diagnosis

Acute

1. Lead poisoning.
2. Arsenic poisoning.
3. Coccidiosis.
4. Copper poisoning.
5. Meningitis.
6. Hypomagnesaemia.
7. Pneumonia.
8. Mercury poisoning.

Chronic

1. Phosphorus deficiency but lesions different.
2. Calcium deficiency but lesions different.
3. Vitamin D deficiency but lesions different.

Treatment

Remove the animals from the source of the problem. Give calcium borogluconate i.v., and gastro-intestinal astringents orally, e.g. kaolin, chalk, etc. Aluminium salts are of use by combining with fluoride and preventing absorption, aluminium hydroxide or aluminium sulphate can be used at a level of 10 - 20 g orally daily. Glucose injections are also recommended.

Control

Remove the cattle from the contaminated pasture or discontinue use of the suspect feed.

Formaldehyde Poisoning

Also known as formalin poisoning.

Aetiology

Due to ingestion of formaldehyde (formalin).

Occurrence

The condition is very unusual and normally arises as the result of lack of available water. It occurs mainly in calves and growing cattle (Mitchell and Law, 1984).

Signs

Severe

There is dullness, abdominal pain, weak pulse leading to coma and death.

Less Severe

Such animals show salivation with inflammation of the gingivae and soft palate.

Necropsy

Oedema of ruminal pillars and abomasal folds is seen. There is enteritis and formaldehyde is present in the ruminal contents.

Diagnosis

1. Access to formaldehyde.
2. Signs (inflammation of oral mucosa).
3. *Post mortem* presence of formaldehyde in rumen.
4. High blood urea levels.
5. Often high serum aspartate aminotransferase levels (AST;SGOT).

Differential diagnosis

1. Foot-and-mouth disease.
2. Actinobacillosis.

Treatment

There is no specific treatment and so all therapy is symptomatic, using multivitamin injections and cardiac-respiratory stimulants.

Control

Ensure that there is no access to formaldehyde, and that water is always available to cattle.

Reference

MITCHELL, G B B and LAW, J M (1984) Veterinary Record 115, 283-284.

Iodine Poisoning

Also known as iodism.

Aetiology

This is usually due to overuse of sodium or potassium iodide salts in the therapy of iodine deficiency, actinobacillosis, and, in the past, ringworm.

Occurrence

The condition is now uncommon as iodine is little used in therapy these days.

Signs

These depend on the method of administration.

Intravenous - the animal can show considerable discomfort with dyspnoea, staggering and tachycardia.

Subcutaneous - there is swelling following injection for about two days and local discomfort for about two hours after administration.

Oral - the coat becomes stary, with a scaly skin, often with a fine white dandruff. There is excessive lachrymation and nasal discharge with, in some cases, a degree of inappetance.

Abortion

Abortion has been recorded in heavily pregnant animals following sodium iodide injection.

Treatment and Control

If problems with i.v. therapy, give the iodine subcutaneously or orally. Following toxicity with oral therapy, iodine treatment should be discontinued.

Lead Poisoning

Aetiology

It is the most common type of poisoning in growing cattle and is due to the ingestion of lead.

Occurrence

Although the commonest form of cattle poisoning, it is still relatively unusual. The common source of lead is still paint, usually in the form of painted doors, walls or partitions, although lead-free paints have been available for many years. Other sources include car batteries, putty, roofing felt and engine sump oil. Many cases occur soon after turnout and are due to the inquisitive nature of cattle. Sometimes the condition is seen following access to bonfires where the remains of paint may be found in the ashes. Conditions of underfeeding, overcrowding, lack of roughage or boredom can tend to increase the amount of licking activity and thereby predispose to lead poisoning. Environmental pollution by the effluent from factories or pasture contaminated with car exhaust fumes can also occasionally result in poisoning. Much lead will pass unchanged in the faeces, although the acid conditions in the reticulo-rumen allow some conversion to soluble lead acetate. A single dose of lead acetate at 200 - 400 mg/kg BW has been lethal. The signs are due to alimentary disturbance and degeneration of the brain and central nervous tissue. The most common form of the condition is acute. Mortality in untreated cases is often high and can approach 100 per cent.

Signs

Acute

The signs may well be delayed several days after ingestion. As animals may die within 12 - 24 hours of first becoming ill, often cattle are found dead with no premonitory signs. Those found alive tend to be restless, bellow and sporadically grind their teeth. Blindness is present with muscular twitching of the head, neck and ears. The pulse and respirations are fast and the temperature is normal or just ½ - 1°C (1 - 2°F) up. Hyperexcitability may occur with collapse, clonic-tonic convulsions and bellowing. Other nervous signs include maniacal walking around the box with a stiff, jerky action, trying to climb up the walls and falling over. Some cattle are very difficult to handle and may attack people when approached. Death occurs due to respiratory paralysis while in a convulsion.

Subacute

These animals remain alive longer - up to five days - and tend to be depressed. There is again evidence of teeth grinding, anorexia, abdominal pain, bellowing, salivation, ruminal stasis and diarrhoea which is often black and rancid. As with the acute phase, there is blindness, lack of a palpebral reflex, muscular tremors, incoordination with hyperaesthesia to stimuli. Ophthalmoscopic examination reveals congested blood vessels and oedema of the optic disc. The animal will tend to stand still for long periods. Later recumbency and death occur, although others die in accidents.

Necropsy

Gross signs are usually absent in acute cases. In the subacute condition the reticulo-rumen can be examined for traces of lead, e.g. paint flakes, etc. and there may be abomasitis and enteritis. The liver tends to show fatty degeneration as the animal will have been anorectic and there is kidney degeneration. Haemorrhages may be found on the omentum, rumen, liver, kidney and epicardium. The lungs show congestion. In the brain there is congestion of the meningeal and cerebral blood vessels with meningeal haemorrhages in some cases.

Diagnosis

1. Finding a source of lead.
2. Nervous signs, including blindness and a lack of a palpebral reflex (in cerebrocortical necrosis the reflex is normal).
3. Ruminal stasis.
4. *Post mortem* kidney lead levels are better than those of the liver. A kidney level of 25 ppm in wet tissue is diagnostic.
5. The liver tissue levels are usually 10 - 20 ppm wet tissue.
6. Anaemia may be present which is microcytic and hypochromic.
7. The blood lead level will be higher than the normal of 0.05 - 0.25 ppm.
8. The faecal lead estimation will be above the normal which is up to 35 ppm.
9. γ-aminolaevulinic acid dehydratase in the blood is reduced and urinary levels are increased.

Differential diagnosis

1. Hypomagnesaemic tetany.
2. Tetanus.
3. Vitamin A deficiency.
4. Meningitis.
5. Cerebrocortical necrosis.
6. Anthrax.
7. Mercury poisoning.
8. Polyarthritis.
9. Muscular dystrophy.

Treatment

The animal should be kept quiet and sedation with chloral hydrate or xylazine can be of use. Calcium versenate (calcium disodium ethylene diamine acetate) can be given slowly by i.v. injection in doses of 33 - 110 mg/kg BW using a 12½ *per cent* solution and repeating after six to eight hours. Too quick an injection causes muscular fasciculation and increased heart and respiratory rates. The solution can be given s.c. but to avoid pain it should be diluted to a one to two *per cent* solution with glucose. Usually there is an improvement in 24 hours and the animal is able to stand in 48 hours with recovery from all signs except for blindness in five days. However, the blindness may remain for up to three weeks. There is still probably lead in the alimentary tract and the use of magnesium sulphate (Epsom salts) given as a saturated solution twice daily for three or four days is of use. As it is a saline purgative, diarrhoea will occur.

The use of parenteral glucose saline will help prevent dehydration and prophylactic antibiotics should be given to prevent pneumonia following the congestion of the lungs.

Nursing

The animal must be kept quiet and in a darkened box. Good quality feeds should be used to try to encourage the animal to eat.

Control

The source of lead should be found and removed. Ensure all paints used in buildings and on equipment are lead-free. As the condition is more likely to occur in poorly-fed animals, ensure that there is adequate feed of good quality available and that there is adequate trough space per animal.

Linseed Poisoning

Aetiology

Linseed contains linamarin, a cyanogenetic glycoside and an enzyme, linase. When these two react, glucose, acetone and hydrocyanic acid are formed. Reaction between the glycoside and enzyme only occurs in warm, moist conditions, a temperature of 38°C (100°F) being ideal. At lower temperatures the quantities of hydrocyanic acid are only slowly produced.

Occurrence

At one time much linseed was used in gruels for calves. The condition is only rarely seen today, although linseed is still used in some concentrate feeds. If linseed cake is fed as a warm mash or wet linseed cake is used, the hydrocyanic acid dissolves in the water. On entry to the abomasum it is released as a gas which is rapidly absorbed. The condition is often worse if the linseed is wetted and allowed to stand for half-an-hour. When linseed cake is fed dry only a small amount of hydrocyanic acid is released, which is unharmful.

Signs

Peracute

About 15 to 45 minutes after feeding the animal will start to stagger, bellow and go into convulsions. There is involuntary evacuation of the faeces, but without diarrhoea and opisthotonus. There is dyspnoea and the mucous membranes become bright red. Nystagmus and dilated pupils later occur and the pulse is rapid, weak and ultimately results in cyanosis. Death occurs in convulsions.

Acute

There is dullness, dyspnoea and staggering. In some animals there may be hyperaesthesia and muscle tremors which start with the head and neck and later they involve the rest of the body. Normally the animal will recover in about an hour of the start of signs, but it may appear dazed. There are no lasting ill effects.

Necropsy

In most cases the blood is dark red due to anoxia, but it may be bright red. The blood may be slow to clot and there are subepicardial and subendocardial haemorrhages. There may be congestion and haemorrhage in the trachea, lungs, abomasum and small intestines. A bitter almond smell may be present in the abomasum or rumen.

Diagnosis

1. Feeding linseed cake.
2. Sudden onset after eating.
3. The blood has a bright red colour.
4. There may be nervous signs.
5. Hydrocyanic acid can be tested for by putting some feed material into a test tube with a little water and a few drops of chloroform. This should be gently warmed for five minutes with sodium picrate paper which turns from yellow to red when hydrocyanic acid is present.

Differential diagnosis

1. Anaphylaxis.
2. Nitrate poisoning.

Treatment

Intravenous injection with 1 g sodium nitrite and 2.5 g sodium thiosulphate in 50 ml water is a help. Etamiphylline camsylate injections may also be useful.

Control

If linseed mashes are to be fed they should be boiled for at least ten minutes. Otherwise linseed cake or linseed meal must be fed dry.

Male Fern Poisoning

Aetiology

The ingestion of the male fern *Dryopteris felix mas*.

Occurrence

The condition is very uncommon but can occur in animals kept outside and being partially starved. It is most likely to occur at the start of the spring and will often involve ingestion of rhizomes.

Signs

Animals tend to be dull with a normal temperature. There is usually a degree of blindness with the pupils dilated and unresponsive to light.

Prognosis

Some animals may become permanently blind.

Treatment

Remove cattle from the source of the plant.

Mercury Poisoning

Aetiology

Most cases occur as the result of the ingestion of seed grain which has been dressed with a fungicide such as phenyl mercuric chloride (PMC) or phenyl mercuric acetate (PMA). Organic mercurial fungicides are now banned.

Occurrence

At the present time this form of toxicity is extremely rare. When cases occur they are due to the accidental ingestion of fungicide-treated grain. The signs tend to be chronic and a daily intake of 10 mg/kg BW is required for toxicity to occur. The mercury causes degeneration of the mucosa and after absorption there is capillary damage of the mouth, colon and kidney.

Signs

Peracute

Death occurs in a few hours after marked abdominal pain and severe diarrhoea, and is due to dehydration and shock.

Acute

There is usually marked salivation, abdominal pain, followed by intense straining with diarrhoea or dysentery. The temperature is often raised and there are increased pulse and respiratory rates. In some animals nervous signs occur with blindness, posterior paralysis and terminally, convulsions.

Chronic

The animal loses condition, and it is dull, inappetant and often the gait is stiff. The mouth may show a diffuse stomatitis with an offensive odour present. The teeth may become loose and if the animal survives they drop out. Alopecia and skin lesions may be seen around the anus and vulva. Occasionally there are muscular tremors, incoordination, convulsions and dyspnoea.

Necropsy

There is inflammation of the abomasum, small and large intestine. The liver and kidneys are swollen and the lungs show oedema and haemorrhages. In chronic cases a stomatitis is present. Histologically there are degenerative changes in the kidney, brain and spinal cord.

Diagnosis

1. There is often a history of access to mercury compounds.
2. The signs of abdominal pain, diarrhoea, dysentery, stomatitis, dehydration and nervous signs are helpful.
3. The *post mortem* mercury levels in the kidneys are high - often in the region of 100 ppm.
4. The urinary values for alkaline phosphatase and gamma glutamyl transpeptidase are raised.

Differential diagnosis

1. Fluorosis.
2. Arsenic poisoning.
3. Lead poisoning.
4. Copper poisoning.
5. Molybdenum poisoning.

Treatment

As protein is coagulated by mercury then the use of albumen in the form of eggs or milk is of use. Intestinal astringents such as kaolin, and chalk, should also be given. Sodium thiosulphate at a level of 2 - 2.5 g in about 25 ml of water i.v. can be injected, followed by oral doses of 5 - 7 g four times daily. British Anti-Lewisite (BAL) can be injected i.m. at a dose rate of 4.0 mg/kg BW (2.0 mg/lb) or more every four hours if the condition is caught early. The injections can result in considerable reaction as well as pain.

Control

All feed and seed grain should be kept separately. If it is necessary to feed seed grain then it should comprise less than 10 per cent of the diet.

Molybdenum Poisoning

Aetiology

This occurs in areas with high soil molybdenum levels, i.e. 10 ppm or greater.

Occurrence

The condition is relatively common in growing cattle in some areas and is also occasionally seen in young suckler calves. It only occurs where there is a high molybdenum status to the soil such as in the teart areas of Somerset. Plants can then contain 3 - 10 ppm molybdenum. There is a relationship with copper and sulphur in that high sulphur and low copper levels exacerbate the condition. Under such conditions levels of 1 ppm can be toxic but on more normal pastures levels under 3 ppm are acceptable. Clovers take up more molybdenum than grasses and levels tend to be high in the spring and autumn. The condition is really one of secondary copper deficiency resulting from interference with copper storage.

Signs

A profuse, persistent diarrhoea, yellow-green to black in colour with an inoffensive odour occurs at pasture. The tail is often not elevated when the faeces are passed and so it and the buttocks become matted with faeces. The animals tend to be dull and lose condition although appetite is good. Depigmentation of the hair may be seen and bone changes involving rarefaction, thickening of the carpal and tarsal joints can occur and a stiff gait develops.

Necropsy

The carcase is usually in poor condition and dehydrated. Other signs are few but there is no enteritis and if secondary copper deficiency is present in the liver, spleen and kidney may contain haemosiderin deposits. There may be synovial capsule thickening of the carpal and tarsal joints as well as bone rarefaction.

Diagnosis

1. The areas where the condition occurs are well-defined.
2. The animals are at pasture.
3. The signs of diarrhoea, bone changes and hair depigmentation.
4. Plasma copper values can be determined; the normal is over 15 mmol/l (100 μg/100 ml).
5. The blood molybdenum level is high, the normal value is about 0.05 ppm.
6. Liver copper levels are low and in normal animals they are usually more than 100 ppm DM.
7. Haemoglobin levels are low, they are normally in the range 8.0 - 15.0 g/100 ml.
8. The erythrocyte count is low (the normal range is 5 - 10 million/μl).
9. There is a response to copper therapy.

Differential diagnosis

1. Salmonellosis.
2. Winter dysentery.
3. Arsenic poisoning.
4. Coccidiosis.
5. Fluorosis.
6. Salt poisoning.

Treatment

The cattle can be treated orally with weekly doses of 1.5 - 4 g copper sulphate, according to age. However, in most outbreaks today therapy is administered by injection. Methionine copper complex can be used to give 40 - 100 mg copper i.m. or copper calcium edetate provides 50 - 100 mg copper s.c., or diethylamine copper oxyquinoline sulphonate at a level of 12 mg/50 kg BW s.c. Copper sulphate can also be given i.v. to cattle at a level of 200 mg - 1 g copper sulphate (50 - 250 mg copper) in a dilute solution.

Control

The copper content of the diet should be kept at about 10 ppm. Oral dosing with about 1.5 g copper sulphate weekly will prevent the problem, as will injections of methionine copper complex or diethylamine oxyquinoline sulphonate or calcium copper edetate. These parenteral treatments should be given at intervals dependent on the lowering of copper levels in routine blood samples. Recently oral cupric oxide needles have been suggested as being useful (Suttle, 1981a). They contain about 80 per cent copper in gelatin capsules and dosage is dependent on the degree of copper deficiency. The provision of copper sulphate in the drinking water supplied by a proportioner has kept blood copper levels normal in cattle grazing molybdenum-rich pastures (Farmer, Adams and Humphries, 1982). Intra-ruminal boluses of soluble glass containing copper are now available.

References

FARMER, P E, ADAMS, T E and HUMPHRIES, W R (1982) Veterinary Record, 111, 193-195.

SUTTLE, N F (1981a) Veterinary Record, 108, 417-420.

Monensin Poisoning

Aetiology

The excessive intake of monensin.

Occurrence

The condition is relatively uncommon as cattle tend to lose their appetites on a feed containing too much monensin. Most cases occur as the result of mistakes in mixing or adding monensin to a diet which the farmer is unaware already contains the compound. Feed should contain 20 to 40 ppm and when fed as a supplement it is given at the level of 125 mg/head/day up to 250 kg (550 lb) BW, 250 mg/head/day from 250 - 450 kg (550 - 990 lb) BW and 360 mg/head/day over 450 kg (990 lb) BW.

Signs

There is usually some degree of inappetance and this, in severe cases, may lead to a refusal to eat the supplemented feed. There is often lethargy and some cattle show diarrhoea. The heart rate may be increased with marked dyspnoea. Some animals may die.

Necropsy

Signs often include those of heart failure (Wardrope, Macleod and Sloan, 1983). The heart tends to be enlarged and globular and in some cases there are yellow-brown areas of necrosis of the ventricular myocardium but these are hard to detect on the epicardial surface (Van Vleet, Amstutz, Weirich, Rebar and Ferrans, 1983). There may be oedema of various organs including the lungs and mesentery. Fluid may be found in the pericardium, thorax and abdomen. The liver and other organs may be swollen and there may be gastroenteritis. Histologically, the myocardium shows damage of the myocytes with sarcoplasmic vacuolation and necrosis with contraction bands.

Diagnosis

1. History of overfeeding monensin or a change in feed.
2. Dyspnoea and increased heart rate, gastroenteritis.
3. Increased serum levels of SGOT (AST) and CK can occur.
4. Decreased serum levels of sodium, potassium and calcium.
5. Leucocytosis.

Differential diagnosis

1. Acidosis but history should help.
2. Selenium deficiency but other signs usually present.
3. Pneumonia.

Treatment

Therapy is symptomatic but can include etamiphylline camsylate to stimulate the cardiac and respiratory systems. Corticosteroids can be used to reduce pulmonary oedema and counteract shock. Diuretics such as frusemide may be helpful. Prophylactic antibiotics may be required to prevent bacterial invasion of the lungs.

Control

Ensure only recommended dose of monensin is used. Always check rations to ensure that monensin is not already present before supplementation is undertaken.

References

VAN VLEET, J F, AMSTUTZ, H E, WEIRICH, W E, REBAR, A H and FERRANS, V J (1983) American Journal of Veterinary Research, 44, 2133-2144.

WARDROPE, D D, MACLEOD, N S M and SLOAN, J R (1983) Veterinary Record, 112, 560-561.

Nitrate Poisoning

Aetiology

This is caused by nitrate which is converted in the rumen to nitrite.

Occurrence

Poisoning is uncommon but its incidence may well rise with increasing levels of nitrogen usage on grass, etc. Plants with more than 1.5 *per cent* nitrate in the dry matter are potentially toxic. Nitrate levels can be high in well or pond water polluted with leaves or other rotting organic matter, cereals and turnips. Cases can occur following uneven spreading of nitrogen on grass either when eaten at the time or following its conversion to hay. Poorly fed animals are more susceptible and a diet rich in fermentable carbohydrate is thought to reduce nitrate production. Nitrates in the feed are converted in the rumen to nitrites and both nitrites and nitrates can be absorbed into the blood. Cattle can successfully deal with some quantities of nitrite which enter the blood and then are passed out in the urine via the kidney. However, with over a certain amount of nitrite entering the blood, toxic levels rapidly result. Nitrate is caustic to the alimentary mucosa whereas nitrite, after absorption, causes methaemoglobin formation and vasodilation.

Signs

Acute

The animals tend to die in about 12 to 24 hours. They show anoxia, dyspnoea, and nervous signs such as muscle tremors, weakness, staggering gait and, eventially, convulsions. There is abdominal pain and diarrhoea. The mucous membranes tend to be bluish and there is a fast pulse with a normal or subnormal temperature. Methaemoglobinuria occurs. Animals which recover usually do so very rapidly.

Chronic

Long term ingestion of nitrite was at one time considered to be a cause of abortion and increased requirement of vitamin A, although this has been discredited.

Necropsy

The carcase putrefies quickly and has a brown colour, as does the blood which fails to clot quickly. Sometimes the myocardium is blanched. *Post mortem* specimens should ideally be taken within an hour of death.

Diagnosis

1. The short duration of illness.
2. The evidence of a possible exposure to a source of nitrate.
3. The signs are helpful, including dyspnoea, methaemoglobinuria and nervous signs.
4. The blood is a dark red or brown colour.
5. The blood methaemoglobin value is high - the normal is 0.12 - 0.2 g/100 ml and samples for such estimations should be collected in formalin or chloroform.

6. Urine samples also have a high methaemoglobin content and should again be collected in formalin, chloroform or diluted 1:9 with water.

7. The ingesta or suspect feed should be analysed for nitrate levels.

Differential diagnosis

This is often difficult and it involves all cases of sudden death.

1. Anthrax - all cases of sudden death of unknown origin are suspect. Blood smears should be obtained and stained with polychrome methylene blue to ensure anthrax organisms are absent.

2. Bloat.

3. Hypomagnesaemia.

4. Copper poisoning.

5. Arsenic poisoning.

6. Anaphylactic reactions.

7. Pulmonary oedema.

8. Lightning strike.

Treatment

The oral use of formalin, tungsten or antibiotics may help prevent the formation of nitrite. Methylene blue can be administered i.v. as a one *per cent* solution at a dose rate of 20 mg/kg BW. Etamphylline camsylate can be used i.m. or s.c. at a dose of 7 - 10.5 mg/kg every eight hours.

Control

Ensure that water drinking troughs, ponds, etc. have organic matter removed from them. If a feed is suspect then it should be analysed and the aim should be to have a total level of nitrate intake of 0.6 *per cent*. Several different samples of feed should be looked at as nitrogen concentration tends to fluctuate greatly.

Oak Poisoning

Also called acorn poisoning.

Aetiology

Overingestion of oak (*Quercus robur*) leaves or acorns, in which the toxic principle has not been identified.

Occurrence

Cattle are able to eat acorns and oak leaves satisfactorily if they only form a small part of the diet. Occasionally, in autumn when other feed is reduced, large numbers of acorns may be consumed. Tannin is found in the oak and may be part of the cause of the problem. More poisoning occurs after dry summers.

Signs

There is usually abdominal pain with constipation followed by diarrhoea with blood and mucus in it. There may be polyuria and ventral oedema.

Necropsy

There is nephrosis and severe gastroenteritis.

Diagnosis

1. History of eating acorns or oak leaves.
2. Signs.
3. Blood urea and creatinine levels raised.

Treatment

The addition of calcium hydroxide to the ration can help overcome the problem.

Control

Ensure that cattle receive adequate feed besides the acorns.

Organophosphorus Poisoning

Aetiology

Organophosphorus compounds partially combine with the cholinesterase molecule, thereby inhibiting the activity of the enzyme.

Occurrence

Most of the organophosphorus compounds used in cattle are for the treatment or prevention of warble fly. In the past, several anthelmintics contained the compounds. Some insecticides have an organophosphorus base and in other countries they are used in dips. Occasionally toxicity can result from accidental exposure to crops or orchards sprayed with the compounds.

The activity of acetyl choline is potentiated in tissues at four sites. There is increased activity at (a) the post-ganglionic parasympathetic nerve fibres (muscarinic effects - increases secretions, stimulates smooth muscle, slows heart and peripheral vasodilation); (b) ganglia, both sympathetic and parasympathetic; (c) adrenal medullary chromaffin cells; (d) neuromuscular junction between voluntary nerves and skeletal (striated) muscle. Stimulation at (b), (c) and (d) is described as the nicotinic effect and signs include neuromuscular fasciculation and paralysis.

Route of entry

Ingestion, inhalation or via the skin.

Signs

True toxicity

Signs appear soon (30 minutes to 12 hours) after exposure to the organophosphorus compound. They include increased excitability, muscle tremors and stiffness, dyspnoea, diarrhoea and salivation. Useful signs in making a diagnosis are constriction of the pupil size (miosis) and bradycardia. Death is rare.

True anaphylaxis

Reactions can occur following the destruction of warble fly, with marked respiratory distress, sweating, muscle fasciculations, urticaria, pruritis. These occur 24 to 48 hours after treatment.

Toxic shock reaction

This is thought to be due to the release of toxic materials from dead or dying larvae. These occur 24 to 48 hours after organophosphorus use. Signs include salivation, muscle tremors, lachrymation, kicking, erythema and oedema of the ears and perianal region.

Local reactions

These can follow the killing of larvae and can involve bloat, partial or complete posterior paralysis. The signs are usually delayed one to several days after treatment.

Necropsy

True toxicity produces no specific lesions but material can be used for cholinesterase estimations. In cases of local reactions, haemorrhages or dead warbles may be found in the oesophageal wall or the spinal canal fat.

Diagnosis

1. History - exposure to organophosphorus compounds.
2. Signs - muscle tremors, salivation, miosis, bradycardia.
3. Cholinesterase levels.

Differential diagnosis

1. Fog fever.
2. Hypomagnesaemia.

Treatment

True toxicity

Atropine sulphate counteracts the muscarinic action and should be given intravenously in severe cases. The dose is variable and one of 30 to 60 mg or 0.04 mg/kg BW is usually advised, although doses up to 1 mg/ kg BW have been suggested. 2-pyridine aldoxine methiodide (PAM) overcomes the nicotinic effect and is used at 50 mg/kg. It is administered subcutaneously suspended in 100 - 250 ml of physiological saline, but only 50 ml should be given at one place.

True anaphylaxis

Antihistamines or corticosteroids are recommended.

Toxic shock reaction

Antihistamines or corticosteroids are recommended.

Local reactions

Treatment is symptomatic but antihistamines or corticosteroids may be useful.

Control

Ensure cattle are given the correct dose of the drug.

Ragwort Poisoning

Aetiology

Ingestion of ragwort (*Senecio jacobaea*) which contains various alkaloids including retrosine.

Occurrence

Although uncommon, it is the third most frequently diagnosed form of poisoning in cattle examined at Veterinary Investigation Centres. The plant itself tends to be avoided by cattle unless they are very hungry. It can be incorporated in hay, silage, etc., when it is often more acceptable to the animal. Poisoning results in megalocytosis of the liver parenchyma and also a proliferation of the endothelium of the centrilobular and hepatic veins, leading to their occlusion.

Signs

Signs may occur any time after ragwort ingestion.

Acute

The animals are dull with a sudden loss of condition, diarrhoea and straining, often with rectal prolapse. There is usually marked excitability with a staggering action of the hind limbs and the feet not being lifted off the ground during walking. Some animals walk in circles and have partial blindness. There is often abdominal pain. The mucous membranes may be pale and in some cases there is jaundice or photosensitisation. Death may occur in a few days to a few weeks.

Subacute/Chronic

These animals tend to be dull with, in some cases, signs of photosensitisation with a loss of the white areas of skin over the back.

Necropsy

There is a progressive destruction of hepatic cells and their replacement by fibrosis.

Acute

There is abomasal inflammation with haemorrhages throughout the tissues and viscera. There is also acute hepatic degeneration.

Subacute/Chronic

The liver becomes shrunken with fibrosis. There is ascites and anasarca. Some animals show jaundice or photosensitisation.

Diagnosis

1. History of access to ragwort, plants may be in field, hay or silage.
2. Signs of a nervous nature, plus diarrhoea, rectal prolapse, shuffling gait, with no fever.
3. Liver biopsy shows the hepatic changes.

Differential diagnosis

1. Lead poisoning.

Treatment

This is of limited value. The main object is to aid the liver to recover. Intravenous glucose, glucose saline and multivitamins may be helpful.

Control

Cutting ragwort has little effect on the future plant levels. Remove the weeds either by pulling (but this is a laborious task and will need repeating) or by use of a selective weedkiller. Otherwise graze the area with a less susceptible species such as sheep. The best chemical for control is 2,4 D with MCPA also being very efficient. Spraying should take place between late April to late May and if the grass is to be used for conservation it should have been sprayed the previous autumn, i.e. mid-September to November. Keep stock out of the field for at least three weeks after any spraying. The grassland must be improved to reduce ragwort levels.

Rhododendron Poisoning

Aetiology

Ingestion of rhodododendron (*Rhododendron ponticum*) which contains andromedotoxin.

Occurrence

The condition is very uncommon but can occur if cattle break out into woodland in autumn or winter and are hungry. The leaves contain the toxin.

Signs

Projectile vomiting is usually present and there is often abdominal pain, weakness, staggering and collapse. Death occurs in a few days.

Diagnosis

1. History of access to rhododendrons.

2. Signs, projectile vomiting.

Treatment

The use of purgatives may be helpful.

Control

Ensure cattle do not have access to rhododendrons.

Selenium Poisoning

Aetiology

This occurs following the over-enthusiastic treatment or prophylactic use of selenium in deficiency cases.

Occurrence

This appears to be very rare particularly considering that selenium deficiency is at present an "in vogue" diagnosis. However, with the increasing use of selenium supplements on top of which therapy may also be given, accidents are likely to occur. Injections of 1.2 mg/kg BW selenium are lethal and feeds containing over 5 ppm can be dangerous, as also is the daily intake of 0.25 ppm/kg BW.

Signs

Acute

Nervous signs predominate with blindness and head pressing. There may be evidence of colic, depraved appetite and paralysis. Death is due to respiratory failure (Blood *et al*, 1983).

Chronic

These cases show emaciation, dullness and a staring coat with alopecia, particularly at the base of the tail. Separation of the hoof and swelling of the coronary band occur with resultant lameness.

Necropsy

Acute

The rumen is impacted and the abomasum and small intestines may show necrosis and hyperaemia with ulceration in some cases. Congestion of the kidney and liver are present and the liver shows necrosis. There may be epicardial haemorrhages. Histologically there is damage to the liver, lungs and myocardium.

Chronic

Foot deformities include separation and horn separation. There is a mild enteritis, cirrhosis and liver atrophy, glomerulonephritis and myocardial degeneration (Rosenfeld and Beath, 1964*b*).

Diagnosis

1. History of supplementation either orally or by injection.
2. Blood levels of 3 ppm selenium are evidence of poisoning.
3. Urine levels of 4 ppm are also evidence.
4. Reduced haemoglobin values occur and are often about 7g/100 ml.

Differential diagnosis

1. Lead poisoning.
2. Meningitis.
3. Vitamin A deficiency.
4. Liver insufficiency.

Treatment

Remove the source of selenium. A level of 0.1 ppm selenium in the diet is adequate to prevent deficiency. High protein levels should be used if poisoning has occurred (Rosenfeld and Beath, 1964a). The addition of 0.01 per cent arsanilic acid may assist in reducing toxic effects if of dietary origin particularly when linseed oil is also present.

References

BLOOD, D C, RADOSTITS, O M and HENDERSON, J A (1983) "Veterinary Medicine", 6th edition. Bailliere Tindall, London. pp. 1102-1104.

ROSENFELD, I and BEATH, O A (1964a) American Journal of Veterinary Research, 7, 52-56.

ROSENFELD, I and BEATH, O A (1964b) American Journal of Veterinary Research, 7, 57-61.

Sodium Chloride Poisoning

Aetiology

This is either directly due to excess salt intake or indirectly to a reduced water consumption.

Occurrence

It is uncommon in Great Britain, and growing and beef cattle are less susceptible than milking cows. It can, however, be seen in herds grazing salt marshes in East Anglia and a few other areas which cattle use in summer and which are flooded in winter. Thus it can occur in calves of suckler herds where the dam produces little milk and so the calf is forced to graze early. Otherwise it is seen occasionally when concentrate diets are fed and there is an interruption in the water supply, or when diets are deliberately high in salt and are being fed to prevent urolithiasis but without free access to water. Milk replacer diet containing large amounts of whey can cause problems. High levels of salt cause alimentary irritation and the increased osmotic pressure of the gut contents results in dehydration.

Signs

Acute

This is the only syndrome present in Britain. Animals show excessive thirst. There is marked intestinal irritation resulting in diarrhoea, dehydration and loss of condition. Other signs can be seen, referrable to central nervous system dysfunction. They include hyperaesthesia, nystagmus, blindness and paresis (Pearson and Kallfelz, 1982). Animals can die within a day of onset of signs.

Necropsy

The main lesions are of omasal and abomasal mucosa congestion. Animals which survive a few days may show hydropericardium and skeletal muscle oedema.

Diagnosis

1. History which includes access to excess salt or water deprivation.
2. Signs are helpful, such as excess thirst, diarrhoea and dehydration.
3. There is a rise in the serum sodium levels (normal values are 130 - 150 mmol/l; 130 - 150 mequ/l).
4. Analysis of the feed.

Differential diagnosis

1. Arsenic poisoning.
2. Molybdenum poisoning.
3. Mercury poisoning.
4. Salmonellosis.
5. Coccidiosis.

Treatment

If the source of the salt is the diet then it should no longer be fed. Access to water should be provided but cattle should be allowed it "little and often" and they should not be able to engorge themselves. The use of isotonic fluids parenterally may be helpful as also may be astringents such as kaolin, chalk, etc.

Control

If diets high in salt are to be fed then there must be free access to water at all times.

Reference

PEARSON, E G and KALLFELZ, F A (1982) Cornell Veterinarian, 72, 142-149.

Sodium Monochloroacetate Poisoning

Aetiology

Poisoning with sodium monochloroacetate (a halogenated acetic acid).

Occurrence

The condition is unusual. The compound is a contact herbicide (Herbon Somon, Cropsafe; Monoxone, ICI). It tends to cause problems if cattle have access to fields which have recently been sprayed, if there is spillage of the chemical or access to drainage effluent (Quick, Manser, Stevens and Bolton, 1983). The fatal dose is 17 - 68 mg/kg BW.

Signs

Peracute

Sudden death.

Acute

The cattle usually show nervous signs with increased aggressiveness and hyperexcitability. There is then lateral recumbency with muscle tremors, convulsions and paralysis of the extensor muscles of the limbs. Death normally occurs within 24 hours of exposure.

Necropsy

There is usually marked venous congestion of the neck and thorax, particularly ventrally. Affected tissues tend to show multiple haemorrhages of the subcutaneous tissues and muscles. The epicardium and endocardium show multiple haemorrhages.

Diagnosis

1. History of exposure to sodium monochloroacetate.

2. *Post mortem* examination.

3. Detection of herbicide by gas chromatography, mass spectrometry analysis.

Control

Always follow the manufacturer's instructions.

Reference

QUICK, M P, MANSER, P A, STEVENS, H and BOLTON, J F (1983) Veterinary Record, 113, 155-156.

Staggers

Aetiology

The cause is a tremorgenic mycotoxin - penitrem A - produced by *Penicillium puberulum*.

Signs

Early

There is excitability with a fine muscle tremor which increases with excitement. It can proceed so that the animal eventually stands like a rocking horse with its legs stiff and wide apart. There may be periods of ataxia, the gait is stiff and the animal may fall over. There is sometimes profuse salivation and nystagmus.

Late

If the condition progresses there is lateral recumbency, opisthotonus and a severe tremor.

Diagnosis

1. Signs.

Treatment

Take animals off likely source of penitrem A. Give pentobarbitone until tremor ceases.

Sweet Vernal Grass Poisoning

Aetiology

Excessive intake of sweet vernal grass (*Anthoxanthum odoratum*).

Occurrence

The plant usually only forms 5 to 10 *per cent* of the sward. Poisoning is uncommon and only occurs if the plant predominates in the sward, and in most cases it has been made into hay (Pritchard, Markson, Brush, Sawtell and Bloxham, 1983). It is mainly found on unimproved pastures where there is little use of nitrogenous fertilisers and little or no liming. The grass contains high levels of coumarins which can be converted to 4-hydroxycoumarin by fungi such as *Aspergillus fumigatus* and *A. nigur*. Atmospheric formaldehyde then results in conversion to dicoumarol.

Signs

Peracute

Sudden death. There may be petechial haemorrhages on mucous membranes, ulcerations in the mouth and massive haematomas from trauma.

Acute

The animal is dull, lethargic and weak. The mucous membranes tend to be pale or blanched and there is tachycardia and tachypnoea.

Necropsy

Animals tend to show extensive haemorrhages throughout the viscera and carcase. There may be ulcerations in the region of the cheek teeth with diphtheresis of the larynx.

Diagnosis

1. History of feeding hay containing much sweet vernal grass.

2. Signs of haemorrhages.

3. Increased prothrombin time (normal animals take less than 20 seconds).

4. Haematological examination gives normal cell numbers, but there is anaemia and leucopaenia close to death.

Differential diagnosis

1. Anthrax.

2. Bracken poisoning.

3. Blackleg.

4. Pasteurellosis.

Treatment

The oral administration of 1 g vitamin K daily will help. In severe cases blood transfusions can be given.

Control

If hay contains much sweet vernal grass, feed one part of the hay with two parts of ordinary hay. Repeatedly feeding the sweet vernal hay for two weeks and then stopping for two weeks is another way of tackling the problem.

Reference

PRITCHARD, D G, MARKSON, L M, BRUSH, P J, SAWTELL, J A A and BLOXHAM, P A (1983) Veterinary Record, 113, 78-84.

Urea Poisoning

Aetiology

Toxicity following ingestion of urea.

Occurrence

The condition is uncommon although urea is often used as a non-protein nitrogen source for cattle, particularly those over six months old. When problems arise they are normally due to poor mixing, feeding large quantities when the animals are unaccustomed to it or where the cattle gain access to the powder or concentrated liquid. Starving cattle are more susceptible to poisoning. When cattle are used to consuming urea, large quantities can be fed without deleterious effect. However, the tolerance is lost three days after the urea is withdrawn. Signs normally develop within 20 to 30 minutes of ingesting the urea. Large quantities of ammonia are produced in the rumen and these are absorbed into the blood. It is the high levels of ammonia in the blood which cause the signs.

Signs

There is usually muscle twitching, severe abdominal pain with excessive bellowing, salivation, bloat, dyspnoea and ataxia. Death can occur from 30 minutes to four hours after ingestion. The death rate tends to be high in those cases where signs occur.

Necropsy

There are no characteristic lesions although most organs show generalized congestion and haemorrhage. There is usually marked pulmonary oedema.

Diagnosis

1. History of feeding urea.
2. Signs with early death in those severely affected.
3. High blood ammonia nitrogen levels (often they reach 0.7 - 0.8mg/ 100 ml).
4. Rumen ammonia levels high (normal 6 mg/100 ml).
5. Rumen alkalinity high (normal pH 6.9).

Differential diagnosis

1. Nitrite poisoning - methaemoglobin present.
2. Anthrax - possible haemorrhages from extremities.
3. Blackleg - crepitation in affected muscles.

Treatment

Usually of little help. It may be best to perform rumen lavage with a wide bore tube. Pump in warm water until the left sublumbar fossa bulges, then drain by gravity. Repeat until the rumen is empty. Otherwise the pH can be reduced by giving four litres (one gallon) of vinegar. This may alleviate the signs but they tend to return half-an-hour or so after therapy and so the treatment should be repeated. Besides vinegar, various acids can be used, such as five per cent acetic acid, dilute lactic acid or dilute sulphuric acid.

Prevention

Ensure that cattle are introduced to diets containing urea slowly. When urea is added to a diet, ensure adequate mixing. It is unsafe to have more than 25 per cent of nitrogen in the diet as urea.

Yew Poisoning

Aetiology

The yew tree (*Taxus baccata*) contains an alkaloid taxine which has a strongly depressant action on the heart.

Occurrence

The condition is very uncommon but can occur following the break-out of cattle into churchyards, etc. Other cases follow the disposal of yew clippings into fields grazed by cattle.

Signs

Peracute

There is sudden death with few obvious signs.

Acute

In some animals there is dyspnoea with muscle tremors, weakness and collapse.

Necropsy

Usually nothing significant is found but there may be pieces of yew in the rumen.

Diagnosis

1. Access to yew.
2. Presence of yew in the rumen *post mortem*.

Treatment

Large doses of glucose and hydroxycobalamin intravenously have effected recovery.

Control

Keep cattle away from yews.

CHAPTER 8

OTHER CONDITIONS

Anaphylaxis

Aetiology

It is the result of antigen antibody reaction and when severe it can result in anaphylactic shock.

Occurrence

The condition is usually very uncommon. Most cases follow the parenteral injection of drugs or biological products such as blood. Occasionally the problem can arise through exposure via the alimentary tract or lungs. Cases can involve signs in the system exposed or they may be generalised. Most cases follow the introduction to the blood of an antigen to which the animal has already been sensitised, but occasionally reactions occur where the animal is not known to have been exposed previously. More anaphylactic reactions occur in some herds and families of cattle than others. Reactions are particularly prevalent in Channel Island breeds. Initial reactions tend to be largely of a respiratory nature, but other areas affected can be the alimentary tract and skin.

Signs

In many cases the reactions occur about 20 minutes after the introduction of the antigen. The animal exhibits a sudden, pronounced dyspnoea with, on auscultation, bubbling and emphysematous sounds. Muscle tremors often occur which may cause pyrexia to 40°C (104°F). Other reactions can include bloat, diarrhoea, increased salivation, urticaria and rhinitis. Very occasionally laminitis occurs. Death is due to anoxia. Following intravenous blood transfusion there are usually hiccoughs and then dyspnoea, muscle tremors, salivation, coughing, lachrymation and fever.

Necropsy

Usually only the lungs are involved in acute cases with marked pulmonary oedema and vascular engorgement; some animals develop emphysema. Longer-standing cases show hyperaemia and oedema of the abomasum and small intestines.

Diagnosis

1. History of recent introduction of an antigen to which the animal may have previously been exposed.
2. Signs - sudden, severe dyspnoea, urticaria, etc.
3. Haematological examination shows increased packed cell volume, leucopaenia and thrombocytopaenia.
4. Biochemically there is a hyperkalaemia and blood histamine levels are raised in some cases.
5. Response to therapy.

Differential diagnosis

1. Acute pneumonia but usually there is toxaemia and lesions are more pronounced in the arterio-ventral parts of the lungs.

Treatment

The most effective method of treatment is an intramuscular injection of adrenaline (4 - 5 ml of 1 in 1,000 solution) and if necessary a fifth of the dose (0.2 - 0.5 ml) can be given intravenously diluted to about a two per cent solution. Otherwise, corticosteroids can be administered or they may be given immediately following adrenaline as they potentiate the latter's activity. Antihistamines give variable results, partly because most histamine is released early in the reaction and also there are other mediators of the anaphylactic reactions. Various other compounds have been shown to alter the reaction of mediators and these include sodium meclofenamate, acetylsalicylic acid and diethylcarbamazine.

Control

Once a reaction has occurred in an animal, the antigen providing the problem should not be reintroduced. If a blood transfusion is given, introduce up to 200 ml in a 450 kg (990 lb) animal and wait for about 10 minutes before injecting the remainder.

Laminitis

Aetiology

Damage to the sensitive laminae in the hoof, which may be the result of bacterial toxins produced after an alimentary disorder such as over-eating cereals, etc.

Occurrence

The acute condition is not as common as cases of acidosis or liver abscess. Most disease occurs sporadically and usually in animals which are placed on increased levels of carbohydrate feeding. In cattle, most cases occur up to six months old when the cereal diet is being introduced. Some cases follow other illnesses such as mastitis, metritis, etc. There is an inherited form of laminitis which is mainly seen in Jerseys and Guernseys. Cattle without sufficient exercise are more prone to the condition. The chronic form of laminitis, which results in a deformed hoof, is much more likely to be seen than the acute form.

The cause is still not completely resolved. At one time the condition was thought to be due to histamine release resulting in engorgement of the vascular bed of the foot. Lactic acid production has been incriminated as well as a change in ruminal flora resulting in a release of bacterial endotoxins. It has also been suggested that the main problem is one of epidermal hoof formation causing a reduction in the bond between the sensitive laminae and the horn. It is, however, currently thought that the vascular changes are probably primary. Following the production of toxins there is stagnation of blood within the foot. This is thought to be the result of the arterial blood passing by anastomosis vessels to the venous return and thereby by-passing the corium capillaries. The result is stagnation of blood, hypoxia and functional ischaemia in the laminae. The deficient blood supply to the corium results in insufficient nutrients, especially methionine, cysteine and cystine, being provided for the keratin-producing cells. Poor quality keratin is produced which allows separation of the laminae from the digital corium.

Signs

Acute

There is pain in all four feet, or otherwise only the front feet are affected. The animal develops uncharacteristic stances with either all four feet under it or the front feet placed forward with the hind feet under the body. The animal tends to have an arched back and is reluctant to move. When it does, it has a shuffling gait. The animal shows signs of pain as each foot is placed on the ground. In some cases the front feet show a cross-legged gait. It has difficulty in lying down and once down it is reluctant to stand.

There are often muscular tremors, a rapid, shallow respiratory rate of up to 90 to 100 per minute, a rectal temperature of 39.5°C (103°F) or more and a pulse rate often of 120 to 130 per minute.

Subacute

Some animals show only a few signs or following an acute episode there are bouts of signs of a minor nature. Again the animal shows some pain when putting down its feet, a shuffling gait and is reluctant to move.

Chronic

This may follow an acute episode or be seen separately. The hoof wall tends to develop marked horizontal ridges, the slope of the anterior wall becomes greater and concave. The solar horn becomes thinner, soft and waxy.

Necropsy

The condition is unlikely to result in death.

Acute

There may be large amounts of cereal in the rumen. The sensitive laminae of the digital cushion show engorgement of the blood vessels. Histologically there is often vascular engorgement, oedema and necrosis. There is an absence of the keratogenic structures of the inner zone of cornification of the epidermal laminae.

Subacute and chronic

There are usually changes in hoof shape with thinning of the sole, horizontal ridging, and in some cases there is pedal bone rotation.

Diagnosis

1. Diet - high levels of carbohydrate.
2. Signs - in acute cases the signs and stance are helpful.
3. Eosinophilia occurs in some cases.
4. Blood histamine levels are raised in some animals.
5. In some cases, radiography will show rarefaction of the pedal bone with osteophyte formation at the heel and on the pyramidal processes.

Differential diagnosis

1. Foul of the foot - signs help distinguish.
2. Liver abscess - signs help distinguish.
3. Muscular dystrophy - signs should help, raised CPK and SGOT levels.
4. Blackleg - usually animals are dead, or signs should help.

Treatment

Acute

In the early stages, large doses of corticosteroids may be useful. In the past, antihistamines were used but they appear to be of limited value. Animals should be encouraged to eat roughage or bran and concentrates should not be given. As the animal improves, it should be encouraged to walk but obviously on soft ground. There is controversy as to whether or not the feet should be bathed and, if so, with hot or cold water. It would seem probable that bathing the feet with hot water should assist in dilating the arterioles and reducing hypertension. Injections of acepromazine may be of use as a hypertensive and analgesic agent. Mild purgatives can be helpful in removing toxins and these include liquid paraffin and Epsom salts. In some cases the use of phlebotomy to remove 3 to 5 litres of blood from a 450 kg animal (½ to 1 gallon per 1000 lb) can bring considerable relief. Animals should be given 10 g of methionine daily for a week to improve hoof quality.

Prevention

Ensure that all changes in feed are undertaken slowly. All potentially toxic conditions, e.g. metritis, mastitis, should be adequately treated and promptly. There should be adequate access to forage. Free access to iodised or rock salt should be allowed as this will assist in increasing the flow of saliva and thereby act as a natural buffer. The provision of grass or lucerne can help reduce problems, as also can the inclusion of one per cent sodium bicarbonate in the rations. Exercise should always be provided for the cattle.

Lightning Strike/Electrocution

Aetiology

Exposure to high voltage electric currents, either natural or generated by man.

Occurrence

The condition is uncommon but it is often of interest as it is one of the few problems which farmers have usually insured against. Problems arise from lightning, exposure of electrical wires or faulty wiring or earthing in farm buildings. Cases may be single or a group. In many cases damp ground or floors help to conduct the electricity. Low voltages of 110 - 220 volts are sufficient to kill cattle. Outside, some trees such as oak, poplar, elm and conifers are all prone to lightning strike.

Signs

Severe

Animals die without a struggle. Burns or singeing may be seen because of the severity and often they involve the muzzle and feet. Death is usually due to paralysis of the medullary centre, accompanied in some cases by ventricular fibrillation.

Less severe

The animal becomes unconscious for a varying time and there is usually some sign of a struggle. Following regaining consciousness, there may be dullness, blindness, paralysis of one or more legs, and surface hyperaesthesia. The signs may persist or slowly disappear over a period of up to two weeks. If burns are present, sloughing of the skin in the area is seen.

Minor

The animal may jump, be restless, show periodic convulsions or be knocked down.

Necropsy

In lightning strike the animal is usually close to a fence, barn, trees or a pond. Often there are signs of burning affecting these objects. The animal itself may show singeing of the hair or burn marks on the muzzle and feet. Half-chewed food may be present in the mouth. The animal quickly becomes distended with gas and decomposes. Blood often exudes from the nostrils, rectum, vulva. The pupils are dilated and the anus relaxed. There tend to be petechial haemorrhages throughout the body and the viscera are congested. The superficial lymph nodes are often haemorrhagic.

Diagnosis

1. History of a storm, position of animal near trees, etc. and sudden death of a group of animals.
2. Signs - singeing of the hair, burns on muzzle and feet. Evidence of sudden death.

Differential diagnosis

1. Anaphylaxis but marked pulmonary involvement.
2. Acute heart failure but engorgement of visceral veins and macroscopic or microscopic myocardial lesions.
3. Brain trauma but usually a haemorrhagic lesion of brain.
4. Nitrate/nitrite poisoning but methaemoglobin present.
5. Anthrax, but stained blood smears assist.
6. Bloat, but congested front part of animal, distended rumen and some froth.
7. Blackleg - swelling and dark with organism present.

Treatment

Usually the cattle are better or dead before any therapy can be administered. Central nervous system stimulants can be given. Artificial respiration may be helpful.

Control

Although nothing can be done about lightning strike, all electrical installations should be fitted properly and earthed.

Photosensitisation

Aetiology

The condition is the result of photodynamic substances concentrating in the skin resulting in dermatitis following exposure to light.

Occurrence

The condition is not common but can be the result of many different problems.

Primary photosensitisation

This is due to the ingestion of preformed photodynamic substances such as St John's Wort (*Hypericum perforatum*), phenothiazine, perloline from perennial ryegrass (*Lolium perenne*), rose bengal and acridine dyes.

Hepatogenous photosensitisation

A normal end product of photosensitisation, phylloerythrin accumulates in the body rather than being excreted in the bile. This is usually the result of liver impairment, whether from hepatitis caused by plants such as ragwort (*Senecio jacobaea*) or chemicals, e.g. carbon tetrachloride, or following obstruction of the bile duct system.

Aberrant pigment synthesis

Congenital porphyria in cattle can result in excessive production of porphyrins which are photodynamic. The condition is inherited.

Uncertain aetiology

There are many different compounds and plants which can on occasion result in photosensitisation, including kale, rape and lucerne. Many cases occur at pasture where no photodynamic substance is identified.

The lesions only occur if light can penetrate into the deeper layers of the skin and so they are only present in the unpigmented areas with little hair cover. There is then histamine liberation with cell death and tissue oedema.

Signs

The lesions occur in the unpigmented areas of the body and tend to be more severe in the parts most exposed to light, such as the dorsal part of the body, ears, face, muzzle, eyelids and areas exposed when the animal lies down such as the sides of the teats, vulva and perineum. There is firstly reddening, followed by oedema, exudation, lifting and sloughing of the skin. There is often irritation with rubbing of the skin. Some animals become hyperaesthetic and can show other signs such as depression, blindness or posterior paralysis.

Necropsy

Most lesions are confined to the unpigmented areas and show varying degrees of dermatitis. In the hepatogenous form there may be liver lesions. In congenital porphyria there is a purple colouring to the bones and teeth.

Diagnosis

Aetiology is often very difficult to determine.

1. Signs of lesions affecting the unpigmented skin.
2. In liver damage, biochemical testing to demonstrate raised liver enzyme levels can be helpful, such as raised SGOT (AST), SAP.

Differential diagnosis

1. Mycotic dermatitis, but lesions are usually more focal.

Treatment

Keep the animal out of direct sunlight. Laxatives may assist in removing toxic material. Corticosteroids or antihistamines can be administered to reduce the inflammatory reaction but when the former is used, antibiotic should be given to cover the chance of infection.

Control

This is often difficult, but on some occasions problems occur in the same fields at a given time each year and in such cases animals should be kept off the pastures during the period.

Spastic Paresis

There is an extension of the stifle and tarsal joints of one or both hind limbs. The condition is seen in the Friesian, but other breeds can be affected. Signs are not usually present until the animal is several weeks or months old and signs then progress. Contraction of the Achilles' tendon, gastrocnemius and superficial flexor tendons overstraighten the hock joint, so that the os calcis is moved cranially towards the tibia. Usually one leg is affected more than the other and this limb may appear shorter. In the later stages of the severe cases, the leg may swing backwards and forwards like a pendulum. The condition is considered to be inherited, but, where only small numbers of an A.I. bull's offspring are affected and the animal is of high genetic merit, it has been suggested that it should still be used as a sire. Surgery can relieve the condition but the animals should not be used for breeding. Recently analysis of cerebrospinal fluid concentrations of homovanillic acid, the main metabolite of dopamine, has shown levels to be lower in spastic paresis calves than normal contemporaries. The possibility of a disorder in dopamine metabolism has therefore been suggested as a possible cause of the condition (Dewulf and de Moor, 1982).

Reference

DEWULF, M and de MOOR, A (1982) Proceedings of Twelfth World Congress on Diseases of Cattle, International Congrescentrum RAI, Amsterdam, The Netherlands. September 7-10th, 1982. Volume II, pp. 760-762.

Progressive Ataxia

The condition has been recorded in the Charolais in Britain and subsequently in France. The signs do not develop until the animal is about a year old and they are seen as a progressive ataxia. The animal has increasing difficulty in rising until it may become permanently recumbent. Histologically there is a myelin degeneration of the white matter of the cerebellum and internal capsule.

Mannosidosis

The condition has been recorded in Aberdeen Angus and Murray Grey cattle in New Zealand, Australia and recently Britain. It is inherited as an autosomal recessive trait and is a deficiency of a specific lysosomal hydrolase enzyme called alpha mannosidase and this causes the accumulation of mannose and glucosamine in secondary lysosomes. The signs develop from one to 15 months old and most animals die by one year. There is at first slight hind leg ataxia, then a fine lateral head tremor, slow vertical head nodding, aggression and loss of condition. Diagnosis is based on reduced tissue and plasma levels of alpha mannosidase.

Histologically, accumulations of mannose and glucosamine are seen in the nerve cells, fixed macrophages and epithelial cells of the viscera. Normal tissue and plasma levels of alpha mannosidase are about half the normal in heterozygous animals and so they can be detected. This fact has allowed a genetic screening programme in Angus and Murray Grey breeds in New Zealand which has been successful (Jolly, 1982).

Reference

JOLLY, R D (1982) Proceedings of Twelfth World Congress on Diseases of Cattle. International Congrescentrum RAI, Amsterdam, The Netherlands. September 7-10th, 1982. Volume II, pp. 1146-1150.

Colobomata

Occurrence

These problems appear to have a high prevalence in the Charolais. There is an absence of part of one or more of the structures of the eye. The condition occurs during early gestation, when the eye is developing. Although always bilateral, it may not be symmetrical and it is usually found associated with the optic disc and the tapetum nigrum below the disc. The retina is involved and in some animals the choroid and sclera are also affected. The condition is present at birth and does not progress. The mode of inheritance has been debated, but a dominant gene with incomplete penetrance, autosomal recessive or polygenic inheritance have all been suggested.

Signs

These are usually not apparent although an ophthalmoscopic examination will reveal the lesion. The very severely affected animal can be blind, and a few others are considered to be hyperexcitable due to the defective vision.

APPENDIX A

TABLE A 1

Some of the Causes of Diarrhoea in Growing Cattle and their Differentiation

Condition	Group or Single Problem	Frequency of Occurrence	Epidemiology History	Presence of Blood	Attitude	Acute or Chronic Signs	Pyrexia	Diagnosis
Acidosis	Group or single	Common	Access to excess carbo-hydrate	No	Dull	Acute	No	Signs, history
Actinobacillosis of reticulorumen	Single	Uncommon	Intermittent diarrhoea ± bloat	No	Normal	Chronic	No	History intermittent diarrhoea
Actinomycosis of reticulorumen	Single	Uncommon	Intermittent diarrhoea ± bloat	No	Normal	Chronic	No	History intermittent diarrhoea
Aflatoxicosis	Group	Uncommon	Diet	Yes	Dullness	Acute	No	Toxin detection
Amyloidosis	Single	Rare	Individual problem,	No	Dull	Chronic	No	Signs, oedema
Anaphylaxis	Single	Uncommon	Injection; oral	No	Variable	Acute	Yes	History
Anthrax - acute	Single	Uncommon	Usually in feed	Sometimes	Dull	Acute	Yes	Signs, history
Antibiotic contamination of feed	Group	Uncommon	New batch of feed introduced	No	Dull	Acute	No	History, ketosis, recovery after feed removal
Arsenic poisoning (acute, subacute)	Group	Uncommon	Area	Yes	Dullness	Acute	No	Urine arsenic levels
Bacillary haemoglobinuria	Single	Rare	Good condition	Usually no	Dull	Acute	Yes	Signs, bacteriology
Bracken poisoning	Single/ few	Uncommon	Usually young bracken	Yes	Dull	Acute	Yes	History, white cell platelet erythrocyte depression

TABLE A 1 (cont'd)

Condition	Group or Single Problem	Frequency of Occurrence	Epidemiology History	Presence of Blood	Attitude	Acute or Chronic Signs	Pyrexia	Diagnosis
Brassica spp. poisoning	Few	Not uncommon	Kale fed for several weeks	Usually no	Dull	Acute	Usually no	History, anaemia, Heinz-Ehrlich bodies
Bunostomiasis (subacute)	Group	Rare	Pasture	No	Variable	Subacute	No	Faecal egg count
Cobalt deficiency	Group	Not common	Area, heavy liming	No	Slight dullness	Chronic	No	Signs, history, plasma vitamin B_{12} levels
Coccidiosis	Group	Quite common	Overcrowding, poor hygiene	Yes	Dull	Acute/ chronic	No	Oocysts in faeces
Copper deficiency	Group	Common	Area, molybdenum presence	No	Slight dullness	Chronic	No	Signs, history, plasma and liver copper
Copper poisoning (acute, chronic)	Single or group	Uncommon	Diet, injections	Yes	Dullness	Acute or chronic	No	Plasma copper levels
Dicrocoelium dendriticum infestation	Group	Uncommon	Pasture	No	Slight dullness	Chronic	No	Faecal egg count
Ergot poisoning	Single	Rare	Diet	No	Depression	Acute	No	Presence of ergots
Fascioliasis	Group	Not uncommon	Wet area where snail host survives	Yes (acute) No (chronic)	Dull	Acute/ chronic	No	Faecal egg count
Fluorosis	Group	Uncommon	Diet, area	No	Variable	Acute	No	Blood fluorine levels
Haemonchosis (subacute) (diarrhoea uncommon)	Group	Quite common	Pasture	No	Slight dullness	Acute	No	Faecal egg count
Hypomagnesaemia	Group	Common	Diet, pasture, weather	No	Hyper-aesthetic	Acute	Yes	Serum magnesium levels

TABLE A 1 (cont'd)

Condition	Group or Single Problem	Frequency of Occurrence	Epidemiology History	Presence of Blood	Attitude	Acute or Chronic Signs	Pyrexia	Diagnosis
Lead poisoning	Group	Common	Paint or other source of lead	Sometimes	Hyper-excitable	Acute	Usually	Kidney and liver lead levels
Linseed poisoning (acute)	Single or group	Rare	Diet	No	Dullness	Acute	No	Signs, history
Listeriosis (septicaemic)	Single/ small group	Uncommon	Silage feeding	No	Depression	Acute	Yes	Signs, bacteriology, serology
Malignant catarrhal fever	Single	Uncommon	Often association with sheep, deer	Usually no	Depression	Acute	Yes	Signs
Mercury poisoning	Single or group	Rare	Diet	Yes	Hyper-aesthesia	Acute and chronic	No	Signs, post mortem
Molybdenum poisoning	Group	Common	Area	No	Slight dullness	Chronic	No	Plasma copper levels
Monensin poisoning	Group	Rare	Overfeeding monensin	No	Dull	Acute	No	History
Mucosal disease	Single or group	Common	Usually over 6 months	Sometimes	Depression	Acute and chronic	Yes	Virus isolation, serology
Oak poisoning	Single/ few	Rare	Acorns being eaten	Yes	Dull	Acute	No	History
Oesophagostomiasis	Group	Rare	Pasture	No	Variable	Subacute	No	Faecal egg count
Organophosphorus poisoning	Single	Rare	Use of organophosphorus compounds	No	Hyper-excitable	Acute	Some	History, blood cholinesterase levels

TABLE A 1 (cont'd)

Condition	Group or Single Problem	Frequency of Occurrence	Epidemiology History	Presence of Blood	Attitude	Acute or Chronic Signs	Pyrexia	Diagnosis
Parasitic bronchitis (unusual or early sign)	Group	Common	Pasture	No	Dull	Relatively acute	No	Faecal larval count
Parasitic gastroenteritis	Group	Common	Pasture grazed previously by infested animals	No	Dull later	Usually chronic	No	Faecal egg count
Ragwort poisoning	Few	Uncommon	Access, usually in hay	Usually no	Dull	Acute/ chronic	No	History, liver biopsy
Redwater fever	Group	Common	Tick area	No	Slight dullness	Acute	Yes	Signs, organism present
Salmonella dublin infection	Single	Common	Carrier animal	Often	Dull	Acute	Yes	Faecal swab, serum agglutination test
Salmonellosis	Single/ group	Common	Contaminated feed or water	Often	Dull	Acute/ chronic	Yes	Faecal swab, serum agglutination test
Selenium deficiency	Group	Not common	Area	No	Often normal	Chronic	No	Low glutathione peroxidase blood level
Sodium chloride poisoning	Single/ group	Rare	Diet	No	Hyper-aesthesia	Acute	No	Serum sodium levels
Tapeworm infestation	Group	Common but disease unusual	Pasture	Occas-ional	Bright	Chronic	No	Proglottids and eggs in faeces
Vitamin A deficiency	Group	Uncommon	Diet	No	Often normal	Chronic	No	Plasma vitamin A and carotene levels
Winter dysentery	Group	Common	Area problem	Yes	Slightly dull	Acute	Slight	History, bacteriology

TABLE A 2

Differential Diagnosis of Respiratory Problems in Growing Cattle

Condition	Single or Group Problem	Occurrence	Signs	Aids to Diagnosis
Acidosis	Single or group	Common	Temperature low or normal, ruminal stasis, tachycardia, yellow diarrhoea	Signs, history
Acute exudative pneumonia	Single	Fairly common	Pyrexia, some moist sounds, pleuritic rub	Signs
Anaphylaxis	Single	Uncommon	Dyspnoea, muscle tremors, urticaria, diarrhoea	History, hyperkalaemia, leucopaenia
Aspiration pneumonia	Single	Rare	Toxaemia, moist rales, often areas of dullness	History of drenching, leucopaenia, neutropaenia
Avian tuberculosis	Single	Uncommon	Cough	History, comparative tuberculin test
Bacillary haemoglobinuria	Single	Rare	Dyspnoea, terminally diarrhoea	Signs, history, post mortem findings
Bovine nasal granuloma	Single	Uncommon	Dyspnoea, stertor, mucopurulent oculo-nasal discharge, sneezing	Occurs in summer months
Chronic suppurative pneumonia	Single	Common	Loss of condition, thoracic pain, intermittent pyrexia	History, signs
Dusty feed rhinotracheitis	Group	Fairly common	Coughing following feeding, oculo-nasal discharge, bright	Follows introduction of dusty or dry feed
Ethylenediamine hydroiodide poisoning	Group	Rare	Lachrymation, some coughing, pyrexia, nasal discharge	History
Fluorosis	Group	Uncommon	Dyspnoea, diarrhoea, constipation, muscle tremors, weakness	Signs, blood fluorine levels
Fog fever	Group	Fairly common	Dyspnoea, no coughing, dullness	History of suckler cows in autumn

TABLE A 2 (cont'd)

Condition	Single or Group Problem	Occurrence	Signs	Aids to Diagnosis
Haemophilus somnus infection	Single or group	Not uncommon	Tachypnoea, hyperpnoea, conjunctivitis	Signs, bacteriology, serology
Infectious bovine rhinotracheitis	Group	Common	Pyrexia, conjunctivitis, explosive cough, nasal lesions	Many affected, virus isolation from nasal swabs
Inhalation pneumonia	Single	Rare	Toxaemia, moist rales, often areas of dullness	History of drenching, leucopaenia, neutropaenia
Laryngeal diphtheria	Single	Uncommon	Stertor, dyspnoea, painful cough, painful laryngeal region	History, signs
Linseed poisoning	Single or group	Rare	Dyspnoea, staggering, dullness, muscle tremors	Signs, history
Malignant catarrhal fever	Single	Uncommon	Dyspnoea, stertor, nervous signs, lymph node enlargement	Signs, history, *post mortem* histology
Monensin poisoning	Group	Rare	Dyspnoea, diarrhoea, dullness	History
Mucosal disease	Single or group	Common	Mucopurulent discharge from nostrils, diarrhoea	Signs, virus isolation, serology
Organophosphorus poisoning	Single	Uncommon	Dyspnoea, salivation, diarrhoea, lachrymation, miosis, bradycardia	Signs, use of organophosphorus compounds, blood cholinesterase levels
Parasitic bronchitis	Group	Common	Loss of condition, dyspnoea, paroxysmal coughing	Signs, history, faecal larval count
Shipping fever	Group	Common	Dullness, pyrexia, tachypnoea	Signs, history, bacteriology
Summer snuffles	Single	Uncommon	Dyspnoea, stertor, mucopurulent oculo-nasal discharge, sneezing	Occurs in summer months

TABLE A 2 (cont'd)

Condition	Single or Group Problem	Occurrence	Signs	Aids to Diagnosis
Thrombosis of caudal/cranial vena cava	Single	Uncommon	Haemoptysis, tachypnoea, melaena, thoracic pain	History, signs
Tuberculosis (bovine)	Small groups	Uncommon	Soft chronic cough, tachypnoea, hyperpnoea, dyspnoea	History, tuberculin test
Urea poisoning	Group	Rare	Dyspnoea, bloat, abdominal pain	Signs, history, blood ammonia levels
Vitamin E/ selenium deficiency	Group	Common	Hyperpnoea, dyspnoea, myoglobinuria	Signs, vitamin E and glutathione peroxidase blood levels
Yew poisoning	Small groups	Rare	Dyspnoea, muscle tremors, weakness, collapse	Signs, post mortem findings

TABLE A 3

Differential Diagnosis of Skin Conditions in Growing Cattle

Disease	Pruritus	Alopecia	Lesions	Main Sites	Diagnosis
Aujeszky's disease	Yes	Yes	Marked nervous signs with mutilation of the affected area	Lesion where virus entered	Signs
Bovine malignant catarrh	No	No	Necrosis	Teats, vulva, muzzle, feet skin-horn junction	Signs, necropsy
Chorioptic mange	Yes	No	Small scabs	Base of tail, legs, udder, escutcheon	Skin scraping for parasites
Copper deficiency	No	No	Depigmentation of hair	Body then periorbital area	Plasma copper level, liver copper level
Demodectic mange	Little	Occasionally	Nodules and pustules	Shoulder, forearm, brisket, lower neck	Mites in pus
Ergot poisoning (chronic)	No	No	Loss of tissue	Tips of ears, tail	Presence of ergot in feed
Inherited parakeratosis	No	Yes	Parakeratosis	Limbs, muzzle underside of jaw	Serum zinc levels
Iodine deficiency	No	Yes	Alopecia	Variable	Low blood protein, blood iodine
Iodism	No	No	Stary coat, much dandruff	Whole body	Use of iodine
Mercury poisoning	Yes	Yes	Scabby lesions	Anus, vulva	Exposure to mercury

TABLE A 3 (cont'd)

Disease	Pruritus	Alopecia	Lesions	Main Sites	Diagnosis
Molybdenum poisoning	No	No	Depigmentation of hair	Body, then periorbital area	Plasma copper level
Mucosal disease	No	No	Scabbiness	Body, vulva, scrotum, perineum	Virus isolation, serology
Mycotic dermatitis	No	Yes	Matting of hair	Back, sides of legs, back of udder	Presence of organism
Papillomatosis	No	No	Papillomas	Muzzle, head, neck	Biopsy
Pediculosis	Yes	Yes	Self-inflicted lesions	Shoulders, upper part of neck, head	Lice isolation, presence of eggs
Photosensitisation	Yes	No	Reddening, oedema, exudation and sloughing of skin	Unpigmented areas of skin exposed to sun	Signs
Psoroptic mange	Yes	Yes	Papules, scabs	Withers, neck, base of tail	Skin scraping for parasites
Ringworm	No	Sometimes	Thick grey-white encrustations	Eyes, neck, head, perineum	Hair sample for spore presence
Sarcocystosis	No	Yes	Loss of hair	Variable	Other signs, presence of organism

TABLE A 3 (cont'd)

Disease	Pruritus	Alopecia	Lesions	Main Sites	Diagnosis
Sarcoptic mange	Yes	Yes	Thickened, wrinkled skin	Inside thighs, axilla, underside of neck	Skin scraping for parasites
Vitamin A deficiency	No	No	Bran scales	Back, mane	Plasma vitamin A level, liver vitamin A level
Warble fly	Little	No	Larvae in subdermal tissue	Back	Larvae in lesions
Zinc deficiency	No	Yes	Parakeratosis	Limbs, muzzle, vulva	Serum zinc levels

TABLE A 4

Differential Diagnosis of Central Nervous Problems in Growing Cattle

Disease	Blindness	Dullness	Hyper-Aesthesia	Pyrexia	Other Signs	Other Nervous Signs	Response to Therapy	Diagnosis
Acidosis	Apparent	Yes	Yes	No	Ruminal stasis, tachycardia	Head deviation, circling, staggering gait, muscle tremors	Variable	Signs, history
Aflatoxicosis	Yes	Yes	No	No	Teeth grinding, jaundice, diarrhoea, tenesmus	Walk in circles	Limited value	Use of groundnut or other feed
Arsenic poisoning	No	Very	Usually No	No	Abdominal pain, foetid diarrhoea	Incoordination, muscle tremors	Variable	Urine sample
Aujeszky's disease	No	No	Yes	Yes	Respiratory distress, salivation	Pruritus, licking, chewing	None	Signs
Brain abscess	Often	Yes	Yes	Some	Variable	Nystagmus, ataxia, circling, head deviation	Variable	Leucocytosis, suppurative lesion elsewhere
Botulism	No	Yes	No	No	Recumbency later	Incoordination, ataxia, progressive paralysis	No use	Signs
Cerebrocortical necrosis	Yes	Less Severe Cases	Yes	No	Normal ruminal movements	Muscle tremors, opisthotonus, pupils respond to light, recumbency	Good if early	Age (usually over 6 months), signs, histology, brain fluorescence
Coccidiosis	No	Slight	Yes	No or Slight	Diarrhoea/ dysentery	Strabismus, tetany, opisthotonus	Poor	Faecal oocyst count

TABLE A 4 (cont'd)

Disease	Blindness	Dullness	Hyper-Aesthesia	Pyrexia	Other Signs	Other Nervous Signs	Response to Therapy	Diagnosis
Coenurosis	Unilateral	Yes	Yes	No	Loss of condition	Head deviation, circling, ataxia, head pressing	Surgical - often good	Signs, area
Ergot poisoning	At times	At times	At times	No	Diarrhoea	Drowsiness, convulsions	No therapy	Presence of sclerotia in feed
Fluorosis	No	Yes	No	Some	Dyspnoea, diarrhoea, constipation	Muscular tremor, tetany	Variable	Blood fluorine levels
Furazolidone poisoning(acute)	No	No	Yes	No	Few other signs	Convulsions	Limited value	History of usage
Haemophilus somnus infection	Unilateral	Yes	Yes, later	Yes	Recumbency	Eyes often partly closed, ataxia, convulsions	Variable	Signs, neutro-paenia, bacteriology
Hypomagnesaemia	No	No	Yes	Yes	Increased loud heart rate	Opisthotonus, paddling movements	Good if early	Low blood magnesium levels
Infectious bovine rhinotracheitis (nervous)	No	Inter-mittent	Inter-mittent	Yes	Anorexia	Incoordination	No therapy	Viral isolation, paired serology
Infectious necrotic hepatitis	No	Yes	Some	Yes	Painful liver, tachypnoea	Hyperaesthesia	Poor	Signs, history, bacteriology
Lead poisoning	Yes	No	Yes	No or Slight	Ruminal stasis, diarrhoea	Bellowing, tonic-clonic convulsions, lack of palpebral reflex	Some success	Blood lead levels, liver and kidney *post mortem*

TABLE A 4 (cont'd)

Disease	Blindness	Dullness	Hyper-Aesthesia	Pyrexia	Other Signs	Other Nervous Signs	Response to Therapy	Diagnosis
Lightning strike/ electrocution	Yes	Yes	Yes	No	Paralysis	Paralysis of one or more limbs	Little use	Signs, history
Linseed poisoning	No	Yes Acute	Yes	No	Cyanosis, dyspnoea	Opisthotonus, nystagmus	Variable	Linseed feeding
Listeriosis	Often	Yes	No	Yes	Hypopyon, panophthalmitis	Head pressing, circling, head deviation, unilateral facial paralysis	Often poor	Signs
Louping ill	Apparent	No	Yes	Yes	Variable	Jerky stiff movements, incoordination	Variable	Serology
Male fern poisoning	Yes	Yes	No	No	Poor condition	Partial blindness	Variable	History, signs
Malignant catarrhal fever	Yes	Yes	Yes	Yes	Scleral congestion, lymph node enlargement	Muscle tremors, nystagmus, incoordination	Hopeless	Signs
Mannosidosis	No	Slight	Yes	No	Loss of condition	Fine lateral head tremor, vertical head nodding	None	Low tissue alpha-mannosidase
Meningitis	No	At times	At times	Yes	Anorexia	Opisthotonus, spasm of neck muscles, paddling movements	Good if early	Cerebro-spinal fluid cell count

TABLE A 4 (cont'd)

Disease	Blindness	Dullness	Hyper-Aesthesia	Pyrexia	Other Signs	Other Nervous Signs	Response to Therapy	Diagnosis
Mercury poisoning	Yes	Yes	No	No	Abdominal pain, diarrhoea	Terminal incoordination, convulsions, recumbency	Variable	*Post mortem* kidney mercury levels, history, faeces, urine
Middle ear disease	No	Yes	No	No	Respiratory signs	Head rotation	Often poor	Signs, previous respiratory infection
Nitrate poisoning	No	Yes	No	No	Dyspnoea, diarrhoea, cyanosis	Muscle tremors, staggering gait	Some success if early	Methaemoglobin
Organophosphorus poisoning	No	Yes	No	Yes	Dyspnoea, diarrhoea, salivation, bradycardia	Miosis, muscle tremors, stiff gait	Good	Signs, history
Otitis (non-discharging)	No	Yes	No	No		Head rotation, incoordination	Often poor	Signs, bacteriology
Photosensitisation	Some	Some	Some	No	Skin lesions of unpigmented parts exposed to the sun		Good	Signs, history
Progressive ataxia	No	No	No	No	Usually none	Progressive ataxia	None	Signs, breeding, histology
Ragwort poisoning	Yes	Yes	No	Yes	Rectal prolapse, diarrhoea, straining	Frenzy, staggering gait, circling	Usually little value	Signs, history, histology

TABLE A 4 (cont'd)

Disease	Blindness	Dullness	Hyper-Aesthesia	Pyrexia	Other Signs	Other Nervous Signs	Response to Therapy	Diagnosis
Selenium poisoning	Yes	Yes Chronic	Yes Acute	No	Colic, depraved appetite, chronic loss of condition	Head pressing, paralysis	Limited success	Blood and urine levels
Sodium chloride poisoning	Sometimes	Slight	No	No	Excessive thirst, diarrhoea abdcminal pain	Paresis, fetlock knuckling	Usually good if early	Serum sodium levels
Sodium mono-chloroacetate poisoning	No	No	Yes	Variable	Few other signs	Hyperexcitability, aggressiveness, convulsions, paralysis	Little	History, use of herbicide
Spastic paresis	No	No	No	No	Over-straight hock	Abnormal gait	Surgical - good	Signs
Staggers	No	No	Yes	Variable	Profuse salivation	Nystagmus, rocking-horse gait	Good	Signs
Tetanus	No	No	Yes	Yes	Bloat, difficulty in swallowing	Stiff gait, hyperaesthesia, erect ears, raised tail base	Poor	Signs
Urea poisoning	No	No	Yes	Yes	Bloat, dyspnoea	Muscle twitching	Variable	Signs, blood and rumen ammonia levels
Urolithiasis	No	Yes	No	No	Straining		Good if early	Signs
Vitamin A deficiency	Yes	No	No	No	Diarrhoea, bran skin scales	Convulsions, syncope	No use if congenital, good if post-natal	Low plasma and liver levels

TABLE A 5

Differential Diagnosis of Sudden Death in Growing Cattle

Condition	Likely Duration of Signs Before Death	Clinical Signs	Post Mortem Signs	Diagnosis
Abomasal ulceration	2-24 hours	Pale mucous membranes, abdominal pain	Abomasal ulcer, haemorrhage	Lesion
Acidosis	12-24 hours	Recumbent or staggering gait, diarrhoea	Reticulo-ruminal contents have a fermentation odour with epithelial sloughing	History, post mortem findings
Aflatoxicosis	24-48 hours	Jaundice, diarrhoea, abdominal discomfort	Jaundice, swollen liver, ascites	Feed level
Anaphylaxis	Minutes	Dyspnoea, muscle twitching, nystagmus, cyanosis	Pulmonary oedema, vascular engorgement	History of injection
Anthrax*	1-48 hours	Pyrexia, dyspnoea, congested mucosa, collapse, haemorrhages from orifices	No rigor mortis, tarry unclotted blood, multiple haemorrhages in tissues	Blood smears
Antimony poisoning	24-72 hours	Arched back, depressed, colic	Thickened abomasum with inflammation	Antimony in faeces
Aortic stenosis	Very quickly	Dyspnoea, systolic murmur	Aortic stenosis	Post mortem examination
Arsenic poisoning (peracute)	48-72 hours	Abdominal pain, ruminal stasis, diarrhoea, teeth grinding	Rapid putrefaction, garlic odour, haemorrhages in abomasum and caecum	Arsenic levels in liver and kidney
Aspiration pneumonia	Minutes - 72 hours	Dullness, cough, respiratory signs	Acute exudative or gangrenous pneumonia	History

*Always check for evidence of anthrax in cases of sudden death.

TABLE A 5 (cont'd)

Condition	Likely Duration of Signs Before Death	Clinical Signs	Post Mortem Signs	Diagnosis
Aujeszky's disease	Few hours	Excessive licking, pyrexia, pruritus	Central nervous system congestion, local skin lesions	Signs
Blackleg	12-36 hours	Pyrexia, depression	Haemorrhage and emphysema in muscles	Signs, history, bacteriology
Bracken poisoning	1-5 days	Dysentery, haemorrhages from orifices	Widespread haemorrhages, necrosis of gut mucosa, kidney, liver	History, presence of plant
Brassica spp. poisoning	Few hours	Pale mucous membranes, haemoglobinuria	Anaemia, jaundice	History, anaemia, Heinz-Ehrlich bodies
Coccidiosis	24 hours to several days	Dysentery, normal temperature, ? nervous signs	Congestion and haemorrhagic enteritis of large intestine	Many oocysts in faeces
Coenurosis (migratory)	Few days	Convulsions, frenzy	Cyst on brain surface	History, signs, *post mortem* findings
Copper poisoning (acute)	24 hours	Diarrhoea, abdominal pain, jaundice, haemoglobinuria	Friable yellow liver, jaundice, abomasitis	Kidney and liver copper levels
Copper poisoning (chronic)	24-48 hours	Jaundice, anorexia, depression	Friable yellow liver	Kidney and liver copper levels
Electrocution/ lightning strike	Minutes	Loss of consciousness, struggling, shock	Burn mark, congested viscera, multiple haemorrhages	History
Fascioliasis (acute)	Few days	Pale mucous membranes, abdominal pain	Swollen liver, blood-stained fluid in peritoneal cavity	History, area, *post mortem* findings

TABLE A 5 (cont'd)

Condition	Likely Duration of Signs Before Death	Clinical Signs	Post Mortem Signs	Diagnosis
Fluorosis (acute)	6 hours	Nervous signs, constipation, diarrhoea	Abomasitis, enteritis, liver, kidney degeneration	Fluoride levels in bones and teeth
Fog fever	24 hours or more	Dyspnoea, tachypnoea, dullness, no cough	Swollen, heavy lungs, emphysema, haemorrhages in respiratory tract	Signs, history, post mortem findings
Furazolidone poisoning (acute)	48 hours	Hyperexcitability, convulsions	Few	Feeding history
Furazolidone poisoning (chronic)	48 hours	Dysentery, mouth necrosis	Haemorrhages, necrosis of intestines, serosal haemorrhages	Feeding history
Haemonchosis (acute)	Few days	Pale mucous membranes	Pale carcase, helminths in abomasum	Signs, history, post mortem findings
Haemophilus somnus infection	Few hours	Pyrexia, nervous signs	Focal or diffuse meningitis	Signs, serology, Pandy globulin test on CSF
Hypomagnesaemia	½-6 hours	Nervous signs, convulsions, increased heart rate and sounds	Congestion and haemorrhages in various organs	Calcium : magnesium levels
Infectious bovine rhinotracheitis (nervous)	48 hours	Pyrexia, incoordination, nervous signs	Non-suppurative encephalitis	Virus isolation
Infectious bovine rhinotracheitis (respiratory)	24 hours	Pyrexia, coughing, respiratory signs, conjunctivitis	Extensive obstructive bronchiolitis	Virus isolation
Infectious necrotic hepatitis	24-48 hours	Depression, weakness	Liver dark and swollen	Signs, history, bacteriology

TABLE A 5 (cont'd)

Condition	Likely Duration of Signs Before Death	Clinical Signs	Post Mortem Signs	Diagnosis
Inhalation pneumonia	Minutes - 72 hours	Dullness, cough, respiratory signs	Acute exudative or gangrenous pneumonia	History
Lead poisoning	12-24 hours	Blindness, bellowing, abdominal pain, tooth grinding, diarrhoea, ruminal stasis	Abomasitis, enteritis, fatty degeneration of liver, abdominal haemorrhages, meningeal and cerebral vessel congestion	Liver and kidney lead levels
Lightning strike/ electrocution	Minutes	Loss of consciousness, struggling, shock	Burn mark, congested viscera, multiple haemorrhages	History
Linseed poisoning	15-45 minutes	Staggering, bellowing, convulsions, nervous signs, dyspnoea	Dark or bright red blood, subepicardial and endocardial haemorrhages	Hydrocyanic acid in feed
Listeriosis	Few hours	Pyrexia, nervous signs	Meningeal vessel congestion, microabscesses in brain stem	Histology, serology, bacteriology
Malignant oedema	12-48 hours	Erythema and swelling at site of infection, pyrexia	Rapid putrefaction, skin gangrene, oedema of area	Signs, history, bacteriology
Mercury poisoning	4 hours	Abdominal pain, dehydration, diarrhoea	Intestinal ulceration, swollen liver and kidney	Kidney and urine mercury levels
Monensin poisoning	Several days	Lethargy, dullness, diarrhoea	Heart enlarged, oedema of lungs and mesentery, swollen liver, gastro-enteritis	Signs, history
Mucosal disease	48 hours	Pyrexia, depression diarrhoea	Necrosis and erosions of alimentary mucosa	Viral isolation lesions and faeces

TABLE A 5 (cont'd)

Condition	Likely Duration of Signs Before Death	Clinical Signs	Post Mortem Signs	Diagnosis
Multiple cardiac lesions	Very quickly	Stunted growth, often cyanosis, heart murmurs	Ventricular septal defects, other lesions	*Post mortem* examination
Nitrate poisoning	½-24 hours	Anoxia, muscle tremors, dyspnoea, nervous signs	Rapidly putrefying carcase	Ingesta nitrate levels and urine methaemoglobin level
Organophosphorus poisoning	10 minutes - 24 hours	Miosis, bradycardia, muscle tremors, salivation, ataxia	No gross signs	History, tissue cholinesterase levels
Pneumonia (acute)	24-48 hours	Pyrexia, respiratory signs, coughing	Lung consolidation, oedema, emphysema, congestion	Bacterial and viral identification
Rhododendron poisoning	Few days	Projectile vomiting, abdominal pain	Gastroenteritis	Signs, history
Ruminal tympany	½-12 hours	Distended reticulo-rumen and/or abomasum	Distended reticulo-rumen and/or abomasum	Distended abdomen
Salmonellosis	24-48 hours	Depression, injected mucous membranes, increased heart and respiratory rates	Often few, subserosal and submucosal haemorrhages	Culture of swabs from intestinal wall and contents, spleen, heart blood, mesenteric lymph nodes, gall bladder
Selenium poisoning	48 hours	Blindness, circling, head pressing	Necrosis of abomasum and small intestine, congestion and necrosis of liver	Blood and urine selenium levels
Shipping fever	Few hours	Pyrexia, mucopurulent discharge, tachypnoea	Consolidation in lungs and emphysema	History, *post mortem* findings

TABLE A 5 (cont'd)

Condition	Likely Duration of Signs Before Death	Clinical Signs	Post Mortem Signs	Diagnosis
Sodium chloride poisoning	24 hours	Diarrhoea, loss of condition, dehydration, blindness	Congestion of omasum and abomasum, hydro-pericardium	Brain and liver sodium levels
Sodium monochloroacetate poisoning	Up to 24 hours	Hyperexcitability, aggressiveness	Venous congestion of neck and thorax, haemorrhages in tissues	History, detection of herbicide
Summer mastitis	Few days	Pyrexia, swollen udder	Inflammation of udder	History
Sweet vernal grass poisoning	Variable	Lethargy, tachypnoea, tachycardia	Petechial haemorrhages on mucous membranes, haematomas	History, presence of plant
Thrombosis of caudal/ cranial vena cava	Few hours	Haemoptysis, blood in front of animal	Intrapulmonary haemorrhages, thrombosis of vena cava	Signs, history
Tickborne fever	12-24 hours	Lethargy, pyrexia	No gross lesions	History, tick area
Ventricular septal defects	Very quickly	Decreased exercise tolerance, heart murmur	Ventricular septal defect	Post mortem examination
Vitamin E/selenium deficiency	½ minute - 18 hours	Dull, recumbency, conscious calf, fast heart rate	Pallor of myocardium or pale skeletal muscle	Kidney and liver selenium, liver tocopherol
Yew poisoning	Few hours	Dyspnoea, weakness	No gross signs, yew in rumen	History, post mortem findings

TABLE A 6

Differential Diagnosis of Gradual Loss of Condition in Growing Cattle

Condition	Signs	Diagnosis
Actinobacillosis (lingual)	Shrunken tongue	Signs, bacteriology
Actinobacillosis (visceral)	Intermittent bloat, indigestion, intermittent diarrhoea	Signs, bacteriology
Actinobacillosis (soft tissue)	Bloat, diarrhoea	Signs, *post mortem* findings
Actinomycosis (bone)	Enlargement of bone	Signs, bacteriology
Amyloidosis	Anasarca, enlarged kidney, polydipsia	Signs
Arsenic poisoning (chronic)	Dullness, poor coat, erythema of mucous membranes	Signs, urine arsenic levels
Avian tuberculosis	Cough	History, comparative tuberculin tests
Calcium deficiency	Lameness	Signs, low bone ash
Chronic suppurative pneumonia	Thoracic pain, intermittent pyrexia, tachypnoea	Signs, history
Cobalt deficiency	Diarrhoea, progressive fatigue, infertility	Signs, history, anaemia, serum vitamin B_{12} levels
Coccidiosis	Diarrhoea often with blood in it, tenesmus	Signs, oocysts in faeces
Contagious bovine pyelonephritis	Polyuria with blood and pus in urine. Enlarged kidney.	Signs, bacteriology
Copper deficiency	Diarrhoea, lameness, hair colour loss	Signs, history, plasma and liver copper levels
Dicrocoelium dendriticum infestation	Mainly loss of condition	History, faecal egg count

TABLE A 6 (cont'd)

Condition	Signs	Diagnosis
Fascioliasis	Diarrhoea, anaemia	Signs, history, faecal egg count
Fluorosis	Mottling of teeth, lameness	Signs, history, blood fluorine levels
Foot-and-mouth disease	Vesicles in mouth and on feet, pyrexia earlier	Signs, virus isolation
Hypoderma spp. infestation	Presence of subdermal swellings on the back	Signs, larval presence
Liver abscess	Reduced appetite, intermittent digestive disturbances	Signs, history, haematology
Manganese deficiency	Poor coat formation	Signs, blood and liver manganese levels
Molybdenum poisoning	Diarrhoea, hair depigmentation, bone rarefaction	Signs, history, plasma copper levels
Mucosal disease	Intermittent diarrhoea, inappetance	Signs, virus presence
Oesophagostomiasis	Loss of condition, anaemia	Signs, history, faecal egg count
Parasitic bronchitis	Cough	Signs, history, faecal larval count
Parasitic gastroenteritis	Diarrhoea	Signs, history, faecal egg count
Phosphorus deficiency	Progressive stiffening of gait, enlarged joints	Signs, serum phosphorus levels
Ragwort poisoning	Dull, photosensitisation	Signs, liver biopsy
Salmonellosis (chronic)	Variable appetite, intermittent diarrhoea and pyrexia	Signs, bacteriology

TABLE A 6 (cont'd)

Condition	Signs	Diagnosis
Selenium deficiency	Diarrhoea, responds to selenium therapy	Glutathione peroxidase blood level
Selenium poisoning (chronic)	Dullness, staring coat, alopecia, hoof horn separation	Signs, blood selenium levels
Sodium chloride deficiency	Excessive licking, urine drinking	Signs, serum sodium levels
Sporadic bovine leucosis (adult multicentric)	Generalised lymph node enlargement	Signs, biopsy
Sporadic bovine leucosis (generalised)	Depression, general lymph node enlargement	Signs, biopsy
Tapeworm infestation	Dull, staring coat, constipation occasional anaemia, dysentery	Signs, proglottides, eggs in faeces
Tuberculosis	Chronic soft cough, dyspnoea	Signs, comparative tuberculin test
Vitamin A deficiency	Incoordination of gait, night blindness, brown scales in coat	Signs, plasma vitamin A and carotene levels
Vitamin D deficiency	Lameness, enlargement of limb joints, arched back	Signs, serum phosphorus and calcium levels
Zinc deficiency	Alopecia	Signs, parakeratosis, serum zinc levels

Note: Management factors have not been included in this table.

TABLE A 7

Causes of Abortion in Heifers and their Differentiation

Condition	Occurrence	Time of Abortion	Other Signs	Placenta	Foetus	Diagnosis
Avian tuberculosis	Rare	Any stage	-	Organism present	-	Bacteriology, comparative tuberculin test
Bacillary haemoglobinuria	Rare	Variable	Haemoglobinuria, diarrhoea, abdominal pain, pyrexia	-	-	Signs, bacteriology
Brucellosis	Uncommon	Over 6 months	Usually none	Cotyledon necrosis, oedematous placenta with leathery plaques. Organism present	Pneumonia in some, organism in foetal stomach	Bacteriology (including milk, uterine discharge), Rose Bengal Plate Test, serum agglutination test, complement fixation test
Epizootic abortion	Rare	6-8 months	Occasional mastitis	Necrotic cotyledons, brown gelatinous intercotyledonary area	Liver degeneration, ascites, anasarca, oesophageal and tracheal haemorrhages	Presence of chlamydia. Complement fixation test
Foot-and-mouth disease	Rare	Variable	Pyrexia, vesicles on mouth, lameness	-	-	Virus presence, tissue culture
Fungal (*Aspergillus* spp., *Absidia* spp., *Mucor* spp.)	Common	3-7 months	None	Often yellow areas on cotyledons. Raised yellow leathery inter-cotyledonary area, organism present	Raised soft skin lesions, Organism in foetal stomach	Organism isolation

TABLE A 7 (cont'd)

Condition	Occurrence	Time of Abortion	Other Signs	Placenta	Foetus	Diagnosis
Haemophilus somnus infection	Uncommon	Variable	Pyrexia, dullness, nervous signs	-	-	Signs, bacteriology, serology
Infectious bovine rhinotracheitis	Common	6-8 months	Weeks after respiratory disease	Organism present	Autolysis, organism in foetus	Presence of virus, serum neutralisation test
Iodine deficiency	Uncommon	6-9 months	-	-	Thyroid enlarged	Thyroid enlargement, blood protein iodine level
Iodism	Uncommon	5-9 months	Scaly coat, excessive lachrymation and nasal discharge	Cotyledon necrosis	-	Signs, history
Leptospira hardjo infection	Common	Over 6 months	Abortion usually weeks after flabby bag syndrome	Oedematous placenta, yellow-brown cotyledons	Organisms in pleural fluid, kidney and liver	Bacteriology (including urine), serum agglutination test, complement fixation test
Leptospira infections (e.g. canicola and ictero-haemorrhagiae)	Uncommon	Usually over 5 months	Pyrexia	-	Organism isolated	Bacteriology (including urine)
Listeriosis	Uncommon	6-9 months	Pyrexia	Organism present	No abnormality, organism present in foetal stomach	Organism presence (including uterine discharge), serum agglutination test

TABLE A 7 (cont'd)

Condition	Occurrence	Time of Abortion	Other Signs	Placenta	Foetus	Diagnosis
Mucosal disease	Common	Variable	-	-	Stunted growth, congenital abnormalities	Organism present
Q fever	Rare	Variable	Anorexia	-	Organism present	Organism isolation
Redwater fever	Uncommon	Variable	Haemoglobinuria, diarrhoea, pyrexia	-	-	Signs, organism presence
Salmonella dublin infection	Quite common	About 7 months	Often none	-	-	Bacteriology
Salmonella typhimurium infection	Quite common	Any time	Pyrexia, enteritis	-	-	Bacteriology
Other Salmonella spp. infections	Quite uncommon	Any time	Pyrexia, enteritis	-	-	Bacteriology
Sarcocystosis	Rare	Variable	Anorexia, anaemia, muscle tremors, diarrhoea	-	-	Organism present
Summer mastitis	Occasional	Over 5 months	Pyrexia, mastitis	-	Reduced growth	Bacteriology
Tickborne fever	Uncommon	7-9 months	Pyrexia, tachy-pnoea	-	-	Signs, organism in host's monocytes
Trichomoniasis	Probably not present	2-4 months	Others show infertility	Uterine exudate contains floccules	Macerated foetus, organism in foetal stomach	Organism isolation (including uterine discharge), cervical mucus agglutination test

TABLE A 7 (cont'd)

Condition	Occurrence	Time of Abortion	Other Signs	Placenta	Foetus	Diagnosis
Tuberculosis	Rare	Any stage	Often metritis	Organism present	-	Bacteriology, comparative tuberculin test
Vibriosis (*Campylobacter fetus* variety *veneralis*)	Uncommon	5-7 months	Others show irregular dioestrus, early embryonic death	Semi-opaque petechial haemorrhages, organism present	Pus on peritoneum, organism in foetal stomach	Bacteriology (including uterine exudate), blood agglutination test
Vitamin A deficiency	Rare	Variable	Diarrhoea, bran skin scales	-	Reduced growth	Low plasma and liver levels

APPENDIX B

Approximate Doses for Some Compounds Used to Treat Growing Cattle

Note: The doses given below are only suggestions. It is recommended that the manufacturer's literature is consulted before the administration of any particular compound to cattle. Dosage also often has to be altered according to the disease being treated, the severity of the condition and whether a calf is a ruminant or non-ruminant at the time. Some of the drugs listed are not yet licensed for use in cattle.

COMPOUND	ROUTE OF ADMINISTRATION	DOSAGE (on weight basis)	
Acepromazine	Injection	0.05-0.10 mg/kg	0.03-0.05 mg/lb
Acetyl salicylic acid (aspirin)	Oral	7-100g according to size	0.25-3.0 oz according to size
Adrenaline 1 in 1000	Injection	0.1-0.5 ml/50 kg	0.1-0.5 ml/cwt
Albendazole	Oral	7.5 mg/kg	3.5 mg/lb
Aluminium hydroxide	Oral	100-200g/500 kg	3-7 oz/1000 lb
Aluminium sulphate	Oral	100-200g/500 kg	3-7 oz/1000 lb
Amicarbalide isethionate	Injection	5-10 mg/kg	2.5-5 mg/lb
Amoxycillin	Injection	7 mg/kg	3.5 mg/lb
Ampicillin	Injection	2-7 mg/kg	1-3.5 mg/lb
Amprolium	Oral	10 mg/kg	5 mg/lb
Bambermycin	Oral	1.5 mg/10kg	1.5 mg/20 lb
Betamethasone	Injection	10-40 mg/animal	
Bismuth carbonate	Oral	20-40 g/animal	0.5-1 oz/animal
British Anti-Lewisite	Injection	4 mg/kg	2 mg/lb
Bromhexine hydrochloride	Oral Injection	0.2-0.5 mg/kg 0.2-0.5 mg/kg	0.1-0.25 mg/lb 0.1-0.25 mg/lb
Caffeine	Injection	0.3-1.5 mg/kg	0.15-0.75 mg/lb
Calcined magnesite	Oral	15-60 g according to size	0.5-2 oz according to size
Calcium versenate	Injection	33-110 mg/kg	16.5-55 mg/lb
Catechu	Oral	10-20 mg/kg	5-10 mg/lb

COMPOUND	ROUTE OF ADMINISTRATION	DOSAGE (on weight basis)	
Chalk	Oral	0.3-0.5 mg/kg	0.15-0.25 mg/lb
Chloral hydrate			
(sedation)	Oral	40-80 mg/kg	20-40 mg/lb
(anaesthesia)	Injection	120-160 mg/kg	60-80 mg/lb
Chloramphenicol	Injection	4-10 mg/kg	2-5 mg/lb
Clenbuterol*	Oral	8 μg/kg	4 μg/lb
	Injection	8 μg/kg	4 μg/lb
Cod liver oil	Oral	15-60 ml	0.5-2 fl oz
Copper calcium edetate	Injection	100 mg/animal over 100 kg	100 mg/animal over 220 lb
Copper methionine complex	Injection	40-100 g/animal	
Copper sulphate	Oral	4g/animal/week	0.1oz/animal/week
	Injection	0.5-1 g/animal	
Cortisone	Injection	Up to 1000 mg/animal	
Dexamethasone	Injection	10-30 mg/animal	
Dichlorophen	Oral	500 mg/kg	250 mg/lb
Diethylcarbamazine citrate	Oral	90 mg/kg	45 mg/lb
	Injection	90 mg/kg	45 mg/lb
Diethylamine copper oxyquinoline sulphate	Injection	0.24 mg/kg	0.12 mg/lb
Di-iodohydroxy-quinoline	Oral	22 mg/kg	11 mg/lb
Diprophylline*	Injection	2.5-10 mg/kg	1.3-5 mg/lb
Erythromycin	Injection	2.5-5 mg/kg	1.3-2.5 mg/lb
Etamiphylline camsylate	Injection	3-6 mg/kg	1.1-3 mg/lb
Febantel	Oral	7.5 mg/kg	3.5 mg/lb
Fenbendazole	Oral	7.5 mg/kg	3.5 mg/lb
Flumethasone	Injection	1.25-2.5 mg/animal	
Framycetin	Injection	5 mg/kg	2.5 mg/lb
Furazolidone	Oral	10 mg/kg	5 mg/lb
Griseofulvin	Oral	7.5-10 mg/kg	3.5-5 mg/lb
Hydrocortisone	Injection	Up to 750 mg/animal	
Hyoscine hydrochloride	Injection	40-100 mg according to size	

COMPOUND	ADMINISTRATION	DOSAGE (on weight basis)	
Imidocarb dihydrochloride	Injection	1 mg/kg	0.5 mg/lb
Iron dextran	Injection	10 mg/kg	5 mg/lb
Ivermectin	Injection	200 μg/kg	100 μg/lb
Kaolin	Oral	50-250 g	1.75-8 oz
Lead arsenate	Oral	0.5-1.5g per growing animal	
Levamisole hydrochloride	Oral Injection "Pour On"	7.5 mg/kg 7.5 mg/kg 10 mg/kg	3.5 mg/lb 3.5 mg/lb 5 mg/lb
Lincomycin*	Injection	5-11 mg/kg	2.5-5.5 mg/lb
Liquid paraffin	Oral	200-1000 ml or more/animal	7 fl oz - 2 pints or more/animal
Magnesium carbonate	Oral	1 g/kg	2 oz/cwt
Magnesium oxide	Oral	1-2 mg/kg	0.5-1 mg/lb
Magnesium sulphate	Oral Injection	0.1-1 kg/animal Up to 400 ml of 25% solution/ animal	1-2 lb/animal
Meclofenamic acid*	Oral	2.2 mg/kg	1.1 mg/lb
Methscopolamine bromide	Oral	0.04-0.12 mg/kg bid	0.02-0.6 mg/lb bid
Methylene blue	Injection	20 mg/kg	10 mg/lb
Monensin sodium	Oral	3.15mg/100 kg	3.15 mg/200 lb
Neomycin	Injection	5-10 mg/kg	2.5-5 mg/lb
Niclosamide	Oral	75 mg/kg	38 mg/lb
Nitrofurazone	Oral	10 mg/kg	5 mg/lb
Nitroxynil	Injection	10 mg/kg	5 mg/lb
Oxfendazole	Oral	4.5 mg/kg	2 mg/lb
Oxibendazole	Oral	10 mg/kg	5 mg/lb
Oxyclozanide	Oral	10 mg/kg	5 mg/lb
Oxytetracycline	Injection	5-10 mg/kg	2.5-5 mg/lb

COMPOUND	ROUTE OF ADMINISTRATION	DOSAGE (on weight basis)	
Parbendazole	Oral	20 mg/kg	10 mg/lb
Penicillin	Injection	8000-20000 units/ kg	4000-10000 units/ lb
Phenamidine isethionate	Injection	13 mg/kg	7.5 mg/lb
Phenylbutazone*	Oral	4.4 mg/kg	2.2 mg/lb
	Injection	4.4 mg/kg	2.2 mg/lb
Phthalylsulpha-thiazole	Oral	0.1-0.2 g/kg bid	0.05-0.1 g/lb bid
Potassium iodide	Oral	Up to 16 g/animal	Up to ½ oz/animal
Prednisolone	Injection	50-200 mg/animal	
Quinuronium sulphate	Injection	75-100 mg/100kg up to 300 mg	0.5 mg/lb up to 300 mg
Rafoxanide	Oral	7.5 mg/kg	3.7 mg/lb
	Injection	3.0 mg/kg	1.5 mg/lb
Sodium bicarbonate (1.3 per cent)	Injection	150 ml/kg bid	75 ml/lb bid
Sodium bicarbonate	Oral	150-200 g/animal	5-7 oz/animal
Sodium iodide	Injection	1 g/12 kg	1 g/25 lb
Sodium selenate	Injection	0.1-0.15 mg/kg	0.05-0.08 mg/lb
Sodium thiosulphate	Oral	30-60 g/animal	1-2 oz/animal
	Injection	8-12 g/animal	
Spectinomycin	Injection	11-30 mg/kg	5 -15 mg/lb
Spiramycin	Injection	20 mg/kg	10 mg/lb
Streptomycin	Injection	10-15 mg/kg	5-7.5 mg/lb
Sulphadiazine	Oral		
	-Initial	0.2 g/kg	0.1 g/lb
	-Maintenance	0.1 g/kg bid	0.05 g/lb bid
	Injection		
	-Initial	0.2 g/kg	0.1 g/lb
	-Maintenance	0.1 g.kg bid	0.05 g/lb bid
Sulphadimidine (Sulphamethazine)	Oral		
	-Initial	0.2 g/kg	0.1 g/lb
	-Maintenance	0.1 g/kg bid	0.05 g/lb bid
	Injection		
	-Initial	0.2 g/kg	0.1 g/lb
	-Maintenance	0.1 g/kg bid	0.05 g/lb bid

COMPOUND	ROUTE OF ADMINISTRATION	DOSAGE (on weight basis)	
Sulphaguanidine	Oral	0.1-0.3 g/kg	0.05-0.15 g/lb
Sulphamerazine	Oral		
	-Initial	0.2 g/kg	0.1 g/lb
	-Maintenance	0.1 g/kg bid	0.05 g/lb bid
	Injection		
	-Initial	0.2 g/kg	0.1 g/lb
	-Maintenance	0.1 g/kg bid	0.05 g/lb bid
Sulphamethyoxy-pyridazine	Injection	22 mg/kg	11 mg/lb
Sulphapyrazole	Injection	0.02-0.08 g/kg	0.01-0.04 g/lb
Sulphapyridine	Oral		
	-Initial	0.15 g/kg	0.08 g/lb
	-Maintenance	0.07 g/kg bid	0.04 g/lb bid
	Injection		
	-Initial	0.15 g/kg	0.08 g/lb
	-Maintenance	0.07 g/kg bid	0.04 g/lb bid
Theobromine	Oral	20-40 mg/kg	10-20 mg/lb
Thiabendazole	Oral	66 mg/kg	33 mg/lb
Thiamine hydrochloride	Injection	5-10 mg/kg	2.5-5 mg/lb
Thiophanate	Oral	60-140 mg/kg	30-70 mg/lb
Thyroid extract	Oral	1-6 mg/kg bid	0.5-3 mg/lb bid
Triamcinolone acetonide	Injection	Up to 20 mg/animal	
Trimethoprim and sulphadiazine	Injection	15 mg/kg	7.5 mg/lb
Trimethoprim and sulphadoxine	Injection	15 mg/kg	7.5 mg/lb
Tylosin	Injection	4-10 mg/kg	2-5 mg/lb
Vitamin A	Injection	Up to 5000 iu/kg	Up to 2500 iu/lb
Vitamin B_{12}	Injection	5-10 µg/kg	2.5-5 µg/lb
Vitamin D	Injection	3000-5000 iu/kg	1500-2500 iu/lb
Vitamin E (as α-tocopherol)	Injection	6-20 iu/kg	3-10 iu/lb
Xylazine	Injection	0.05-0.3 mg/kg	0.03-0.15 mg/lb
Zinc oxide	Oral	5-10 g/animal	0.25-0.3 oz/animal
Zinc sulphate	Oral	20-30 g/animal	0.5-1 oz/animal
	Injection	10-20 g/animal	0.3-0.6 oz/animal

*Not recommended by the manufacturers for use in cattle.

REFERENCES

ALLCROFT, T R and LEWIS, G (1963) Groundnut toxicity in cattle: experimental poisoning of calves and a report on clinical effects in older cattle. Veterinary Record, 75, 487-493.

ALLEN, W M, LITTLE, W and SANSOM, B F (1978) Selenium supplementation. Veterinary Record, 102, 222-223.

ALLEN, W M and MALLINSON, C B (1984) Parenteral methods of supplementation with copper and selenium. Veterinary Record, 114, 451-454.

ANDERSON, L and TORNQUIST, M (1983) Toxic effects of ethylenediamine hydroiodide treatment in Swedish calves. Veterinary Record, 113, 215-216.

BEDFORD, P G C (1976) Infectious bovine keratoconjunctivitis. Veterinary Record, 98, 134-135.

BLOOD, D C, RADOSTITS, O M and HENDERSON, J A (1983) 'Veterinary Medicine' 6th edition. Bailliere Tindall, London. pp. 257-259, 798-804, 879-885, 1098-1102, 1102-1104, 1031-1034.

BRITISH FRIESIAN JOURNAL (1982) Infectious bovine rhinotracheitis. 64, (May), No. 3, p.222.

BROWNLIE, J, CLARKE, M C and HOWARD, C J (1984) Experimental production of fatal mucosal disease in cattle. Veterinary Record, 114, 535-536.

BUSWELL, J F, BYWATER, R J and HEWETT, G R (1982) Benzathine cloxacillin as a single topical treatment for keratoconjunctivitis. Proceedings Twelfth International Congress Diseases of Cattle, International Congrescentrum RAI, Amsterdam, The Netherlands. 7-10th September, 1982. Vol.II, pp. 1122-1126

COWIE, R (1978) Selenium supplementation. Veterinary Record, 102, 267-268.

DARCEL, C I R Q and DORWARD, W J (1975) Recovery of infectious bovine rhinotracheitis virus following corticosteroid treatment of vaccinated animals. Canadian Veterinary Journal, 16, 87-88.

DEWULF, M and de MOOR, A (1982) Surgical and biochemical research on spastic paralysis. Proceedings Twelfth World Congress Diseases of Cattle, International Congrescentrum RAI, Amsterdam, The Netherlands. 7-10th September, 1982. Vol. II, pp. 760-762.

DONE, J T, TERLECKI, S, RICHARDSON, C, HARKNESS, J W, SANDS, J J, PATTERSON, D S P, SWEASEY, D, SHAW, I G, WINKLER, C E and DUFFELL, S J (1980) Bovine virus diarrhoea - mucosal disease virus: pathogenicity for the fetal calf following maternal infection. Veterinary Record, 106, 473-479.

DUBEY, J P and FAYER, R (1983) Sarcocystosis. British Veterinary Journal, 139, 371-377.

EDWIN, E E, MARKSON, L M, SHREEVE, J, JACKMAN, R and CARROLL, P J (1979) Diagnostic aspects of cerebrocortical necrosis. Veterinary Record, 104, 4-8.

ELLIS, W A, O'BRIEN, J J, NEILL, S D, FERGUSON, H W and HANNA, J (1982) Bovine leptospirosis: microbiological and serological findings in aborted foetuses. Veterinary Record, 110, 147-150.

FARMER, P E, ADAMS, T E and HUMPHRIES, W R (1982) Copper supplementation of drinking water for cattle grazing molybdenum-rich pastures. Veterinary Record, 111, 193-195.

FOSTER, P D (1983) Outbreak of malignant catarrhal fever in British cattle. Veterinary Record, 113, 477.

FRERICHS, G N, WOODS, S B, LUCAS, M H and SANDS, J J (1982) Safety and efficacy of live and inactivated infectious bovine rhinotracheitis vaccines. Veterinary Record, 111, 116-122.

GARTLEY, C, OGILVIE, T H and BUTLER, D G (1981) Magnesium oxide contraindicated as a cathartic for cattle in the absence of rumen acidosis. Proceedings Thirteenth Annual Convention of American Association Bovine Practitioners, 19th-22nd November, 1980. Toronto, p. 17-19.

HAGGARD, D L, STOWE, H D, CONNER, G H and JOHNSON, D W (1980) Immunologic effects of experimental iodine toxicosis in young cattle. American Journal of Veterinary Research, 41, 539-543.

HONG, C, LANCASTER, M B and MICHEL, J F (1981) Worm burdens of dairy heifers in England and Wales. Veterinary Record, 109, 12-14.

HOWARD, J L (1981) Ruminal metabolic acidosis. Bovine Practitioner, No. 12, 44-53.

ISMAY, W S (1980) Use of modified live infectious bovine rhinotracheitis in the field. Veterinary Record, 107,. 511-512.

JARRETT, W F H, URQUHART, G M and BAIRDEN, K (1980) Treatment of bovine parasitic bronchitis. Veterinary Record, 106, 135.

JENSEN, R and MACKEY, D R (1971) 'Bovine pancreolithiasis' in 'Diseases of Feedlot Cattle', 2nd edition. Lea and Febiger, Philadelphia. p.299.

JENSEN, R, MAKI, L R, LAUERMAN, L H, RATHS, W R, SWIFT, B L, FLACK, D E HOFF, R L, HANCOCK, H A, TUCKER, J O, HORTON, D P and WEIBEL, J L (1983) Cause and pathogenesis of middle ear infection in young feedlot cattle. Journal of the American Veterinary Medical Association, 182, 967-972.

JOLLY, R D (1982) Mannosidosis. Proceedings Twelfth World Congress Diseases of Cattle. International Congrescentrum RAI, Amsterdam, The Netherlands. 7th-10th September, 1982. Vol. II, pp. 1146-1150.

JULIAN, R J, HARRISON, K B and RICHARDSON, J A (1976) Nervous signs in bovine coccidiosis. Modern Veterinary Practice, 57, 711-719.

LAMONT, H H and HUNT, B W (1982) Haemophilus somnus and conjunctivitis. Veterinary Record, 111, 21.

LEECH, A, HOWARTH, R J, THORNTON, I and LEWIS, G (1982) Incidence of bovine copper deficiency in England and the Welsh Borders. Veterinary Record, 111, 203-204.

LONG, S E and DAVID, J S E (1981) Testicular feminisation in an Ayrshire cow. Veterinary Record, 109, 116-118.

McCAUSLAND, I P, BADMAN, R T, HIDES, S P and SLEE, K J (1984) Multiple apparent Sarcocystis abortion in four bovine herds. Cornell Veterinarian, 74, 146-154.

MacKELLAR, J C (1962) The application of blood transfusion in cattle with particular reference to redwater (Babesia bovis). Veterinary Record, 74, 763-765.

MAHMOUD, D H and FORD, E J H (1981) Injection of sheep with inorganic injections of copper. Veterinary Record, 108, 114-117.

MARQUARDT, W C (1976) Some problems of host and parasite interactions in cattle. Journal of Protozoology, 23, 287-290.

MARSHALL, A B (1981) 'Summer mastitis' in 'Mastitis Control and Herd Management'. National Institute for Research in Dairying, Reading and Hannah Research Institute, Ayr. Technical Bulletin No. 4. pp. 81-94.

MINISTRY OF AGRICULTURE, FISHERIES AND FOOD/WELSH OFFICE AGRICULTURAL DEPARTMENT/DEPARTMENT OF AGRICULTURE AND FISHERIES FOR SCOTLAND (1976) Animal Salmonellosis Annual Summaries, pp. 1-19.

MINISTRY OF AGRICULTURE, FISHERIES AND FOOD/WELSH OFFICE AGRICULTURAL DEPARTMENT/DEPARTMENT OF AGRICULTURE AND FISHERIES FOR SCOTLAND (1977) Animal Salmonellosis Annual Summaries, pp. 1-27.

MINISTRY OF AGRICULTURE, FISHERIES AND FOOD/WELSH OFFICE AGRICULTURAL DEPARTMENT/DEPARTMENT OF AGRICULTURE AND FISHERIES FOR SCOTLAND (1978) Animal Salmonellosis Annual Summaries, pp. 1-24.

MINISTRY OF AGRICULTURE, FISHERIES AND FOOD/WELSH OFFICE AGRICULTURAL DEPARTMENT/DEPARTMENT OF AGRICULTURE AND FISHERIES FOR SCOTLAND (1979) Animal Salmonellosis Annual Summaries, pp. 1-24.

MINISTRY OF AGRICULTURE, FISHERIES AND FOOD/WELSH OFFICE AGRICULTURAL DEPARTMENT/DEPARTMENT OF AGRICULTURE AND FISHERIES FOR SCOTLAND (1980-81) Animal Salmonellosis Annual Summaries, pp. 1-58.

MINISTRY OF AGRICULTURE, FISHERIES AND FOOD/WELSH OFFICE AGRICULTURAL DEPARTMENT/DEPARTMENT OF AGRICULTURE AND FISHERIES FOR SCOTLAND (1982) Animal Salmonellosis Annual Summaries, pp. 1-38.

MINISTRY OF AGRICULTURE, FISHERIES AND FOOD/WELSH OFFICE AGRICULTURAL DEPARTMENT/DEPARTMENT OF AGRICULTURE AND FISHERIES FOR SCOTLAND (1983) Animal Salmonellosis Annual Summaries, pp. 1-69.

MINISTRY OF AGRICULTURE, FISHERIES AND FOOD/WELSH OFFICE AGRICULTURAL DEPARTMENT/DEPARTMENT OF AGRICULTURE AND FISHERIES FOR SCOTLAND (1984) Animal Salmonellosis Annual Summaries, pp. 1-60.

MITCHELL, G B B and LAW, J M (1984) Formaldehyde poisoning in cattle. Veterinary Record, 115, 283-284.

MYLREA, P J and BYRNE, D T (1974) An outbreak of acute copper poisoning in calves. Australian Veterinary Journal, 50, 169-170.

NETTLETON, P F and SHARP, J M (1980) Infectious bovine rhinotracheitis virus excretion after vaccination. Veterinary Record, 107, 379.

OAKLEY, G A (1982) Comparison of protection against lungworm infection between levamisole treated and vaccinated calves. Veterinary Record, 111, 23-31.

PEARSON, E G and KALLFELZ, F A (1982) A case of presumptive salt poisoning (water deprivation) in veal calves. Cornell Veterinarian, 72, 142-149.

PETRIE, L, ARMOUR, J and STEVENSON, S M (1984) Type 2 ostertagiasis in milking dairy heifers. Veterinary Record, 114, 168-170.

PIRIE, H M (1979) 'Respiratory Diseases of Animals. Notes for a Post-graduate Course'. Edited by Pirie, H M. Glasgow University, Glasgow. pp. 41-42, 71-74.

PRITCHARD, D G, MARKSON, L M, BRUSH, P J, SAWTELL, J A A and BLOXHAM, P A (1983) Haemorrhagic syndrome of cattle associated with the feeding of sweet vernal (Anthoxanthum odoratum) hay containing dicoumarol. Veterinary Record, 113, 78-84.

QUICK, M P, MANSER, P A, STEVENS, H and BOLTON, J F (1983) Sodium monochloroacetate poisoning of cattle and sheep. Veterinary Record, 113, 155-156.

ROEDER, P L and DREW, T W (1984) Mucosal disease of cattle: a late sequel to fetal infection. Veterinary Record, 114, 309-313.

ROSENFELD, I and BEATH, O A (1964a) The influence of protein diets on selenium poisoning I. American Journal of Veterinary Research, 7, 52-56.

ROSENFELD, I and BEATH, O A (1964b) The influence of protein diets on selenium poisoning II. The chemical changes in the tissues following selenium administration. American Journal of Veterinary Research, 7, 57-61.

SNOWDON, W A (1975) The IBR-IPV virus: reaction to infection and intermittent recovery of virus experimentally in treated cattle. Australian Veterinary Journal, 41, 135-141.

SORENSEN, G H (1978) Bacteriological examination of summer mastitis secretions. The demonstration of Bacteroidaceae. Nordisk Veterinaermedicin, 30, 199-204.

STOCKDALE, P M G (1977) The pathogenesis of the lesions produced by Eimeria zuernii in calves. Canadian Journal of Comparative Medicine, 41, 338-344.

STUART, P, BUNTAIN, D and LANDRIDGE, R G (1951) Bacteriological examination of secretions from cases of summer mastitis and experimental infection of non-lactating bovine udders. Veterinary Record, 63, 451-453.

SUTTLE, N F (1981a) Effectiveness of orally administered cupric oxide needles in alleviating hypocupraemia in sheep and cattle. Veterinary Record, 108, 417-420.

SUTTLE, N F (1981b) Comparison between parenterally administered copper complexes of their ability to alleviate hypocupraemia in sheep and cattle. Veterinary Record, 109, 304-307.

TAYLOR, S M (1983) Assessment of prevalence of clinical babesiosis in cattle in Northern Ireland. Veterinary Record, 112, 247-256.

TAYLOR, S M, KENNY, J, MALLON, T R, ELLIOTT, C T, McMURRAY, C and BLANCHFLOWER, J (1984) Efficacy of pyrethroid impregnated ear tags for prophylaxis of tick-borne diseases of cattle. Veterinary Record, 114, 454-458.

VAN VLEET, J F, AMSTUTZ, H E, WEIRICH, W E, REBAR, A H and FERRANS, V J (1983) Clinical, clinicopathologic and pathologic alterations in acute monensin toxicosis in cattle. American Journal of Veterinary Research, 44, 2133-2144.

VETERINARY RECORD (1979) Infectious bovine rhinotracheitis. 105, 3-4.

VETERINARY RECORD (1981) Proposed new feeding stuffs regulations. 109, 148.

WARDROPE, D D, MACLEOD, N S M and SLOAN, J R (1983) Outbreak of monensin poisoning in cattle. Veterinary Record, 112, 560-561.

WARREN, W A (1976) Flies are first to spot summer mastitis. Farmers' Weekly, 84 (17), 44-45 (letter).

WHITELAW, A and FAWCETT, A R (1982) Biological control of liver fluke. Veterinary Record, 110, 500-501.

WISEMAN, A, GIBBS, H A and McGREGOR, A B (1982) Bovine nasal granuloma (atrophic rhinitis) in Britain. Veterinary Record, 110, 420-421.

WISEMAN, A, MSOLLA, P M, SELMAN, I E, ALLAN, E M and PIRIE, H M (1980) Clinical and epidemiological features of 15 incidents of severe infectious bovine rhinotracheitis. Veterinary Record, 107, 436-441.

YEOMAN, G H and WARREN, B C (1984) Summer mastitis. British Veterinary Journal, 140, 232-243.

INDEX

(Note: All major entries to the subject are underlined.)